Riccardo Parboni

Verso

The Dollar and Its Rivals

Recession, Inflation, and International Finance

Translated by Jon Rothschild

British Library
Cataloguing in Publication Data

Parboni, Riccardo
  The dollar and its rivals.
  1. International finance—History—20th century
  I. Title II. Finanza e crisi
  internazionale, *English*
  332.4'5   HG3881

  ISBN 0-86019-046-6 cloth
  ISBN 0-86019-744-4 pbk

First published as
Finanza e crisi internazionale
by Etas Libri, Milan 1980
© Etas Libri S.p.A., 1980

This edition first published 1981
© NLB, 1981
NLB and Verso Editions, 15 Greek Street, London W1

Photoset in 10 on 12pt. Times New Roman by
Servis Filmsetting Ltd, Manchester

Printed in Great Britain by
Billings Ltd,
Worcester

Contents

Preface to the English Edition

When the manuscript of *The Dollar and Its Rivals* was completed in September 1979, new trends in international economic and financial relations had just begun to emerge. In some respects they differ from those considered in the book, but they can be analysed without modifying the basic conceptual approach I have used to reconstruct the international financial turmoil of the seventies and its connection to the deep economic crisis of the industrialized countries. The hub of the thesis that runs through the analysis is that conflict among the major industrialized countries is sharpening.

The post-war period has seen a relative decline of the American economy, while the economies of the other industrialized countries, especially Germany and Japan, have gained in strength. This US decline can be measured by any number of indices. Perhaps the most general one is the course of manufacturing production, depicted in table i. Through 1966, the total value of North American manufacturing production was higher than that of Western Europe and Japan combined. Since 1975, however, it has been lower than that of Western Europe alone (see table ii). This deterioration of the US share of manufacturing production has been accompanied by a slump in the US share of world exports. The American trade surplus was gradually whittled away, eventually becoming insufficient to assure the financing of outflows of American capital for international loans, aid, and direct investment abroad, not to mention the financing of foreign military spending. In order to be able to sustain these outflows of capital, the United States was compelled to rely ever more massively on what are effectively forced loans from the rest of the world, obtained through the special position of the dollar as the principal international reserve currency.

It was inevitable that declining American competitivity and the

7

Table i

Share of Total Manufacturing Production of Ten Industrialized Countries (in %)

	1950	1960	1970	1977
USA	61.9	50.5	43.6	44.0
Canada	3.5	3.3	3.4	3.6
Japan	2.1	6.3	13.1	13.4
Denmark	0.7	0.6	0.7	0.7
France	7.6	8.1	8.9	9.6
Germany	10.1	17.2	17.2	16.0
Italy	2.2	3.1	3.7	4.3
Holland	1.8	2.2	2.3	2.2
Britain	8.2	6.9	5.3	4.5
Sweden	2.0	1.9	1.9	1.6

Source: Us Department of Labor.

Table ii

Share of World Manufacturing Production of Major Areas* (in%)

	1960	1965	1970	1975
Western Europe	31.6	30.1	29.8	27.8
North America	37.8	36.9	30.7	27.0
Japan	3.9	4.8	7.8	7.1
Socialist countries	18.1	19.6	22.6	27.7
Developing countries	6.9	6.9	7.3	8.6

* The table does not include China, whose share should in principle be equal to 100 minus the sum of the other areas; this, however, seems an underestimation of the Chinese share, which, when corrected, would reduce the share of the other areas.

Source: UNIDO.

enhanced role of the rest of the world in long-term financing would eventually trigger a crisis of the dollar, which is just what happened in 1971. *The Dollar and Its Rivals* argues that the United States chose the tempo and form of this crisis, and thus managed to effect a devaluation of the dollar that would not compromise its dominant position as international means of payment. The price paid for this was the destruction of the international monetary system based on fixed exchange rates, which had been established at Bretton Woods in 1944 under the aegis of the United States itself.

The devaluation of the dollar—or rather, the various devaluations that occurred through the seventies—did serve to halt the American economy's loss of competitivity, as is demonstrated by the halt in the decline of the US share of world manufactured exports. Nevertheless, the improvement in American competitivity was not transformed into an increase in industrial accumulation or an acceleration of the growth of industrial productivity. The United States thus appears to be suffering from some of the problems that have long racked the British economy: slow growth of industrial productivity, insufficient accumulation in industry compared with competing countries, mounting weight of the service sector in the national income—in a word, de-industrialization.

In the past several years a discussion has arisen in the United States on the causes of this economic decline, one that again has many affinities with the debate on the causes of the British deterioration. The latter, of course, has been under way much longer, and the initial reasons for it must be sought back in the last quarter of the nineteenth century. Partly because the British decline has been going on for a full century now, discussion about its causes has come to involve not only economists, but also economic historians and students of other social disciplines. Quite a number of explanations have been proposed: the excessive foreign entanglements of the British economy, which allegedly harmed the national economy both by supplanting national with international investments and loans and by long maintaining an unrealistically high value of the pound sterling in order to ensure that the City of London would continue to serve as the world's bank; the composition of aggregate demand, said to be unfavourable for accumulation because of the mounting demand for private and public services, the latter sustained by high public spending; the insufficient aggressivity and commercial spirit of industrial managers, a consequence of the higher social standing accorded careers in the civil service, scientific research, and finance; the role of the trade unions in retarding the application of technological progress.

Some of these themes recur in the American discussion, and the two debates merit serious comparison. Clearly, sociological factors and considerations connected to industrial relations are of scant importance in the United States, for they bear little relation to US reality. There is probably no country in which the drive to make money has exerted such attraction, despite some changes in mass psychology brought about by the youth movement of the sixties. US managers find few equals in aggressivity and career-dedication, and it would be difficult to find trade unions socially weaker or more accommodating in negotiations on the introduction of progress in technology and the organization of the labour process. On the other hand, quite similar arguments have been advanced about the excess of foreign investment, the over-valuation of the dollar until 1971, and the specially high weight of services in the composition of aggregate demand. In addition, the American discussion has seen the formulation of an original argument: that the superior economic performance of the other industrialized countries since the Second World War is the result of both their efforts to make up for lost technological ground and their shift of labour-power from agriculture, where per capita productivity is low, to industry, characterized by higher levels of productivity. As the stock of excess agricultural labour is depleted and the technological gap closed, this argument runs, the economic performance of the rest of the industrialized world will inevitably sink to the American level. In other words, the exceptional feature is not the low US growth rate, but the high growth rate of the rest of the world.

Finally, a number of heterodox interpretations have been tailored to fit both situations, the British and American. According to these hypotheses, the poor performance of the two economies may be traced to their excessive oligopolization, the predominance of finance over industry in the strict sense, and the inadequacy of state involvement in economic planning. A high degree of industrial concentration tends to reduce investment by firms, according to the thesis of A.M. Hansen, defended more rigorously by Steindl.[1] The predominance of finance over industry tends to encourage the sort of investment that yields secure and immediate returns, with obvious positive effects on the value of a company's stock-market shares, and to discourage innovative projects of broad scope but deferred returns. Various forms of direct state intervention to stimulate investment, from direct state management of enterprises to Japanese-style mixed bureaucratic-industrial planning, have been fundamental in all the industrialized countries that have registered high growth rates. Even Germany, with its 'social market economy', has benefited

---

[1] See A.M. Hansen, 'Economic Progress and Declining Population', in American Economic Association, *Readings in Business Cycle Theory*, Philadelphia 1944; J. Steindl, *Maturity and Stagnation in American Capitalism*, Oxford 1952.

from a form of investment planning implemented through the direct participation of the banks (discretely assisted by the state) in the management of the companies they finance.

It is useful to link discussion of whether devaluation is effective in encouraging productive accumulation to discussion about the decline of the mature capitalist economies. If the predominant factors of decline are international in nature, then one would expect that devaluation alone would probably suffice to augment accumulation. If, on the other hand, the predominant factors are oligopolization, the dominance of finance, and insufficient state intervention, then the effectiveness of devaluation would be lower. It is my view (although I must admit that I am not an unprejudiced observer) that despite the undoubted importance of the 'non-international' factors, devaluation, if maintained long enough, would be capable of producing some positive results for the declining economies. But neither Britain nor the United States has succeeded in maintaining devaluation for a period long enough to influence accumulation.

The recent history of the pound is well known and can be summarized briefly. After the hefty devaluation of 1976, the British economy became more competitive relative to the strong-currency economies of Western Europe and to the United States. During the same period, North Sea oil production began to attain high levels, bolstering the trade balance. The pound, which had fallen as low as $1.55 in 1976, rose slightly to about $1.70, around which figure it oscillated throughout 1977 and 1978. In the meantime, the loss of confidence triggered by the new crisis of the dollar induced the holders of liquid wealth to diversify their deposits from the dollar to other currencies. Because of the expectations of high oil income and high interest rates brought about by the deflationary policy undertaken during the last phase of the Labour government, the pound became an attractive currency in which to hold financial resources. To avert revaluation, the authorities could have held oil extraction to a minimum (making it quite clear to the market that Britain would never agree to live on oil) and lowered interest rates, thus discouraging the influx of funds from abroad, and possibly imparting expansionary impulses to the economy in order to reabsorb unemployment. Current-account deficits possibly brought about by expansion would have had to be countered through further devaluations. But the Labour right hesitated to take such measures, preferring to rely on an incomes policy supplemented by deflation through public-spending cuts.

When the Conservatives came to power these trends were accelerated, but a decisive turn in currency policy was also taken. The struggle against inflation was consigned to monetary controls and the revaluation of the pound. Interest rates rose to levels unprecedented until the most recent increases in the American rate. Oil production continued to rise in an effort to achieve self-sufficiency in energy. At the same time, all restrictions on foreign capital movements were lifted. An avalanche of funds seeking refuge from the weak dollar therefore flowed into pounds, lured both by the anticipated improvement of the British trade balance as a result of North Sea oil production and the deflationary policy of import reductions and by the very high interest rates. By October 1980 the pound had risen to $2.42, a revaluation of 55% relative to the 1976 low point, of 40% relative to the quotations that prevailed through most of 1977 and 1978.

The pound also gained relative to the other European currencies; this caused a paralysis of British manufacturing exports and a frightful increase in imports, contributing to the massive rise of unemployment, now approaching 3 million. The revaluation of the pound, together with the high interest rates, is the factor really responsible for the British economic collapse, because the Tories have not yet implemented their policy of reducing the public deficit. Indeed, the budget has continued to show a significant deficit, which contributes to propping up the level of economic activity. There was a slight depreciation of the pound relative to the dollar in the early months of 1981, but this was the result of a rise in the strength of the dollar and not a decline of the pound relative to other currencies.

The Conservatives thus seem to have opted for a strong-currency policy in the manner of the German mark. But Germany's success in maintaining its exports in spite of the revaluation of the mark is a consequence of the intrinsic strength of German industry, which enables it constantly to raise the quality of its products by increasing their technological content. Moreover, Germany has consolidated its position on the markets of the oil-producing countries and in the socialist countries. For an industrialized country, to be an oil producer can be a handicap. Indeed, OPEC members will tend to buy their manufactures from the countries that buy their oil, in order to balance their trade. And Britain's bellicose attitude toward the Soviet Union, and its servile alignment with Washington's various anti-

Soviet initiatives, certainly do not facilitate British trade with the socialist countries. Britain's internal and international conditions are therefore quite different from Germany's. It thus seems inevitable that the maintenance of a strong pound will contribute to British industrial decay. But it is probable that the progressive deterioration of the country's industrial base will lead eventually to forms of massive state intervention in the management of industry and finance, completely inverting the present laissez-faire direction of policy.

One of the main reasons why the British government decided to let the pound appreciate was that the Tories were convinced that the devaluation of the pound was accelerating inflation and that, contrariwise, revaluation would help to bring inflation under control. It is certainly true that devaluation entails a very high inflation potential, for reasons that will be explained in chapter 1. But it is much less true that revaluation lowers the inflation rate. In the case of the United States, on the other hand, the devaluation of the dollar has extremely limited inflationary effects, because of the relatively lesser importance of imports to the US economy. Thus, as I argue throughout this book, the United States was able to resort freely to the competitive weapon of devaluation for much of the seventies. But the inflationary effects of devaluation, while limited in the American case, nevertheless do exist. Moreover, many countries responded to the dollar devaluation with counter-devaluations of their own, in an effort to recover competitivity against the United States. This step was taken by European countries like Italy, Spain, and even Britain and France until 1976; by non-European countries that occupy positions of supreme importance in US foreign trade, like Canada, Mexico, and Brazil; and even, on a more modest scale, by South Korea and many other developing countries. To maintain a given 'real' devaluation—based on a trade-weighted average expressing the devaluation relative to various currencies—the dollar answered counter-devaluation with further devaluation, and not necessarily relative to the currencies that had counter-devalued. The real devaluation produced by this process of devaluation followed by revaluation followed by further devaluation has higher inflationary results, because of what has been called the ratchet effect: the inflation generated by the first devaluation is not eliminated by the subsequent revaluation but is further accelerated by the next devaluation. At bottom, this is a consequence of the fact that in modern economies prices are upward- but not downward-flexible. Slowly but inexorably, the devaluation of the dollar became increasingly inflationary. The sensitivity of inflation to devaluation was further augmented by the behaviour of economic operators, who soon learned to form inflationary expectations in the wake of dollar devaluations. It was yet further exacerbated by the behaviour of exporters to the US market, who invoice in dollars; initially the dollar prices of US imports did not change in the wake of dollar devaluations (except the price of oil), but in the course of years dollar prices increasingly responded to the decline of the dollar in an effort to maintain the real price, thus augmenting the impact of devaluation on US inflation (and also on inflation in other countries that import large quantities of goods invoiced in dollars).

Moreover, from 1975 to 1979 the US government applied a highly expansionary economic policy that had produced one of the longest booms in American economic history. Naturally, this expansion stimulated some inflationary reaction, which compounded the inflation caused by devaluation. It also eroded the American trade balance by increasing imports consequent to the rising demand generated by higher incomes. Little by little, international financial markets began to become convinced that the United States would eventually lose control of the situation. Inflation resulting from devaluation was aggravating inflation of internal origin; the trade balance was deteriorating under the impact both of the increase in national income caused by the policy of expansion and of the loss of competitivity occasioned by inflation. The deterioration of the trade balance seemed to herald yet a new devaluation, which would give further impetus to inflation. In sum, the markets anticipated that American currency would be further weakened and that the authorities would no longer be able to control the process. This sentiment was heightened by news of sharp disagreements about the dollar between the Carter administration and the Federal Reserve System and more generally by the scant confidence in the irresolute and contradictory Carter presidency. Moreover, the spread of monetarist theories tended to aggravate lack of confidence in the dollar, because of the constant growth of US monetary aggregates.

During 1978, especially in the summer, international operators began to protect their funds against potential dollar devaluations (or even began to sell dollars, speculating on its fall), purchasing financial and real assets as alternatives to investments in dollars. Downward pressure on the dollar intensified as funds were shifted to marks, yen, Swiss francs, and pounds. The process of remonetarization of gold, to which the United States is extremely hostile, accelerated as funds were directed to the purchase of gold. Terrible impetus was given to a new rise in raw materials prices, which threatened to trigger a wave of inflation similar to that which swept through the world economy in 1972–73, as funds poured into cash purchases of raw materials (or cover for commodity futures). In sum, in the summer and autumn of 1978 symptoms of a new crisis of confidence in the dollar were taking shape similar to those that had been evident in the past—but of greater scope and, it was feared, with even more sweeping effects. Under the pressure of both the internal financial establishment and the monetary authorities of other countries (especially Germany), and terrified of an influx of funds to the US market and of the threatened rise in raw materials prices, the Carter administration finally decided, in November 1978, to stabilize the dollar, primarily through credit measures. At the same time, monetary co-operation with the governments of other countries was stepped up in order to co-ordinate intervention in exchange markets and to guarantee the formation of a foreign currency reserve, at least temporarily, for the United States.

During the same period, the European Monetary System, which linked all Community currencies (except the pound), and even some non-EEC currencies, to the mark, was coming into being. On the whole, then, 1979 and 1980 were years of substantial stability of exchange rates, which encouraged the most optimistic observers in the hope that the old system of fixed exchange rates, albeit slightly more elastic, could rise from the ashes. The dollar's real quotation did recover slightly in 1979, but not by much, because the devaluation of various non-European currencies was compensated by the significant appreciation of the pound.

It was only in the spring of 1980 that the dollar climbed significantly, under the impetus of the rise in American interest rates (see table iii). The last period of the Carter administration was generally dominated by a policy of dollar stability, which more or less maintained the devaluation that had occurred previously. This devaluation gave strong impetus to American manufactured exports, which in 1979 overtook Germany's and thereby recovered first position in total world exports (manufactures and raw materials).

Table iii

Dollar Quotations in German Marks and Japanese Yen
(at the end of each period)

Year and Quarter	Mark	Yen
1977: 1	2.38	277.5
2	2.33	267.7
3	2.30	265.4
4	2.10	240.0
1978: 1	2.02	222.4
2	2.07	204.7
3	1.93	189.1
4	1.82	194.6
1979: 1	1.86	209.3
2	1.84	217.0
3	1.74	223.3
4	1.73	239.7
1980: 1	1.94	249.7
2	1.75	217.6
3	1.81	212.2
4	1.91	203.0
1981: Jan.	2.12	205.5
Feb.	2.13	209.5
Mar.	2.10	210.8
Apr.	2.21	214.8

Source: IMF.

The positive performance of us exports tended to bolster the trade balance, which was further fortified in 1980 by Carter's decision to abolish price controls on some types of domestic crude-oil production. The increase in internal production, together with a slight fall in consumption caused by the recession that had meanwhile broken out, resulted in a drop of about 2 million barrels per day in us oil imports in 1980. As a whole, then, the consolidation of the dollar coincided with an improvement in the us balance of payments. But the improvement was by no means dramatic, for the American balance of trade remained in deficit, while Germany's and Japan's were in surplus (table iv). On the other hand, the American current-account was in surplus, Germany's and Japan's in deficit. The current-account includes not only items of trade, but also services and transfers. For the United States, services are in surplus because of the enormous profits made abroad by subsidiaries of us multinational

Table iv

Balance of Trade and Current Account for USA, Germany, Japan
(thousands of millions of $)

		1977	1978	1979	1980	1981, 1st quarter
USA	(1)	−30.9	−33.8	−29.5	−25.0	−17.0
	(2)	−15.2	−13.5	−0.3	0.1	n.a.
Germany	(1)	19.3	25.5	17.7	10.0	17.0
	(2)	4.3	8.9	−5.8	−15.5	n.a.
Japan	(1)	17.3	24.6	1.8	0	8.0
	(2)	10.9	16.5	−8.6	−10.8	n.a.

(1) Trade Balance
(2) Balance on Current Account

Source: OECD.

corporations and because of the income from the financial brokerage effected by American banks. For Germany, services and transfers are in deficit, because of spending abroad by German tourists and the remission of money to their countries of origin by immigrant workers in Germany. Japan, on the other hand, registers high outlays for transport costs and for financial and insurance services. Although the important factor for the position of a currency is the overall flow of payments and current entries, for the apparatus of production the export and import of commodities, especially manufactures, are more important. The position of the US economy is therefore less favourable than that of the German or Japanese. Furthermore, as shown in table v, Germany's and Japan's balance of foreign trade is far superior to that of the United States, which is increasingly sustained by its exports of raw materials, especially agricultural products.

The not at all brilliant performance of US foreign trade in manufactures was accompanied by sluggishness of the major productive indicators, especially industrial accumulation and productivity, in both of which categories the United States lies at the bottom of the list of industrialized countries, even behind Britain. The great dollar devaluation served only to bolster the international position of the American economy, halting the erosion of its share of world

Table v

Balances of Items Within Trade Balance, USA, Germany, Japan
(thousands of millions of $)

	United States		Germany		Japan	
	1970	1980s	1970	1980s	1970	1980s
Agricultural products and other raw materials	0.3	26.0	−6.8	−23.0	−8.2	−36.0
Fuels	−1.3	−73.0	−2.4	−34.0	−3.9	−67.0
Manufactures	4.1	25.0	13.1	64.0	12.5	92.0

Source: Morgan Guaranty Trust Co.

manufacturing exports, but it did not halt the dramatic decline in the most important categories: accumulation and productivity. Perhaps—and I repeat, my speculation here is not unbiased—a further devaluation of the dollar could have modified the course of accumulation; there are signs that this is just what is beginning to happen as a consequence of the massive influx of European and Japanese direct investment in the United States, facilitated by the decline of the dollar. Nevertheless, another devaluation would be impractical—except, perhaps, for a minor one—for fear of recreating the sort of lack of confidence that would lead to fresh crises of the dollar.

International constraints, then, require the stability of the dollar, but not its appreciation. Beginning in the last quarter of 1980, however, the dollar rose sharply in a manner reminiscent of the rise of sterling in 1979 and 1980. This was brought about by soaring American interest rates, which began to climb immediately after Reagan's election victory, even before his inauguration. The high interest rates reflect the new monetarist orientation that now prevails in the administration's policy in the struggle against inflation. But they also, along with the reinforcement of the dollar that they bring about, seem to accord with a new US strategic conception of international economic relations.

As the dollar gets stronger, the US economy becomes less competitive, as happened to the British economy before it. In part, the American loss of competitivity is attenuated by the fact that the revaluation of the dollar imparts inflationary· impulses to the European countries: the value, in national currency, of imports invoiced in dollars rises as the dollar goes up; the increase in the cost of imports is then passed on through the domestic price structure. The only way the European economies can offset the inflationary pressures induced by the strong dollar is to accentuate the deflationary character of their economic policies, seeking to prevent the transfer of cost increases by compressing demand.

But it seems probable that US competitivity is affected negatively by the revaluation of the dollar, as has been shown by the course of US exports in the early months of 1981. The loss of competitivity has consequences for the balance of payments that can be contained only if the United States regains self-sufficiency in energy, as Britain did through North Sea oil production. Indeed, Reagan lifted price controls on domestic oil and natural gas precisely in order rapidly to stimulate internal supply. But it seems unlikely that the United States would want to repeat the British experience of replacing a surplus in trade in manufactures with a reduction of the energy deficit.

The American economy has more weapons in its arsenal than the British, for the United States commands unequalled financial and military power. It seems that the United States is now inclined to bring this power to bear to maintain and increase its surplus in trade in manufactures, bending the rules of international competition. Hence the agreements that have been signed with Japan in recent years, leading to Japan's adoption of 'voluntary restrictions' of its exports to the American market, first of steel, then of electronics, and finally of automobiles. At the same time, Japan has had to open its hitherto jealously protected markets to American imports, first of foodstuffs, later of various manufactured products; finally American firms were granted the right to bid for public contracts in telecommunications. These measures have already led to a reduction of the Japanese trade surplus with the United States, which had reached $12 thousand million in 1978. In exchange, the United States supported Japan against the EEC in the Geneva negotiations, the last phase of the Tokyo Round of multilateral trade talks. On that occasion the United States opposed approval of a European proposal to allow the adoption of trade restrictions against a particular country (Japan, in the event) instead of against all countries, as is presently the rule under the General Agreement on Tariffs and Trade (GATT). In other words: mercantilism for the United States, free trade for everyone else—such is the American position.

The whole of US trade policy is now governed by the principle of the total and unconditional assertion of American interests by any means necessary. Numerous initiatives are being taken to keep the Europeans out of Latin America, for in the past decade they have been casting covetous glances at this traditional US preserve. Support to reactionary regimes that can be manipulated by Washington more easily has been stepped up. Through its banking subsidiaries the United States largely controls the Latin American financial system, and the Reagan administration is pressing for the strengthening of organs of financial co-operation like the Inter-American Bank, which is closely overseen by the United States. Control of finance means control of trade flows. As part of the general battle, a great diplomatic contest is now under way for predominance in one of the most promising markets of Latin America: Mexico. In its efforts to keep the Europeans out of the Mexican market, the United States has gone so far as to propose the formation of a North American common market including Canada and Mexico. Mexico has thus far refused, but neither has it accepted urgent European proposals to increase trade, preferring to exert pressure on the United States to obtain trade concessions for its exports and equal treatment for Mexican immigrants to the United States. No European country has yet been able to purchase Mexican oil (with the rather unimportant exception of Spain, linked to Mexico by the bonds of *hispanidad*), because in exchange for oil, Mexico would have to agree to buy European manufactures and foodstuffs.

The Reagan administration has already made it clear that it wants to alter the situation in Sub-Saharan Africa to US advantage too. So far this region has been a virtual EEC monopoly, partly because of the recently renegotiated Lomé Convention with the ACP countries (Africa, the Caribbean, and the Pacific, though in reality the members are almost all African). The Lomé Convention guarantees preferential treatment on European markets for the products of European ex-colonies, in exchange for European predominance on these markets. The United States is now organizing protests by other developing countries that feel excluded by the agreement. But Washington is also moving more heavily toward political and potentially military penetration. The new administration seems not yet to have decided exactly what tack to take, and in particular what should be the role of South Africa, where American investment and trade is rising constantly, in the development of trade relations on the African continent.

In East Asia and Oceania the United States has conspicuously left the field to Japanese penetration, but there are signs that it would like to reappropriate some markets, if not alone then in association with Japan, with the latter subordinate to US interests. There are any number of instances: the opening to post-Mao China; the re-opening, partly in contradiction with policy toward China, of contacts with Taiwan; the continued US commitment in Korea; the pressure brought to bear on all the countries of Southeast Asia to form a free-export zone. India, on the other hand, seems less penetrable by US, and even European, capital, because of its very close trade relations with the Comecon, and with the USSR in particular. But India's need for some high-technology manufactures encourages it to keep its relations with the Western countries open.

But the real focal point of conflict between European and American capitalism is the Middle East. The economic fate of the EEC in the short and medium term will crucially depend on control of the markets of the Arab countries of OPEC. The Community must succeed in selling these countries a quantity of manufactures sufficient to cover European oil imports, or at least a significant portion of them, obtaining automatic credit for the remaining portion. As a whole, the Community has a hefty international payments deficit: the total balance of payments sank from a $15 thousand million surplus in 1978 to a $50 thousand million deficit in 1980. The EEC is in deficit with the United States, Japan, and OPEC; it has modest surpluses with the non-oil-producing developing countries and the socialist countries. If the financial haemorrhage caused by the deficit with the other areas persists, the EEC will find it impossible to finance its foreign trade with the developing countries and the socialist countries, both of which crucially depend on export credits. The first point of attack in reducing the Community deficit is the Middle East: the Europeans must drive the United States out of these markets whatever the cost.

This is what accounts for Europe's general coolness to the Camp David accords between Egypt and Israel, the EEC's growing involvement in the sale of arms to Arab countries, and the unfriendly attitude to the United States assumed by the EEC countries, especially France, throughout the Iranian events.

If the Middle East is the point of maximum intensity of the clash between Europe and America, assuming political and military as well as economic dimensions, trade relations between the Community and the United States and between the Community and Japan reflect the conflict in a less dramatic but more direct way. The EEC has to close its doors to the Japanese commercial invasion, especially after the diversion of Japanese exports from the American to the European market. Nevertheless, Germany, which is more heavily influenced by the United States, is reluctant to accept French and Italian protectionist proposals, in part, perhaps, because Bonn hopes that its industry will not fall victim to the blows of Japanese competition. In the meantime, trade relations between the Community and the United States are developing in a climate of guerrilla warfare, although both rivals are seeking to avert official declarations of war. In 1980 the United States managed to bring its trade surplus with the EEC to a post-war record of $25 thousand million, whereas in 1977 it had been close to zero. This surplus was achieved partly because of the devaluation of the dollar, partly because European exports to the United States were supplanted by goods produced in the United States through direct European investments, and partly because Washington engaged in mercantilist control of trade flows. Customs barriers to aid American steel, differential two-tier pricing of phosphate for fertilizer production by the American multinationals that control the world market, windfalls for the American chemical industry because of the abolition of price controls on national oil production: these are some of the instruments the United States is using against its European competitors. The Europeans are countering with similar manoeuvres. It seems certain that the United States will do all it can to prevent Europe from defending itself against American commercial penetration, although it is difficult to predict the exact moves.

The American strategy is tending to enhance centripetal forces within the European economy, generating a community of interest that may overcome traditional petty antagonisms. Aggressive American mercantilism is stimulating moves toward European protectionist closure through the creation of a reserved economic domain. Just as the United States wants to assure itself complete control of the markets of Latin America and, together with Japan, East Asia and Oceania, so the EEC is striving to consolidate its control of African and West Asian markets. To some extent, these developments would tend to ease the international crisis: the formation of distinct economic blocs whose trade relations would be regulated by official agreements would attenuate competition among the various capitalisms and would permit an economic recovery on regional levels.

Within each bloc it would be easy to organize a system of international payments and transfers so as to avert balance of payments crises in member countries. Moreover, the blocs would be so vast as to assure sufficient economies of scale to establish the highest technology in all industrial sectors, except perhaps in the aerospace industry. Powerful forces on both sides of the Atlantic are pressing in the direction of the formation of autonomous economic blocs, which would entail a more balanced system of international power and would favour the reprise of detente among the capitalist powers. But it seems hard to believe that the more aggressive forces of American capitalism would resign themselves to a solution that would effectively exclude American goods and capital from the Old World.

American policy-makers face a highly complex problem: how to maintain both the unity of the world capitalist market and the supremacy of the declining US economy. Maintenance of supremacy through mercantilist methods tends to undermine the unity of the world market; respect for free trade assures maintenance of that unity, but at the price of a loss of economic influence for US capitalism that could eventually become ruinous and lead to the extirpation of the most obvious advantages the Americans draw from the present order: supremacy of the dollar, control of international monetary and financial mechanisms, and so on.

The new administration seems bent on trying to resolve the dilemma drastically. The economic and social power of American capitalism is being reorganized in accordance with a programme of anti-democratic reaction aimed at destroying the welfare state and reducing the political influence of the trade unions and minorities. The ogre of excessive Soviet power is being conjured up, and under this pretext the maximum effort made to draw Europe and Japan into contingency plans for nuclear attack on the USSR: the notion that 'regional theatres' of nuclear war are possible is the latest theory. The threat of war is making the Europeans careful not to blunder in international and trade policy. The potential war would wreak its greatest destruction in Europe, where the greater portion of NATO's nuclear arsenal is now to be shifted.

May 1981

Preface

Questions of international finance have generally been considered both far removed from pressing national economic problems, themselves largely ascribed to internal factors, and of great technical complexity. The drama of events of the past decade, from the continuing rise in the price of oil to the successive devaluations of the dollar, to mention only the most striking events, has gone a long way to erode the first conviction, and it is becoming ever clearer how enormously difficult it is to control open economies of the type that prevail in Western Europe and North America. Understanding of international financial developments and their connection with the problems of the industrialized economies is nevertheless hampered by the technical difficulties inevitably associated with complex problems often quite remote from the practical experience even of the business leaders of national economies and financial systems.

The theoretical tradition of international monetary studies itself tends to obfuscate genuine understanding of the real evolution of these relations and of their role in the overall development of the capitalist system. Indeed, this tradition is firmly rooted in the assumption that the agents of the international economy are identical to those of the national economies—individual firms and consumers. It follows that the most desirable basis for the international monetary system is that which interferes least in the options of these agents and thereby minimizes the need for government intervention. Thus it was that the gold standard was long considered the best possible international monetary system. Later, after the establishment of the gold-exchange standard, discussion repeatedly focused on the institutional and functional features this system required if it was to operate in the manner most similar to the gold standard. More recently, the floating-exchange system has been put forward as the most appropriate theoretical model under contemporary conditions of fiduciary circulation and the inflexibility of internal prices. Discussion of the merits of the floating-exchange system as compared to the system of fixed exchange-rates under the gold-exchange standard is now the daily bread of international monetary economists.

This point of view has tended to focus attention on those aspects of the international financial system that influence the national economies most heavily—for example, the question of how to settle balances of payments, or the problem of the international transmission of inflation. But it has almost entirely obscured analysis of the factors that shape the evolution of the international monetary system itself—fundamentally the pressure generated by developments in the individual national economies. Indeed, theory has often concealed this problem outright, or has tried to exorcize it by claiming that it results from technical aspects of the international monetary system itself. It is enough to recall the hasty explanations of the end of the gold standard, depicted in more than a few handbooks as the consequence of an inadequate world supply of gold.

Naturally, this commentary on the state of analysis, like all simplifications, is somewhat exaggerated. There has in fact been no lack of heterodox voices and penetrating analyses of the pressures brought to bear on the international monetary system by the exigencies of the development of the various national economies. Indeed, at times this order of problem has stood at the very centre of scientific debate. It is undeniable, however, that we have seen few lucid theoretical frameworks within which these problems could be properly structured. The common element of most innovative positions on international monetary analysis (although it is rarely made explicit) is probably awareness that the protagonists of the international economy consist of national states, and not families and firms. These states seek to inflect the features of the international monetary system in accordance with their efforts to safeguard what, in the absence of any more precise term, we may call the 'national interest'. By shaping the monetary system, states seek to postpone, or even avoid altogether, the necessity to settle their balance of payments, to promote the international use of their own currency, and to garner additional advantages. The ultimate objectives may vary from country to country, and, of course, they change with time: the balance of various interests that determines government policy in the national economy also determines which objectives the state will seek to attain through its action in the realm of international finance. These objectives may be, for example, defence of full employment, maximization of the rate of development, expansion of the share of industrial production in gross national product, protection of investment abroad, and many others. Naturally, the stronger a country is, both economically and politically, the more it will be able to mould the international monetary system in its favour. But weak countries can attempt to intervene in the operation of the monetary system too, and can even form coalitions in their efforts to protect their own interests.

Economic analysis must not halt on the threshold of these problems, but should delve into the varying interests of the countries that participate in international monetary relations. In recent years, moreover, economists have increasingly shifted their thinking about the basic trends that underlie the evolution of the international monetary system and the policies that foster these trends. A few of the more notable economists who have concentrated on these questions are C.F. Bergsten, R.N. Cooper, C. Kindleberger, and M. von Neumann Whitman in the United States, Lord Balogh, Lord Kaldor, A. Schonfield, and the late F. Hirsch in Britain, and many others of similar stature. It should also be recalled that the French school, in particular J. Rueff, has had the distinction of constantly focusing attention on these sorts of problems throughout the post-war period, despite the peculiarities of some of their contentions.

The chapters of the present book consist largely of edited and updated versions of articles that first appeared in the journals *Inchiesta*, *Politica ed economia*, *Quaderni piacentini*, *Quaderni di studi e ricerche dell'Istituto di economia di Modena*. Their aim is to clarify some of the current problems of international economics, viewed from the standpoint of the conflicts of interest among national economies. While I have sought to take proper account of the specialized literature, the themes it emphasizes, and the conceptual structures of which it avails itself, I have deliberately chosen to make sure that the level of exposition is such that the arguments can be understood by non-specialists. At the same time, the discussion is supplemented by a bibliographical apparatus and statistical documentation that will assist those readers who wish to go into the various subjects more deeply. I do hope, however, that my effort to erect a conceptual framework within which the subjects discussed can be placed and through which greater theoretical depth can be attained, will not escape the reader.

The outline of the book is as follows. The first chapter, which analyses the dollar standard, sets out the context in which the main events in the international monetary system during the 1970s should be placed. The second chapter goes on to analyse the various phases of the devaluation of the dollar during the seventies, seeking to assess its effects on the competitivity of the American economy. The third locates the factors responsible for the stagnation of the international economy in the perverse functioning of the international financial order and its practical subordination to private finance. The fourth, which begins with the difficulties encountered by the United States in its efforts to recover commercial competitivity, discusses the strategy adopted by West Germany in defending itself against the depreciation of the dollar and examines both the reasons for Germany's deflationary policy and its effects on the European economy.

The fifth chapter explains why Germany has an interest in promoting the currency union among the European countries, the European Monetary System, and strives to detail the negative consequences this has for the Italian economy, as a case in point. Finally, the sixth chapter extends the analysis to the new tendencies toward industrialization in the Third World, promoted by the industrialized countries through international finance, and examines the financial and structural aspects of the relation between this industrialization and the evolution of the European economic crisis.

I would like to extend my thanks to Professor Federico Caffè, with whom I was able to discuss at length and from whom I received criticisms of earlier drafts of these essays. I would also like to thank my colleagues of the Faculty of Economics and Commerce of the University of Modena for the atmosphere of lively discussion that has impelled the deepening of many of the ideas set out here. Particular thanks are due Salvatore Biasco and Michele Salvati, who encouraged me to publish this book. Naturally, responsibility for what is argued here is mine alone.

University of Modena
September 1979

1
The Dollar Standard

1. The End of Bretton Woods

Discussions of the problems of international finance commonly cite two dates, almost interchangeably, to mark the end of the Bretton Woods system: 15 August 1971 and 19 March 1973. It was in August 1971 that the United States, unilaterally withdrawing from commitments assumed under the Bretton Woods agreement, indefinitely suspended the convertibility of the dollar for gold and other reserve assets.[1] In March 1973 the central banks of the major industrialized countries renounced their commitment to maintain the quotation of their respective currencies within a band of $\pm 2.25\%$ with respect to the dollar.[2] Both these commitments—convertibility of the dollar for gold on the one hand and fixed exchange rates on the other—seemed equally essential characteristics of the old system; so much so that even after the dollar could no longer be converted for gold, many still insisted that the maintenance of fixed exchange rates was sufficient to keep the spirit of Bretton Woods alive.

With hindsight these events can be viewed with greater assurance. It now seems clear that the really essential characteristic of Bretton

[1] For the relevant passage of the speech of then President Nixon, see R. Solomon, *The International Monetary System, 1945–1976*, New York 1977, p. 186.

[2] This decision was made by the central banks of the countries of the Group of Ten plus Switzerland (an associate member), along with the central banks of the smaller members of the European Economic Community (EEC): Ireland, Denmark, and Luxemburg. The Group of Ten is made up of the major industrialized countries—the United States, West Germany, Japan, Canada, Britain, France, Belgium, the Netherlands, Italy, and Sweden—which agreed under the General Agreement to Borrow in December 1961 to extend loans to the International Monetary Fund whenever shortages of liquidity arose.

Woods was not the maintenance of parity but the convertibility of the dollar. Indeed, it is important to understand that exchange rates were not completely fixed even under the Bretton Woods system. Triffin has recently recalled that between 1948 and 1965 no less than ninety-four members of the International Monetary Fund altered the parity of their currencies—many more than once.[3] On the other hand, the present system of exchange rates does not absolutely reflect the rules of free fluctuation: after March 1973, the central banks rapidly discovered that it was simply not possible to abandon exchange rates to market forces completely.

2. Flexible Exchange Rates

The reason for this lack of confidence on the part of the central banks lay in their observation that variations in exchange rates, far from correcting disequilibria in the balance of payments that cause them, could easily stimulate cumulative processes that would tend to aggravate these disequilibria. The sequence of events can be briefly outlined as follows. Trade flows, not to mention flows of many services, do not respond to variations in exchange rates very rapidly.[4] The initial effect of a devaluation is therefore to reduce foreign-currency income, which exerts even greater downward pressure on the exchange rate.[5] (Conversely, the initial effect of an upward

[3] '"Europe and the Money Muddle" Revisited', *Banca Nazionale del Lavoro, Quarterly Review*, March 1978.

[4] By speed of response is meant the degree of elasticity over a brief period, the first three or six months after a change in the exchange rate, for example.

[5] In fact the *physical* quantities of commodities exported and imported do not vary much during the first few months after a shift in the exchange rate, because of rigidity and inertia. Deliveries of exported and imported goods that had been contracted in previous months continue. It takes time before the higher price in national currency brings about a search for domestic substitutes (where these exist) and a consequent diminution of imports in physical terms; it likewise takes time before the lower price of exports in foreign currency generates influxes of new orders from abroad, and even more time to fill these orders and thus increase exports in physical terms. On the other hand, the variation of the exchange rate produces an immediate effect on the *value* in foreign currency of the trade balance. Let us make the restrictive hypothesis that the exports of a country whose money is undergoing a shift in exchange rate are invoiced in the national currency, while all imports are invoiced in foreign currency. Then, if the national currency depreciates, the income in foreign money generated by exports is automatically diminished by a percentage equal to the depreciation of the national currency. Payments for imports in foreign money, on the other hand, are unchanged. The country whose money depreciates thus suffers a worsening of its foreign-trade

revaluation is to augment the inflow of foreign currency, which tends to drive the exchange rate still higher.) The monetary authorities must then intervene to make sure that the cumulative effects of this process do not result in a rapid slide of the exchange rate in the event of a devaluation or an excessive skyrocketing of the rate in the event of a revaluation.[6] Variations in exchange rates, however, do react on domestic price levels very rapidly. Depreciation of a currency accelerates inflation and thus reinforces the trend toward devaluation;[7] appreciation of a currency contains the rise of prices and thus reinforces the tendency toward revaluation. When a national currency depreciates, the cost of imports, as measured in that currency, rises. If these imports consist of primary products or components, the increase in their prices is transmitted to the price of the finished products through increments in the cost of production. An increase in the prices of imported finished goods also produces a rise in price levels, because it 'raises the ceiling' of international competition and thereby enables domestic producers to raise the prices of their own

---

balance as an immediate consequence of devaluation, while the *physical quantities traded* remain unchanged. A symmetrical situation pertains in the case of an appreciation of a national currency. Then the currency income of exports rises by the amount the currency was revalued relative to foreign currencies, while currency payments for imports remain unchanged. Consequently, a country that devalues immediately suffers a decline in its reserves, while one that revalues augments its reserves. This monetary effect of variations in the exchange rate is the less pronounced the more we relax our hypothesis about the currency in which foreign trade is invoiced. In the case of devaluation, the lower the share of exports invoiced in national currency, the smaller will be the reduction of currency income from exports. Account must also be taken of the price policy of companies that (for example, again in the case of devaluation) can decide to raise the price of exported goods in order to widen profit margins, even if they invoice in national currency. Nevertheless, the effect on the trade balance is generally quite considerable in practice. In the scientific literature it is known as the 'J-curve effect', so named because of the shape of the graph representing the foreign-trade balance of a country whose money has been devalued on the y-axis and the time elapsed since the devaluation, measured in months, on the x-axis. Because of the existence of the J-curve, monetary authorities have to increase the volume of their interventions in exchange markets to support their own currency after a devaluation, if a chain-reaction is to be prevented. See F. Hirsch and D. Higham, 'Floating Rates: Expectations and Experience', *Three Banks Review*, June 1974.

[6] For a clear analysis of this sequence of events, see S. Biasco, *L'inflazione nei paesi capitalistici industrializzati–Il ruolo della loro interdipendenza*, Milan 1979, pp. 140–46.

[7] Experience shows that the rapidity with which inflation accelerates after a devaluation tends to rise in successive incidents of devaluation, because the economy 'learns' this effect. The protagonists of the various stages of the process of production thus tend, so to speak, to 'index' the prices of their products to the variations in the rate of exchange.

products. The opposite effect pertains in cases of revaluation of a national currency.[8]

A review of the available data seems to suggest that the speed at which prices respond to depreciation of national currencies is high;[9] the effects on domestic price levels in the event of upward revaluation of the national currency, on the other hand, are relatively slight, because of the rigid price floors of modern economies, as a result of which corporations do *not* transmit decreases in the cost of imports in national currency to final products.[10] Vicious circles are thus quite easily set in motion: devaluation leads to inflation, which leads in turn to further devaluation, and so on. Economies that get trapped in such circles find it quite difficult to break out of them. Virtuous circles are possible too, in principle: revaluation, followed by a slackening of price increases, followed by further revaluation, and so on. Except that since price levels respond less elastically to revaluations, virtuous circles require healthy doses of deflation in order to take hold. The existence of speculation, which can come into play at any point in either process, intensifying whichever inflection of exchange rates is under way, significantly increases the probability of vicious, and not virtuous, circles: the interaction between exchange rates and price levels ensures that speculation in currency markets acts almost

[8] The literature on the interaction of exchange rates and price levels is now quite extensive. For an overall view, see A.D. Crockett and M. Goldstein, 'Inflation Under Fixed and Flexible Exchange Rates', *IMF Staff Papers*, November 1976, and W.S. Salant, 'International Transmission of Inflation', in L.B. Krause and W.S. Salant (eds.), *Worldwide Inflation – Theory and Recent Experience*, Washington 1977.

[9] In the cases of Britain and Italy, unofficial estimates are that 80% of the average devaluation is transmitted to consumer price increases within twelve months. It must also be remembered that in both these economies the effect of devaluation on prices is mitigated by the independence of the prices of major agricultural products because of the mechanism of the 'green pound' and 'green lira'. 'The 'green' exchange rates were introduced in the European Community after the devaluation of some EEC currencies in an effort to avert damage to the operation of the Common Agricultural Policy. Their existence is nevertheless temporary, although continuing devaluations permitted the maintenance of 'green' exchange rates for the lira and the pound at least through the end of 1979. Green money works this way. When the lira is devalued, the Community authorities continue to derive the 'intervention prices' on the Italian market from those fixed for the entire Community in units of account, converting these units into lire at the lira exchange rate *prior* to the devaluation (the 'green lira'). For a discussion of the experience of 'green money' with particular reference to the containment of inflation, see R. Maclennan, 'Food Prices and the Common Agricultural Policy', *Three Banks Review*, September 1978.

[10] On this asymmetry, see M. Goldstein, 'Downward Price Inflexibility, Ratchet Effects, and the Inflationary Impact of Import Price Changes: Some Empirical Tests', *IMF Staff Papers*, November 1977.

exclusively as a destabilizing factor.[11]

Currency authorities in national economies are therefore highly cautious in abandoning exchange rates to market forces. Obviously, this does not mean that devaluations and revaluations do not occur, but it does mean that the mechanism by which exchange rates vary is quite similar to the way official par values operated under the old system. Countries whose exchange rates are out of line—in other words, whose economies are no longer competitive—effect 'snap' devaluations, by abandoning efforts to support their currency on exchange markets and by playing on the differential of interest rates abroad in order to encourage withdrawals of short-term deposits. When the exchange rate has been depressed[12] enough to render the economy competitive again, the authorities intervene massively on the market to defend the new 'par value' and prevent unwanted fluctuations.[13]

This mode of operation of the currency system has been termed flexible, or floating, exchange rates. Now, it turns out that flexible exchange rates function so similarly to fixed exchange rates that reserve requirements have not even been reduced. On the contrary, the demand for international reserves on the part of the industrialized countries has even increased, because of the greater difficulty in stabilizing exchange rates in the absence of coordination with other countries.[14]

There is, nevertheless, a profound difference between the systems of fixed and floating exchange rates: under the new system countries are much more willing to allow variations of the rate. This indulgence of variations is not the result of any neo-mercantilist attitude like that reflected in the 'beggar-thy-neighbour' policy applied in the thirties. Indeed, one of the greatest concerns of the founders of the Bretton

---

[11] P.A. Samuelson stresses this point in his 'Economic Problems Concerning a Futures Market in Foreign Exchange', in *The Futures Market in Foreign Currencies*, International Monetary Market of the Chicago Mercantile Exchange, Inc., n.d.

[12] Sometimes the authorities prefer to devalue the currency even further in order to manoeuvre more easily against speculation when reestablishing a balanced level of exchange.

[13] This was, for example, the experience of the round of devaluations by the industrialized countries in 1976, initiated by the lira (in January), followed by the French franc (March), the pound sterling (April), and the Canadian dollar (November).

[14] See H.R. Heller and M.S. Kahn, 'The Demand for International Reserves Under Fixed and Floating Exchange Rates', *IMF Staff Papers*, December 1978.

Woods system was precisely to avoid any repetition of those policies.[15] Today, however, the need to alter exchange rates arises in part from the desire to attenuate the varying impact of the rise in oil prices on rates of inflation, and therefore on competitivity, in the various economies. In part, however, the industrialized economies are seeking to compensate for the effects of the continuing devaluations of the dollar.[16]

The trouble is that devaluations restore competitivity only temporarily, because of the effects on the rate of inflation described above. A country that wants to maintain a certain level of competitivity becomes enmeshed in a succession of devaluations, and pays the price of a very high inflation rate. In real terms, then, exchange rates have actually varied little, since the variations in nominal exchange rates for nearly all countries have been almost completely counterbalanced by increments in rates of inflation compared to the rest of the world.[17]

The collateral effect of devaluation on inflation renders the current situation completely different from that of the thirties. In the past this effect was quite obvious, because of the lesser extent of foreign economic links, the lower degree of 'indexing', and finally, because of the very strong fall in the prices of raw materials, which markedly diminished the costs of imports for the industrialized countries.

3. The Freedom of the Dollar

Nevertheless, there is one country in the world today for which the inflationary consequences of devaluation are negligible: the United States. The fundamental reason for this is that the American market is much less dependent on foreign trade.[18] In practice, the United

---

[15] On the currency situation in the thirties, see R. Nurkse, *International Currency Experience*, Geneva 1944. On the problems related to the constitution of the Bretton Woods system, see R. Harrod, *The Life of John Maynard Keynes*, London 1951.

[16] In fact, even the wave of competing devaluations of the 1930s was initiated by the devaluation of the most important currencies, the pound sterling in 1931 and the dollar in 1933.

[17] For a description of the indices of rates of exchange and prices employed in evaluating the variation in the competitivity of an economy, see *World Financial Markets*, April 1979, pp. 6–13.

[18] The sum of imports and exports divided by national income hovers around .15 for the United States, compared with .50 for the European economies. The other often-mentioned factor, that American imports are invoiced in dollars, is much less significant, because of the belated adjustment of the prices of raw materials. I will return to this point later.

States is the only country genuinely free to devalue. A typical calculation estimates that approximately 25% of an average dollar devaluation is transferred to consumer prices over a period of two years.[19] It may thus be supposed that a devaluation of the dollar tends to produce greater inflationary pressure in the rest of the world than in the United States itself. Indeed, price quotations for raw materials, exchange of which is invoiced almost exclusively in dollars, are adjusted to the average depreciation of the dollar within a relatively brief period.[20] Because of this distinctive feature of raw materials prices, a country that wants to avert the indirect inflationary pressures generated by the devaluation of the dollar will

[19] On the relationship between devaluation and inflation in the American case, see P. Isard, 'The Price Effects of Exchange-Rate Changes' and S.Y. Kwack, 'The Effect of Foreign Inflation on Domestic Prices and the Relative Price Advantage of Exchange-Rate Changes', both in P.B. Clark, D.E. Logue, and R.J. Sweeney (eds.), *The Effects of Exchange-Rate Adjustment*, OASIA Research Department of the Treasury, Washington 1977. Later and more comprehensive data may be found in P. Hooper and B. Lowrly, *Impact of the Dollar Depreciation on the US Price Level: An Analytical Survey of Empirical Estimates*, Board of Governors of the Federal Reserve System, International Finance Discussion Papers, no. 128, January 1979. According to this review, the maximum estimate obtained for the effect of the devaluation of the dollar on US consumer prices, using bilateral trade weights to assess the depreciation and taking account of the delayed effects of the increase in the price of oil, amounted to about 30% in two years. In other words, on the average, a 10% depreciation of the dollar would add about 3% to inflation over two years. Other estimates yielded lower values.

[20] For the relationship between the dollar exchange rate and the index of raw materials quotations, see the second chapter of the *Annual Report* of the Bank for International Settlements for various years. Useful suggestions in this regard may be gleaned from a comparison between the dollar and pound indices of the quotations, both given in the British journal *The Economist*. The evolution of these indices shows that when sterling appreciates relative to the dollar, the index of quotations in pounds rises less than that in dollars, and vice versa. The behaviour of raw materials prices can be explained by the strong organization of the markets for these materials and the presence of extensive credit facilities for those who operate in this market; it is thus relatively easy to 'hedge'. An economic operator is said to be hedging when he protects himself against unfavourable shifts in the posted prices of a commodity he needs by buying the commodity and then selling it in the futures market, or by contracting a debt that is expected to depreciate. Hedging, then (unlike speculation), entails no risk, since the operator holds a *closed* position. For example, a flour-milling company that has to supply a quantity of flour at some future date, say in six months' time, will guard itself against potential increases in the price of wheat by buying wheat immediately and simultaneously selling the same quantity on the futures market for delivery in six months at the higher price it fears could develop. If the price does actually rise, then the company uses the wheat it acquired to effect the delivery, without resupplying itself. The future sale at the higher price will be satisfied by buying for cash on the market at the future date. Naturally, since all hedgings can be closed, it is virtually indispensable that some speculation be occurring: someone has to assume *open* positions. On these questions, see N. Kaldor, 'Speculation and Economic Stability', in *Essays on Economic Stability and Growth*, London 1960.

have to revalue its own currency relative to the dollar by a percentage *at least equal* to the average depreciation of the dollar relative to all currencies. If a country wants to avert the inflationary pressures arising from a rise in raw materials prices in excess of the average depreciation of the dollar (which rise is provoked by excesses of demand, albeit often speculative, such as occurred in 1972–74), then it will have to revalue its own currency relative to the dollar by a percentage *greater than* the average depreciation of the dollar. This, for instance, is what happened to the German mark during the 1970s. Nevertheless, it is not at all certain that for any particular country the reduction in inflation thus attained will suffice to compensate for the loss of competitivity occasioned by the revaluation of the country's currency. In sum, it is therefore possible that countries for which imports of raw materials represent a significant share of their own gross national product may, as a consequence of a devaluation of the dollar, suffer an increase in inflation equal to—if not greater than— that suffered by the United States itself.

So long as the United States was obligated to exchange dollars for gold, American governments were reluctant to allow the dollar to depreciate. Indeed, the mere possibility of depreciation could have induced countries holding dollar reserves to convert these dollars in an effort to drive their value upward—their value in gold that is, since under the Bretton Woods system the dollar's 'par value' was fixed in gold. Thus, given the massive conversion of dollars into gold, which would have depleted American gold reserves, the role of gold would surely have become predominant, and sooner or later this would have entailed the evolution of the international monetary system toward a structure under which the dollar would cease to be the prevalent means of reserve.[21]

This does not necessarily mean that departure from the gold-exchange standard would have led to a rebirth of the gold standard itself, a system under which all countries, including the United States, would have been compelled to settle their trade deficits by selling off gold. The dethroning of the dollar could have given way to a parity system conferring no particular privileges on any one currency. It

---

[21] This judgement is accepted even by the more open-minded US scholars. See C.F. Bergsten, *The Dilemmas of the Dollar*, New York 1975. Bergsten joined the Carter administration as undersecretary of the Treasury for international monetary affairs.

seems clear that the prototype of this sort of system was the grandiose Keynes Plan for the reconstitution of the international monetary order after the Second World War.[22] The essential element of any such plan is that liquidity be supplied through the issue of a fiduciary international currency such that seigniorage would not be ascribed to any particular country, but indifferently to all countries in proportion to their respective shares of world trade. For a brief period in the seventies it seemed that the creation of Special Drawing Rights (SDRs)[23] signalled the beginning of the transformation of the system in this direction. Had this evolution continued, a system could have emerged under which the legitimate US interest in improving, through devaluation, the declining competitivity of its own economy[24] and the painful recognition of the existence of new economic powers alongside the United States, through their admission to seigniorage over the international money supply, could have been combined. Utopians could well have hoped that under such a system seigniorage would have been allotted to the weaker countries more than proportionally to their economic weight, or even totally, in an effort to accelerate their development.[25]

With the suspension of the dollar's convertibility for gold, the United States managed on the one hand to obtain the freedom to devalue (and we have seen that under present economic conditions, it

[22] See 'Proposals for an International Clearing Union', reprinted in S.E. Harris (ed.), *The New Economics: Keynes' Influence on Theory and Public Policy*, New York 1947.

[23] This was decided by the Rio de Janeiro meeting of the IMF in September 1967. Special Drawing Rights are a fiduciary money created by the IMF and allocated to member countries in proportion to their share of participation in the Fund itself. The value of an SDR, originally set at the equivalent of a dollar's worth of refined gold, is now calculated with reference to the value of a 'basket' of currencies, the composition of which was last modified in July 1978. For more information, see F. Caffè, *Lezioni di politica economica*, Turin 1978, chapter 14. For a quantitative estimate of the share of SDRs in total international liquidity, see below, pp. 62. 'Seigniorage' is a term used in international monetary analysis to refer broadly to the privileges accruing to the country whose money serves as the major international means of payment. The country that holds seigniorage is able to increase the international money supply simply by printing more of its own currency.

[24] This point will be discussed in chapter 2.

[25] This was proposed during the 1970s, by allotting SDRs only to developing countries. On the 'link' between the problem of underdevelopment and the problem of international liquidity, see F. Hirsch, *Money International*, London 1967, chapter 20.

is the only country free to do so),[26] and on the other hand fully to maintain mastery over the world supply of means of payment.

4. The Rise of Dollar Holdings

The situation created once the dollar was no longer convertible for gold has been called the 'dollar standard'. This terminology seems entirely appropriate, although there has been no lack of critics who, emphasizing the literal significance of the word 'standard',[27] deny that the term accurately describes the present international monetary situation. How can the dollar, whose value is constantly shifting, serve as the basis of a system of monetary relations? But the expression does capture one aspect of the situation rather well: the dollar may not be the reference point for other currencies, but it is surely the only point of reference for the dollar itself. Once the threat of the potential conversion of foreign-held dollars into gold had been eliminated, the limits to the injection of dollars into international circulation disappeared as well. After 1971 the world was flooded with dollars. This phenomenon was somewhat belatedly recognized by observers of the financial scene, who, with customary lexical resourcefulness, coined a succession of new expressions—first 'dollar glut', later 'dollar overhang'—during the first half of the past decade. The mass of dollars in international circulation has continued to rise since then, but no need has been felt to mint fresh terms with which to describe a situation that now borders on the absurd.

[26] Recently many observers, for the most part American officials, have maintained that the relative foreign value of the dollar has actually not changed much from its Smithsonian parity (the central exchange rates among industrialized countries established by the Smithsonian agreement of December 1971), the average depreciation of the dollar allegedly being almost entirely compensated for by differential inflation rates unfavourable to the United States. But this aggregate reading of the data is misleading. In reality, the nominal depreciation of the dollar relative to the Japanese yen and the German mark was so high during the 1970s (more than 50%) that the difference in inflation, calculated according to the consumer price index, does not suffice to compensate; it leaves a real devaluation of 20–30%. Many countries in turn devalued their currency relative to the dollar, in particular three that together account for a share of total US foreign trade equal to that of all Western Europe: Canada, Mexico, and Brazil. Consequently, the United States became less competitive relative to countries of a lower level of development, and more competitive relative to countries of levels of development approximately similar to its own.

[27] In the sense of reference point, unit of measure, or that on which a system is founded.

No one, it seems, thought it useful to employ the good old category of seigniorage to analyse the complex reality of today's international monetary system—perhaps because the word is now indelibly associated with De Gaulle's invective against the 'exorbitant privileges' of the United States. But these privileges were actually used with great moderation in the sixties; it would probably be natural to describe American behaviour toward the rest of the world today with more weighty terms perhaps more appropriate to court records than to international finance.

Table 1 shows that during the nineteen years from 1951 to 1969 official US liabilities (meaning liabilities to foreign central banks and international institutions) rose by $12 thousand million, nearly all during the latter part of the 1960s. During the nine subsequent years[28] the growth of this debt soared by $134 thousand million,

Table 1

Evolution of Official US Liabilities and World Reserves
(in thousands of millions of $)

	(1)	(2)	(3)	(4)	(5)
1951/1969	− 19.4	7.3	12.1	30.0	40%
1970	− 10.7			15.7	
1971	− 30.5			32.8	
1972	− 11.1			26.9	
1973	− 5.3			7.0	
1974	− 8.3	8.3	134.3	33.0	50%
1975	− 3.5			17.4	
1976	− 8.7			32.2	
1977	− 33.5			47.1	
1978	− 31.0			52.6	
Total	− 162.0	15.6	146.4	294.7	49%

(1) Deficits on the basis of official settlements of US balance of payments.
(2) Liquidation of official US assets abroad.
(3) Rise of official US foreign liabilities (column 2 minus column 1).
(4) Increase of official world reserves.
(5) Share of increase of world reserves composed of official US liabilities (column 3 divided by column 4).

Sources: Bank of Italy, Bank for International Settlements, Deutsche Bundesbank.

[28] It is preferable to include 1970 in the second series, because that was the year of the beginning of the significant withdrawals of funds from the United States that were responsible for the collapse of the Bretton Woods system; it was also the year of the first fluctuation of the German mark.

which, even if inflation is taken into account, represents a very sizable increase compared with the previous period. World reserves also rose greatly during this period as a result of the American deficits, and the share of these reserves constituted by official US liabilities rose from 10% to 50%. Such statistics, which suggest a strong increase in American seigniorage, are on the contrary considered irrelevant by some financial commentators. In the highly qualified opinion of Michael W. Blumenthal, secretary of the treasury in the Carter administration, there is no longer any sense—if there ever was—in speaking of the privileges of the country that issues the reserve currency, for the following reasons: 'First, because with flexible exchange rates dollar accumulations by other countries are less an automatic result of the operation of the system and more a matter of discretion; second, because with the present large and open capital markets, onshore and off, many other deficit countries [other than the United States] can at any time be borrowing dollars in large amounts and putting them on the [currency] market—with the result that [official] borrowing to finance US deficits is not the major source of growth in the supply of dollars'.[29]

5. Interpretations of Seigniorage

Blumenthal's observations suggest that the American contention is that the link between private and official international liquidity makes it virtually impossible to ascribe seigniorage to any particular country. If we are to isolate the kernel of truth in this assertion, it is opportune to recall the meaning of 'seigniorage'. It refers to the profit that accrues to the country whose currency is used as an international means of payment, and it is equal, quantitatively, to the net amount of money this country places at the disposal of the rest of the world.[30]

[29] 'Remarks Before the International Monetary Conference – Mexico City, Mexico', *Department of the Treasury News*, 24 May 1978.

[30] The literature on seigniorage is vast, even if we concentrate only on the 1970s. See R.Z. Aliber, 'The Costs and Benefits of the US as a Reserve Currency Country', *Quarterly Journal of Economics*, August 1964; H. Grubel, 'The Benefits and Costs of Being the World Banker', *National Banking Review*, September 1964; and the essays collected in R. Mundell and A. Swoboda (eds.), *Monetary Problems in the World Economy*, Chicago 1969. For an analysis of British seigniorage, see B.J. Cohen, *The Future of Sterling as an International Currency*, London 1971.

This profit subsists whether the possession of reserve currency is voluntary, the fruit of an agreement between the issuing country and the others, or obligatory, as it is under the dollar standard. The advantage lies in the fact that the country that issues the reserve currency can finance its own deficits with payments in its own currency, without having to resort to financial assets abroad previously accumulated through foreign surpluses. In other words, the country whose money serves as the reserve currency appropriates either real resources produced abroad (in the event that its balance of payments deficit is a current-account deficit) or claims to future use of these resources (if the deficit is a capital-account deficit. We must also consider the particular case in which the capital-account deficit is the result of an outflow of capital for direct investment abroad; then the residents of the reserve-currency country acquire the right to use foreign resources on foreign territory). It has been widely noted, of course, that the deficits of the reserve-currency country may be caused by this role itself. The reserve-currency country has to supply liquidity to other countries, which need this liquidity in order to augment their own reserves in proportion to the growth of trade. Nevertheless, it is legitimate to regard as deficits induced by the issuing country's reserve-currency role only those deficits that are clearly ascribable to some initiative taken by the authorities in the countries that use the reserve currency, either a bond issue or an effort by foreign governments or their agents to raise funds on the financial markets of the reserve-currency country. Naturally, if the reserve-currency country shows deficits on other items, access to its capital market by other countries will be proportionally reduced, and the other countries will then be in a position to gather the reserves through a corresponding surplus. It is therefore illegitimate to claim that the entire deficit of the reserve-currency country is caused by the desire of other countries to accumulate reserves. It should also be noted that in the 1960s, when the United States began to encounter balance of payments difficulties, restrictions were imposed precisely on capital movements, going so far as to ration official issues on the American market itself.

Nevertheless, so long as the reserve currency continues to be convertible for other assets (gold, for example), the country that issues this currency does come under strong pressure to limit the quantity of its money in circulation, in order to avert the threat of sudden massive conversions into these other assets. In the literature, this is called the 'confidence problem'.[31]

The confidence problem was one of the most hotly contested issues throughout the 1960s, and led to the invention of numerous indices of the international financial position of the United States, the deterioration of which would in practice act as an alarm signal that confidence in the dollar was crumbling.[32]

A restricted interpretation of 'seigniorage' has been evolving in connection with the unfolding discussion of the confidence problem. On this view seigniorage consists in the privilege of the reserve-currency country to accumulate short-term debts in order to finance long-term credits or investments abroad. At the root of this interpretation lies the observation that *through the end of 1970* the United States registered no trade deficits, and during the twenty years between 1950 and 1970 there were current-account deficits in only six years. Through the end of the sixties, then, American deficits could be attributed exclusively to capital movements, and in particular long-term capital movements and foreign investments. Indeed, the base balance (obtained by adding the balances of long-term capital flows and the current-account balance) was consistently in deficit from 1950 to 1970, except for one year, when the account balanced.

It thus seemed plausible to uphold an interpretation of seigniorage according to which the United States accumulates short-term debts by ceding dollars abroad destined to flow into the official reserves of foreign central banks, which would later redeposit them as short-term deposits in the us financial market. Parallel to these short-term foreign debts, the United States acquires long-term credits abroad, or makes direct investments. In other words, the United States acts as an investment bank whose balance-sheet would show short-term debits and non-liquid assets. Seigniorage was then said to consist in the ability to act as financial broker on a world scale, to command sweeping access to short-term credits from foreign countries. But the real gain for the reserve-currency country, namely its appropriation of foreign resources, was said to correspond merely to the difference between the debit and credit account, the equivalent of a bank's brokerage income.[33] Seigniorage in this narrow sense is a patri-

---

[31] The first to raise this problem in regard to the dollar was R. Triffin, *Gold and the Dollar Crisis*, Hartford, Connecticut 1960.

[32] See the review in Bergsten, *The Dilemmas of the Dollar*, pp. 124–174.

[33] For an interpretation of seigniorage along these lines, see R.I. McKinnon, 'Private and International Money: The Case for the Dollar', *Essays on International Finance*, no. 74, April 1969.

monial sort of concept referring to the international financial position of the centre-country, while seigniorage in the broader connotation is more properly a fluid concept relating to inflows and outflows in the balance of payments.

6. The Link Between Private and Official Liquidity

Until the emergence of an international dollar market on a vast scale[34]—the Eurodollar market—the seigniorage the United States derived year after year from its role as the reserve-currency country was uniquely determined by the American balance of payments on the basis of official settlements. Since the only dollars in circulation outside the United States were those held in the official reserves of central banks, this balance, measuring the variation in dollar reserves (that is, the variation in official US debt), automatically indicated how many dollars the American government had released into world circulation. Since the middle of the 1960s, the volume of dollars in circulation worldwide in the hands of private non-residents—called Eurodollars—has been rising. As has often been demonstrated,[35] the mass of dollar-denominated deposits does not correspond exactly to any particular US balance of payments—nor, most important, does it equal the balance as computed on the basis of official settlements.

With the growth of the Eurodollar market there is no longer any equivalence, nor even functional relationship, between variations in official US liabilities and the total dollars held outside the United States. To begin with, an enormous volume of dollars are in private hands.[36] Second, the dollar holdings of the central banks include not only assets deposited in the United States, but also dollar deposits held outside the United States, in Eurobanks. The variation in the volume of official dollar reserves has become greater than that of official US liabilities, the discrepancy caused by the intervention of the

[34] The Eurocurrency market was born in 1957, but by the middle of the 1960s its total dimension had risen to only about $10 thousand million, while at the end of 1978 it had soared to the equivalent of $900 thousand million, two-thirds of which was in dollars, the rest in other currencies.

[35] See G. Dufey and I.H. Giddy, *The International Money Market*, Englewood Cliffs, New Jersey 1978, chapter 3.

[36] A further complication arises from the fact that the Eurodollar market receives funds from and makes loans to American residents; in other words, it brokers for residents.

Eurodollar market. Through this market the central banks recycle dollars among themselves, increasing official dollar reserves without increasing official American liabilities.[37] In addition, central banks can order dollar transfers 'through the back door', thus automatically diminishing both the volume of reserves and the volume of official American liabilities.[38]

Moreover, since the Eurodollar market permits a genuine creation of deposits, similar to what occurs in a national banking system, it enables the central banks to create dollar deposits through operations with the Eurobanks; with these they can feed their own reserves, in addition to facilitating the recycling of the reserves of the central banks themselves,[39] thus permitting a single deposit to function simultaneously as the reserve asset of two or more central banks.

There are now serious indications that the Euromarket coefficient has begun to exceed unity in recent years, thus causing a net creation of deposits.[40] Finally, since the Eurodollar market is in direct communication with the American money market, the demand for funds on the part of central banks can be satisfied by drawing funds from the United States into the Eurodollar market.[41] The loans issued by American banks to central banks through Euromarket

[37] A hypothetical scenario could run this way. The Bank of Italy withdraws a dollar deposit from a US bank and places it in a Eurobank in London. Official Italian dollar reserves are unchanged, but American liabilities are diminished by the amount of the deposit. The Eurobank in London in turn loans the dollar deposit to the Bank of Greece, which redeposits it in the United States. Official Italian dollar reserves are still unchanged, Greek reserves have risen by the amount of the deposit, and official American liabilities have risen, returning to their initial level. The bottom line is that US liabilities are unchanged, but the level of dollar reserves has risen. In 1971, however, the central banks of the Group of Ten agreed to cease depositing funds on the market; the agreement was renewed in 1979.

[38] This happens when a central bank cedes dollars to local commercial banks, which then use these funds for commitments on the Eurodollar market. Italy resorted to this practice in the sixties, Germany and Japan in the seventies, in order to sustain the international expansion of their own banking systems.

[39] See T.D. Willet, 'The Eurocurrency Market, Exchange-Rate Systems, and National Financial Policies', in C.H. Stem, J.H. Makin, and D.E. Logue (eds.), *Eurocurrencies and the International Monetary System*, Washington 1976; and R.J. Sweeney and T. Willet, 'Eurodollars, Petrodollars, and World Liquidity and Inflation', *Journal of Monetary Economics*, supplement 1977.

[40] For an explanation of the transfers of funds that can give rise to the creation of deposits in the Euromarket, see R.N. Cooper, 'Implications of the Euro-Dollar for Monetary Policy and the Us Balance-of-Payments Deficits', in R.Z. Aliber (ed.), *National Monetary Policies and the International Financial System*, Chicago 1974.

[41] It should be recalled that since 1974 all movements of capital to and from the United States, even short-term, have been completely unrestricted.

banks increase the availability of world reserves, but they do not figure among official American debts, unless the central banks redeposit the funds in the American market. In sum, the existence of the Euromarket, with the interconnections it has woven between private and official liquidity, has vastly complicated the process of creation of reserves.

7. Seigniorage in the Seventies

This phenomenon has important consequences for the analysis of seigniorage. As I have pointed out, so long as the only dollars in circulation outside the United States were those held by central banks. the size of seigniorage equalled the annual variations in official US liabilities. The existence of quantities of dollars in private hands, and the ability of central banks to resort to the market of these funds, makes the calculation of seigniorage much less straightforward. The variation of official debt is too narrow a measure, but the variation of official dollar reserves plus the variation of the Eurodollar market is too broad. In principle, it should be possible to calculate the scope of seigniorage even in the new situation. In practice, however, insuperable difficulties arise.[42]

[42] Indeed, in order to determine the quantity of new dollars injected into international circulation during a particular year, it is necessary to exclude three categories not only from the variation in the total of official dollar reserves (whether deposited in the United States or in the Euromarket) but also from the Eurodollar market: all accounting overlaps; brokering for American residents through the Eurodollar market; the duplication (or multiplication) of deposits. Only the second magnitude can be ascertained with any degree of accuracy. As for the third, there is scant agreement even on the mere existence of the multiplication of deposits in the Eurodollar market, and there are no reliable estimates of the value of the multiplier, if any. Finally, the elimination of accounting overlaps raises very complicated problems. These overlaps comprise, in the first place, all deposits between Eurobanks. This sort of sifting of the data on the gross dimension of the market in an attempt to measure its net dimension is done by the Bank for International Settlements, which for several years has been publishing statistics on the net and gross size of the market in its *Annual Report*. It has also been done by the Morgan Guaranty Trust Company, which explained the method employed in its bulletin *World Financial Markets*, January 1979, pp. 9–15. Second, it is necessary to eliminate duplications that arise from the relations between Eurobanks and central banks. This task is quite different, since it is not possible merely to subtract from the net dimension of the market the value of the Eurodollars available in central banks. Only a small portion of transactions between Eurobanks and central banks are effected directly; for the most part they are mediated by many transactions involving both banking and non-banking establishments, which

In sum, in the new situation created by the growth of private international liquidity and its inextricable link to official international liquidity, it becomes impossible accurately to determine the scope of American seigniorage. Variation in official US liabilities is only a faulty approximation of it. Nevertheless, even calculated in this manner, seigniorage was enormous during the 1970s and contributed more than in the past to the formation of reserves.[43]

Some have maintained that the growth of international financial brokerage poses the question of whether there is any sense in continuing to try to define American seigniorage so punctiliously. We have seen that in the sixties some students, basing themselves on the fact that the American deficit resulted from capital outflows, had asserted that seigniorage consisted in the power to act as international financial intermediary, to gather funds in order to issue loans. By extension this interpretation gave rise to another, that seigniorage is merely the power to obtain credit from the rest of the world in order to finance one's own deficits. The expansion of international financial intermediation during the seventies allowed many countries enhanced access to foreign financing compared with the earlier period. According to this view, precisely because of the explosion of American deficits, seigniorage over the world money supply has now been extended to nearly all countries, which by resorting to international financial markets have been able to finance staggering deficits and to add to their own reserves not only assets deposited in the United States, but also a considerable volume of deposits in Eurocurrencies. In 1971 the central banks of the Group of Ten agreed not to deposit their own reserves in the Eurocurrency market, so the rise in official assets deposited in this market (depicted in table 6 below), must be attributed almost entirely to developing

---

in official descriptions of the market are considered 'final suppliers and users of funds' and therefore included in the net dimension of the market. Each of these transactions gives rise to a deposit: simply to eliminate the Eurodeposits of the central banks would threaten to count the deposits of the establishments just mentioned, which in reality are mere accounting duplications and do not correspond to genuine economic transactions. Indeed, behind this problem lurks yet another: the redefinition of the distinction between duplication and multiplication of deposits when the scope of the market is so widened as to include the central banks themselves.

[43] Highly interesting observations on this theme may be found in the volume edited by R. Mundell and J.J. Polak, *The New International Monetary System*, New York 1977, especially in the essay by R. Solomon, 'Techniques to Control International Reserves' and in the comments of R. Triffin about the essay by G. Haberler.

countries, especially OPEC members. But the developed countries have also gained notable advantages from the existence of the Euromarkets, because they are able thus to obtain credits with which to finance their deficits. In other words, the Euromarkets have increased the speed of circulation of official reserves. In the end, since the existence of the Euromarkets (and to some extent the greater openness of national financial markets themselves) has increased the supply of official reserves and accelerated their rate of circulation, it has diminished the inherent privilege enjoyed by the United States as the reserve-currency country. This is the real meaning of the statement of former Treasury Secretary Blumenthal quoted earlier.[44]

The genuinely greater recourse to international credit on the part of various countries encountering balance of payments difficulties, however, must not obscure the enormous difference that still separates the reserve-currency country from all the others. The reserve-currency country is able to tap the resources of the rest of the world virtually without restriction, simply by issuing its own currency.[45] For countries that turn to international financial markets, however, credit is always limited and 'conditional'. In the case of loans issued by supranational bodies like the IMF, credit conditions are governed by norms and principles sanctioned by long practice. But even in the case of private credit, the country going into debt is compelled to settle its balance of payments and to accept certain norms of economic policy—otherwise the closure of bank credit is

---

[44] This is also the opinion of A.D. Crockett, 'Control Over International Reserves', *IMF Staff Papers*, March 1978, p. 21: 'At the time when holdings of reserve currencies were the direct liabilities of the reserve centres, it was clear that any seigniorage element deriving from the issue of international reserves accrued to the reserve-currency country. Now that the ultimate debtor standing behind holdings of currency reserves can be any country with satisfactory credit standing, seigniorage (to the extent that it exists) can be much more widely shared.' The author continues by maintaining that the United States finds it easier to contract dollar debts with other countries. Would this were so, because it would mean that the United States would finance its current deficit with loans from abroad in its favour. On the contrary, in the 1970s the United States recorded a strong current-account deficit alongside a capital-account deficit (including banking funds), as is shown in table 2.

[45] Although, of course, within the limits imposed by the 'confidence problem', which can arise even under a system of non-convertibility.

Table 2

Evolution of Some Items of the US Balance of Payments
(in thousands of millions of $)

	(1)	(2)	(3)	(4)
1960–69	+23.3	+41.2	−23.7	+15.5
1970	+0.4	+2.2	−4.2	−7.4
1971	−2.8	−2.7	−4.9	−9.0
1972	−7.9	−6.8	−3.1	+2.2
1973	+0.4	+0.5	−2.3	−0.7
1974	−3.3	−5.3	−5.3	−1.9
1975	+11.9	+9.0	−4.8	−8.4
1976	−1.4	−9.3	−2.4	−6.9
1977	−15.2*	−31.2	−3.5	−4.2
1978	−15.9*	−34.1	−4.0	−16.6
Total	−33.8	−70.2	−34.5	−52.9

(1) Current-account balance.
(2) Balance of trade (f.o.b.).
(3) Balance of direct investment, of the United States abroad and of foreign investment in the United States, net of dis-investment and reinvestment of earnings.
(4) Variation of the net position abroad of credit agencies.

* As of 1977 the current account includes earnings on direct foreign investment that are reinvested; the unfavourable current-account balance is correspondingly diminished.

Source: As for table 1.

inevitable.[46] Putting this reasoning in its simplest possible form, we may say that no country can allow itself to register negative current-account balances year after year without irremediably losing its credit worthiness. The United States, however, has not been subject to this constraint, as is shown in table 2. In the end, the dollar standard seems to have accentuated American seigniorage. As we shall soon

[46] Analysis of the position of debtor countries has progressed quite a bit in recent years, with the extension to international finance of the concept of financial confidence expressed in the term 'risk country', which has permitted prudent norms of international credit activity to be drafted. See J. Hanson, 'Optimal International Borrowing and Lending', *American Economic Review*, September 1974; Y. Maroni, 'Approaches for Assessing the Risk Involved in Lending to Developed Countries', Board of Governors of the Federal Reserve System, International Finance Discussion Papers, no. 112; and R. Freeman, 'Optimal International Borrowing With Default', ibid., no. 129. Naturally, political considerations predominate in determining international credit policies. See *International Debt, the Banks, and US Foreign Policy*, US Senate, Washington DC, August 1977. On these questions, with particular reference to the debts of developing countries, see chapter 6.

see, unlimited exploitation of seigniorage by the United States could once again raise the confidence problem in relation to the dollar, and thus could encourage the rise of reserve assets alternative to the dollar. Before exploring these possibilities and considering what efforts the United States will make to prevent them from becoming reality, however, let us examine the consequences of the American deficits for world monetary and economic equilibrium.

8. The American Payments Deficits

During the 1970s official American liabilities rose by about $15 thousand million a year, whereas the average annual increase during the previous twenty years had been about $600 million; the annual increase thus soared twenty-five fold. The seventies marked a new phase, both quantitatively and qualitatively, in the exercise of American seigniorage over the supply of reserves.

The post-war period can be conveniently divided into three phases, roughly corresponding to the three decades elapsed. During the first two phases—the fifties and sixties—the advantages that accrued to the United States consequent to its seigniorage were partially neutralized by the profits garnered by the rest of the world. As a recent taxonomy of systems of international economic organization put it, the United States exercised 'leadership' over the world economy.[47] On the one hand, during the period 1950 to 1970 the US always maintained a current-account surplus, in particular in its trade balance. Moreover, the US authorities allowed this surplus to be less than it could have been, permitting their economic partners to devalue their own money relative to the dollar and to maintain discriminatory practices against American goods for long periods. On the other hand, during an initial phase the United States used this trade surplus, and in part its ability to issue international reserve money, to finance the accumulation of reserves by the rest of the

---

[47] See C.P. Kindleberger, 'Systems of International Economic Organization', in D.P. Calleo (ed.), *Money and the Coming World Order*, New York 1976. The author distinguishes the following five systems: altruism, enlightened self-interest, control on the basis of rules, regional blocs, and leadership. The last of these can degenerate and be lost 'if it becomes exploitative and illegitimate; if the leading country, for example, mixes the collective blessing of maintenance of the stability of the system with the private blessing of acquiring enterprises or resources abroad' (p. 34).

world through a programme of transfers through aid and military assistance. In other words, the United States provided the world with the 'collective blessing' of economic stability while extracting no direct advantages for its own economy, but only indirect gains such as those produced by the general political reinforcement of the Western world made possible by the post-war economic boom and the development of trade on a grand scale. During a second phase, which began toward the end of the 1950s, the United States supplied the rest of the world with reserves no longer through transfers in the form of aid, but mainly through direct investment, the expansion of its own industry in foreign markets, especially Canada and the countries of Western Europe.[48] During this second phase, American leadership, which had previously been based on consent, began to evolve into hegemony, and to provoke reactions from other countries that felt excluded from the benefits of seigniorage.[49]

The third phase has been marked by a complete absence of any legitimation of American power. In reality, the United States no longer provides the collective blessing of world economic stability, but instead unhesitatingly pursues its own national interest, and has thus become the principal source of perturbation of the international economy. Table 2 shows that during the first nine years of the 1970s, the United States ran up a current-account deficit of more than $30 thousand million. The current-account deficit depends essentially on the trade deficit, which reached the cumulative total of $70 thousand million, compared with a surplus of $40 thousand million over the preceding twenty years.

An optimistic interpretation of the American trade deficit has recently become fashionable, even in some European economic circles. According to this view, the deficit is the result of a lack of synchronization of the American and European business cycles. While the European economies have not recovered from the 'oil shock' of 1973–74 and have continued to stagnate in the wake of the German economy, whose policy is guided by excessive preoccupation

[48] On direct US investment see F.C. Bergsten, T. Horst, and T.H. Moran, *American Multinationals and American Interests*, Washington 1978.

[49] They were also concerned about the acquisition of predominant positions in their own industry by American multinationals. Britain, where the greater part of American investments are located, has nevertheless distanced itself from this attitude, partly because it is concerned to safeguard the residual reserve role of the pound, an objective for which American support is indispensable.

with inflation, the Americans began priming demand as early as 1976, breathing life into a vigorous expansion that continued until 1979. Without this, it is argued, the world economy would have been even worse off than it actually is.[50] Thus in the second half of the 1970s, Europe grew at an average annual rate of about 3%, while the United States registered average annual growth rates of about 4.5%. The American deficit, this argument runs, is the consequence of this bifurcation of growth rates, since American imports climbed consequent to increases in income, while exports failed to keep pace, because of the stagnation of European outlets.

This point of view does superficially capture some aspects of the situation, but it misses the essential feature of the American deficits: those recorded in the second half of the seventies are too high to be accounted for simply by the elasticity of American foreign earnings.[51]

In reality, the American deficits were caused by large and rising oil imports. In 1971, the United States, which until 1970 had been 90% self-sufficient in energy, began to increase its oil imports consequent to a decline in domestic production that lowered the percentage of total requirements met by national sources to slightly more than 50% by the end of the decade. American oil imports, as shown in table 3, have risen continuously to attain the present figure of 8–9 million barrels a day, or 30% of total OPEC production, a total value of more than $40 thousand million in 1978. Because of their high oil exports, the producing countries are naturally able to sustain an enormous level of imports, of which the United States is the prime beneficiary. Indeed, the United States occupies first place in trade with the OPEC members, supplying something like 15% of their total imports. But despite this, the United States has not managed to cover the value of its oil imports and has thus incurred a large deficit with the OPEC countries. This, in large part, accounts for the overall trade deficit (see table 3).

---

[50] For a more detailed criticism of this optimistic view, see chapter 4.

[51] The relevant data for the analysis may be found in P. Hooper, 'The Stability of Income and Price Elasticities in Us Trade, 1957–77', Board of Governors of the Federal Reserve System, International Finance Discussion Papers, no. 119; G. Stevens, 'A Multi-Country Model of the International Influences on the U.S. Economy: Preliminary Results', ibid., no. 115, December 1977; H. Howe *et al.*, 'Assessing International Interdependence With a Multi-Country Model', ibid., no. 138, April 1979; and R.Z. Lawrence, 'An Analysis of the 1977 U.S. Trade Deficit', *Brookings Papers on Economic Activity*, no. 1, 1978.

The American trade deficit does not impel the world economy forward, but on the contrary is the direct cause of disorder in international financial relations, which in turn gives rise to the imbalance in economic relations and the recession now racking the world economy. Without the enormous US oil imports, the OPEC cartel would be unable to sustain itself. Now, the United States has little difficulty paying for oil imports on the order of $40 thousand million a year (or even more, as prices continue to rise), because it enjoys the privilege of paying for its imports in its own national currency: the United States is therefore not subject to balance of payments constraints. During the sixties, fear of the massive conversion of foreign dollar-holdings prevented the United States from taking advantage of this privilege. In the seventies, however, the introduction of the dollar standard allowed the United States to ignore foreign constraints completely. It is too early to tell whether fear of a possible currency crisis in the eighties triggered by a massive conversion of dollars into alternative reserve assets will once again place limits on the unbridled exercise of American seigniorage.

The ease with which the United States is able to appropriate foreign resources makes a serious policy of energy saving and increases in domestic oil production much less compelling. Indeed, the reduction of crude-oil production in the United States is not the consequence of any decline in the level of estimated reserves, which in 1979 were about the same as they had been at the start of the decade, some 40 thousand million barrels. It was rather brought about by price controls on oil, petroleum products, and natural gas, which were imposed by successive American governments beginning in 1971. The system of federal controls on fuel prices has now gone through a long evolution. In August 1971 the prices of the petroleum derivatives petrol and fuel oil were frozen at their then-current market levels. Since the measure came into effect in the summer, the price of petrol was rather high, boosted by holiday demand, while the price of fuel oil, used primarily for domestic heating, was low. In winter the price of gasoline, frozen by the government, was too low to encourage the oil companies to refine sufficient quantities of gasoline. Given the relative rigidity of the technical coefficients of oil refining, the gasoline shortage also provoked an oil shortage. The companies then resorted to imports. In the meantime, the regulation limiting the import of oil and petroleum products to a minimum share of American requirements, which had been enacted in 1959 in an effort

Table 3

Evolution of the Oil Balance and of the Balance of Trade Between OPEC and the
United States
(in thousands of millions of $)

	(1)	(2)*	(3)
1960–69	−0.9**	−0.2**	2.1**
1970	−1.5	−0.4	3.2
1971	−2.2	−0.3	3.7
1972	−3.2	−0.1	4.5
1973	−6.5	−1.0	6.0
1974	−22.0	−8.9	5.8
1975	−23.5	−6.3	5.7
1976	−32.5	−14.5	7.3
1977	−42.6	−21.6	8.9
1978	−42.0	n.a.	7.9

(1) Balance of imports and exports of oil and oil products.
(2) Balance of trade with the countries of OPEC.
(3) Net US imports of oil and oil products (in millions of barrels per day).

* It should be recalled that the United States also imports enormous quantities of oil
    and oil products from Mexico and Canada.

** Annual average.

Sources: United Nations, OECD, Us Department of Commerce.

to aid national producers and *to bolster the dollar*, then showing the
first signs of difficulty, was repealed. Imports soared in 1972 (see table
3). Later, in March 1973, price controls were also imposed on
domestic crude oil. In August 1973 the system was further refined
with the introduction of 'two-tier pricing'. Oil extracted from wells
that were already functioning as of 1972 had to be sold at a price no
higher than $1.35 per barrel more than the price prevailing on the
market on 15 May 1973, which was about $3 a barrel. Oil produced
by wells that had begun functioning in or after 1973 was exempted
from this control, as was imported oil.

The imposition of a ceiling on the price of 'old oil' discouraged
extraction from existing wells. Indeed, when the tripling of the price
of oil was ordered by OPEC only a few months after the introduction of
two-tier pricing, a mechanism of speculation took hold. Us producers
found it more advantageous to leave the oil in the ground than to sell
it at a price equivalent to about one-third the world-market price.

Extraction diminished, and imports immediately leapt upward yet again, permitting the consolidation of the OPEC cartel. The tendency to hoard oil was further encouraged by two additional factors: the accelerating rate of inflation, which made it less attractive for producers to be paid in money whose value was condemned to decline, for a commodity whose value was likely to rise; and the promise by the American government that the price controls were temporary and would be lifted before the end of 1985. The temporary character of the price freeze reinforced the tendency of producers to hoard, waiting to be able to dispose of their oil freely again.[52]

Later, in 1976, price controls were also imposed on natural gas. The sales price of gas in the producing states, mostly in the South and Midwest, was set at $2 per thousand cubic feet, while a lower price, $1.50 per thousand cubic feet, was stipulated for sales in the consuming states. This led to a decline in deliveries of natural gas to the north-eastern states, which turned to imports to fill the breach, paying prices higher than those permitted for domestic production and thus causing yet another spurt in total imports of oil and petroleum products, which reached an average of 8–9 million barrels a day by 1978–79.

Now, the worldwide increase in the cost of energy sources does not have equal effects on all economies. To begin with, the increases favour the competitivity of American products. Indeed, because of the two-tier pricing of crude, the average cost of oil in the United States was a good 40% below world-market levels as of the first half of 1979. Commodities whose production requires great expenditures of energy or that use petroleum derivatives as a raw material benefit especially from this situation. This enhanced American competitivity—and not only the stagnation of demand caused by the increase in the price of the product relative to possible substitutes—is

[52] The effect of the price-control measures on oil production in the United States was analysed carefully in a study commissioned by the Federal Trade Commission: C.T. Roush, *Effects of Federal Price and Allocations Regulations in the Petroleum Industry*, Federal Trade Commission, December 1976. It concludes: 'Both the cost pass-through requirements of refined products price regulations and the incentives created by the entitlement allocation programme tended to encourage imports above the level that would have resulted in an unregulated market. De-regulation might have contributed to future economic welfare by breaking OPEC and making available competitively priced oil in the world market.' An excursus on federal controls is contained in W.J. Mead, 'The Performance of Government in Energy Regulations', *American Economic Review*, May 1979.

one of the reasons for the crisis in the European synthetic-fibre industry. Moreover, in the long run the continued rise in oil prices renders alternative energy sources economical, and the United States possesses enormous resources in this domain, well in excess of those of all the other industrialized countries, both relatively and absolutely. Apart from uranium and the possible extraction of combustible synthetics from coal (materials with which the United States is richly endowed), we need only recall the potentially recuperable oil contained in shale and bituminous schists, although in geological layers that are difficult to reach. Until recently, extraction of this oil was prohibitively expensive, quite apart from the technical problems involved. Today, however, some of these deposits are beginning to be exploitable. The enormous shale-oil deposits of Athabaska along the Us-Canadian border, the cost of extraction of which amounted to $16 per barrel at 1979 prices, are now competitive with a world-market cost of oil considerably in excess of $20 a barrel. And indeed, production began in 1979. Above all, however, the United States possesses enormous proven reserves of bituminous schists, equivalent to some 700 thousand million barrels of oil, or twice the proven reserves of Saudi Arabia. Recovery of the oil contained in these deposits becomes economical at a cost equivalent to about $25 a barrel at 1979 prices. The American government is well aware of these reserves and has promoted a grandiose plan that entails government expenditure of some $88 thousand million to subsidize and encourage the exploitation of alternative energy sources (besides, of course, encouraging energy saving). Shale oil occupies the prime position in this plan.[53] In the long run, the possibility of tapping these

---

[53] Thus the us government has proposed enormous tax relief in order to accelerate the exploitation of these deposits: 'Recoverable shale oil reserves in the Western United States have been estimated from 400 to 700 billion barrels, several times the size of Saudi Arabia's proven reserves. It is technically possible today to produce shale oil in large quantities. However, it is not yet a financially viable proposition, although the expected cost of producing shale oil, $25 to $35 a barrel, indicates that it will be the first synthetic fuel to compete economically with imported oil. In addition to including oil shale within the mandate of the Energy Security Corporation, the president has proposed a $3 tax credit for each barrel of shale oil produced. . . . It is expected that many companies need only the encouragement provided by this tax credit to begin the construction and operation of major oil shale production facilities. . . . Because the credit is not taxable, the economic subsidy provided by the credit to corporations paying tax at the top corporate marginal rate of 46% is the equivalent of an additional $5.56 added to the sale price of shale oil.' Statement by D.C. Lubick, then undersecretary of the Treasury for tax policy, to the House Ways and Means Committee, *Department of the Treasury News*, 20 July 1979. A brief review of the

energy sources will make the United States completely self-sufficient in energy, while in order to be able to pay for their energy sources the other industrialized countries, with a few exceptions, will have to continue to export massive quantities of manufactured goods to markets that will be increasingly difficult to penetrate because of enhanced American competitivity.

The American deficits are not limited exclusively to items of trade, although the trade deficit probably has the greatest effects on the world economy, by propping up the high price of oil. Table 2 shows that there have also been rising deficits in capital flows for direct investment and in shifts of banking funds. Even though the influx of foreign capital to the United States has risen enormously (to the point that the stock of foreign investments, which had amounted to $13 thousand million in 1970, had risen to $40 thousand million by the end of 1978), the deficit in these capital flows in the 1970s approximately doubled compared with the average level of the 1960s. This testifies to a continuing expansion in American investment abroad. Us capital, while continuing to flow toward its preferred destinations (Canada and Western Europe), is beginning massively to penetrate the manufacturing sector of those developing countries that have attained a certain degree of industrialization.

Finally, movements of bank capital, which were favourable to the United States during the sixties, partly because of the control system, showed a mounting negative balance in the seventies. This reflects the great foreign expansion of the American banking system. The ten largest US banks now derive more than 50% of their profits from international transactions. Since they are freely able to tap their own money markets in order to grant credit abroad, the American banks command a substantial edge over their competitors.[54] Us banks are now using this edge in an attempt to undermine London's role as the principal home of the Eurodollar. Indeed, for several years now the growth sector of the Euromarket has shifted to the 'offshore markets' in Caribbean islands created by subsidiaries of American banks. The scale of what is coming to be called the North American Eurocur-

---

economic feasibility of various alternative energy sources on the basis of the anticipated profit rates may be found in 'Business Brief: Costing Alternatives to Oil', *The Economist*, 6 October 1979.

[54] For some thought about this phenomenon from the European side, see P. Coupaye, 'Le développement des activités internationales des banques françaises', *Eurépargne*, June 1979.

rency market quadrupled between 1973 and 1978, while the size of the London market merely doubled during the same period. Because they have no difficulty supplying funds, the American banks are recovering their absolute supremacy in international financial brokerage, which had been threatened at the beginning of the seventies by the mounting self-assertion of Swiss and German banks, aided by the revaluation of their currency.[55]

A careful reading of the evolution of American balance of payments statements allows us to reconstruct the manner in which seigniorage was unscrupulously exploited to consolidate the power, competitivity, and predominance of the American economy throughout the world. Had the United States been bound by the evolution of its balance of payments the way other countries are, its economy could not have been directed as it was. Solutions to American economic problems would have had to be sought through agreements with other countries in an effort to safeguard the interests of all members of the world community, as well as international economic and monetary equilibrium. To use Kindleberger's terminology, the present system of organization of international monetary relations can no longer be qualified as 'leadership', no matter how degenerate. The United States no longer supplies the collective blessing of economic stability, but instead appropriates the resources of the rest of the world and stands at the root of the imbalances in the world economy that have produced millions of unemployed and losses of accumulation.

Although it would be wrong hastily and automatically to attribute responsibility for the international crisis of the 1970s to the conduct of the United States alone, there is no doubt that analysis of American seigniorage must be an integral part of any effort to interpret the events of the past decade. In monetary analysis there is a sharp counterposition between those who maintain that the only relevant datum is the quantity of money in circulation and those who argue that it is also necessary to consider the manner in which money enters into circulation in the system.[56] This difference of emphasis

---

[55] See R.H. Mills jr. and E.D. Short, 'U.S. Banks and the North American Euro-Currency Market', *International Finance Discussion Papers*, no. 134, April 1979. Revaluation favours the national banks, because it raises the value of their own capital and enables them to grant larger loans and therefore to take greater risks.

[56] See the famous article of N. Kaldor, 'The New Monetarism', *Lloyds Bank Review*, July 1970.

corresponds, more or less, to the distinction between monetarist and Keynesian persuasions. It is deplorable that in recent years studies on the interaction between monetary and real variables in the international economy (and between monetary variables and inflation), whatever the orientation of their authors, thoroughly ignore the channels through which the money or credit aggregates they are considering are created. Despite the wealth of results obtained, and despite the genuine interest of many of the conclusions that have been drawn, the realism of these studies is not recommended by the fact that they speak of an increase in international reserves without bothering to consider how this increase is generated. But why should it be assumed that an increase brought about by the issuing of SDRs is the same thing as an increase in the reserves of the oil-producing countries financed by withdrawals of funds from the United States, whether directly through American purchases of oil or indirectly through the recycling of these funds to other oil-importing countries that lack the benefit of reserve currency?[57]

9. Alternatives to the Dollar

Unlimited US exploitation of its seigniorage over the international money supply was made possible by the practical lack of any alternative to the dollar in its role as reserve currency. The elimination of alternatives to the dollar was a process that began in the sixties, went through ups and downs, and peaked with Nixon's declaration in August 1971 that the dollar was no longer convertible for gold. This process, however, is far from over, at least as concerns some assets the supply of which is not controlled by the United States. It is this that causes the persistence of the confidence problem with regard to the dollar. The events of autumn 1978 and summer 1979 demonstrate that in spite of floating exchange rates, 'exchange crises' can still occur—caused by flights from the dollar similar to those that occurred under the system of fixed exchange rates.[58]

[57] Among the most important studies, see H.R. Heller, 'International Reserves and Worldwide Inflation', *IMF Staff Papers*, March 1976; A.F. Swoboda, 'Monetary Approaches to Worldwide Inflation', in L.B. Krause and W.S. Salant (eds.). Many bibliographical references may be found in G. Falchi and M. Michelangeli, 'Liquidità internazionale, politiche monetarie e inflazione mondiale', *Bancaria*, December 1978.

[58] On the reappearance of currency crises, see O. Emminger, 'The Exchange-Rate as an Instrument of Policy', *Lloyds Bank Review*, July 1979.

The assets alternative to the dollar are three: gold, Special Drawing Rights, and other currencies. In order to formulate hypotheses as to whether any of these assets could replace the dollar and thereby limit American seigniorage, even if only indirectly by compelling the American government to exhibit greater discretion in the international issuing of dollars, we must briefly review the evolution of the status of these assets as international reserves.

Gold

Let us start with gold. The 1971 declaration that the dollar was no longer convertible for gold was neither the start nor the end of the process of demonetarization of this precious metal. To begin with, it must be recalled that the convertibility sanctioned by the Bretton Woods agreement was limited to official non-residents of the United States. As long ago as the 1930s American citizens were forbidden by law to own gold in the United States. In the fifties the stricture was extended to Americans living abroad.[59] Moreover, the Federal Reserve System was committed to hand over gold only upon the presentation of dollars by foreign central banks. In practice, the exclusion of private non-residents from convertibility meant that the United States was always able to exercise a good deal of political pressure on official foreign owners of dollars so as to limit or even prevent conversion. In effect, then, even before August 1971 the convertibility of the dollar was a theoretical more than practical feature of the system, since many countries had renounced the conversion of their dollar holdings, although Germany was the only country to issue a formal statement to that effect.[60]

Nevertheless, private non-residents could always convert their dollar holdings into gold by turning to the gold market, which was reopened, outside the United States, in the mid-fifties. In order to prevent gold prices in the private market from diverging from the gold par value of the dollar stipulated in the Bretton Woods agreement, the central banks intervened in the private market. In

[59] For accounts of gold legislation in the United States, see M. Friedman and A.J. Schwartz, *A Monetary History of the United States, 1867–1960*, Princeton 1963. Nevertheless, in 1975 the private possession of gold was made legal again in the United States.

[60] See the 30 March 1967 letter sent by Blessing, President of the Bundesbank, to William McChesney Martin, then president of the Federal Reserve System (cited in Bergsten).

October 1960 the major industrial countries, including the United States, agreed, first formally and then informally, to intervene with gold from their own reserves in order to stabilize the price of gold. The existence of this 'gold pool' distributed the pressure of official gold sales among various countries, thus protecting American reserves. Nevertheless, in March 1968 the countries of the gold pool, with the exception of France, decided to suspend purchases and sales on the market, although they continued to exchange gold among themselves at the official rate. The effect of this decision was to freeze the gold reserves of the countries concerned, which became reluctant to exchange gold at a price well below that of the free market.[61] The declaration that the dollar was no longer convertible, coming on top of the cessation of state intervention in the free gold market, seemed to signify the elimination of any further monetary role for gold.

This was confirmed with the approval of the second amendment to the Articles of Agreement of the International Monetary Fund in April 1976. The amendment, which went into effect in April 1978, abolished the official gold price; it barred the IMF from accepting gold from any member country to cover contributions, except on the approval of an absolute majority; finally, it forbade member countries from fixing the value of their currencies in terms of gold.[62] In addition, in August 1975 an agreement was reached[63] among the countries of the Group of Ten (plus Switzerland and Portugal) on the basis of which the aggregate amount of gold possessed by the Ten and the IMF was not allowed to increase. As a result of this agreement and the amendment to the IMF Articles, the major industrial countries can exchange gold among themselves at whatever price they choose, but they can sell gold only to private citizens and cannot buy any.[64] This two-year agreement among the Ten, however, was not renewed when it expired in January 1978.[65]

The present status of gold as a reserve asset is highly problematic. On the one hand, in the absence of interventions by the central banks,

[61] On the functioning of the gold pool, see G. Stammati, *Il sistema monetario internazionale*, Turin 1973.

[62] See *IMF Annual Report 1978*, p. 56.

[63] Which in substance confirmed the Zeist agreement of the previous year among members of the European Community.

[64] See B. Tew, *The Evolution of the International Monetary System, 1945–77*, London 1977, pp. 206–7.

[65] Bank for International Settlements, *48th Annual Report*, Basle 1978, p. 138.

the free-market price has risen significantly, exceeding $300 an ounce in the summer of 1979; this demonstrates that gold remains a private reserve asset.

On the other hand, the highness of the price can itself discourage acceptance of gold by creditors, who could well fear incurring capital losses. Practically speaking, there has been no lack of indications in the past several years that gold continues to perform a monetary function. Portugal, for example, has several times sold gold reserves on the free market, and repaid one American loan by relinquishing gold. Moreover, gold has been used as collateral in obtaining international credit, even though no loans are expressed in gold, or even indexed to the price of gold.[66]

In reality, the greatest obstacle that would have to be overcome to fully restore gold's monetary function would be the determination of its price. So long as no agreement on the price of gold is reached, even informally, it will be quite difficult for gold to function as money, because of the possible capital losses that could be occasioned by its possession. It is quite true that possession of currency can also lead to great capital losses, but these are at least partially amortized by the interest generated by currency and by the lower administrative costs. Given the size of the US gold stock, it seems improbable that any agreement on the price of gold could be reached without American participation. Indeed, the United States would always be able to throw the market out of kilter by selling its own gold.[67] Nor does an agreement to allow limited circulation of gold again seem likely, as was demonstrated by the experience of the settlement of intervention balances in the agreement on the joint float of European currencies.[68]

---

[66] Recently, moreover, there has been a partial cession of gold and currency reserves against the European unit of account in the European Monetary System. See chapter 5.

[67] As the Treasury has done in recent years, but in greater scope. Nevertheless, the major obstacle is political, because American reserves would probably be insufficient to control the market.

[68] In the European currency snake, deficits brought about by interventions in support of a currency in difficulty by the central banks of the other countries had to be settled by the debtor country in proportion to the composition of its own reserves. Italy, which proportionally had more gold than the others, would have had to settle its debts by ceding a percentage of gold. The expectation of a revaluation of gold led Italy to request a modification of the mechanism for the settlement of balances. Thus, it is uncertainty about the price, whether upward or downward, that inhibits the circulation of gold. See Bank of Italy, *Relazione all'Assemblea*, Final Considerations, Rome 1973, pp. 392–93.

Special Drawing Rights

Special Drawing Rights are a form of interest-bearing fiduciary money issued by the IMF and allocated to member countries in proportion to their share of participation in the Fund. From an abstract point of view, SDRs represent the best solution to the problem of the creation of international liquidity. Indeed, their quantity can be strictly regulated by the IMF, and can even be linked automatically to one or more variables of the world economy (for example, the rate of growth of world trade). The creation of SDRs does not entail absorption of resources, and seigniorage can be distributed equitably—at least it is subject to international negotiation. Precisely these characteristics, which make SDRs a real alternative to the dollar, have always left American governments cold. The United States decided to permit the creation of SDRs during the sixties in an effort to ward off the formation of a coalition around a French proposal to restore the role of gold.[69] The first issue of SDRs, the creation of which was decided at the IMF assembly in Rio de Janeiro in 1967, occurred between January 1970 and January 1972. A total of about 9 thousand million SDRs were issued, equivalent to about 7.5% of official world reserves at the time. In subsequent years, industrialized and developing countries striving to enhance the role of SDRs in the international monetary system have encountered firm American opposition. The United States was opposed both to substituting SDRs for dollars in international circulation[70] and to supplying increased international liquidity by issuing new SDRs. Only at the end of 1978 did the *ad interim* committee of the IMF decide to issue new SDRs. A total of 13

[69] For a wide-ranging recapitulation of the discussion about the international monetary system during the sixties, see S. Strange, 'International Monetary Relations', in A. Schonfield (ed.), *International Economic Relations of the Western World 1959–1971*, vol. 2, London 1976, and R. Triffin, *Our International Monetary System*, New York 1969.

[70] The United States was thus opposed to the opening of an IMF 'substitution account' into which dollars could be placed in exchange for SDRs in order to reduce the 'dollar overhang'. Taking advantage of divisions among the other countries, the US also opposed the opening of a substitution account for gold. On these questions, and more generally for an analytical account of discussions during the early seventies about reform of the international monetary system, see J. Williamson, *The Failure of World Monetary Reform, 1971–74*, Middlesex 1977. Nevertheless, in March 1979 the *ad interim* committee of the IMF mandated the executive directors of the Fund to study the possibility of creating an SDR substitution account against deposits of dollars and other currencies.

thousand million were authorized, and the first slice, amounting to 4 thousand million, was issued in January 1979. Total SDRs issued thus exceeded 13 thousand million in 1979. Nevertheless, in relative terms SDRs represent barely 4% of world reserves, and the completion of the new issue will just about permit the reconstitution of the original proportion of 7.5% of world reserves.[71]

Other Currencies

American refusal to concede SDRs a greater role in the monetary system has been provoking, although to a rather limited extent, the assertion of various national currencies other than the dollar as reserve assets. This development, although it obviously entails advantages for the countries whose currencies are so used, does not distribute seigniorage equitably, as could be the case for issues of SDRs.

To start with, is the United States in favour of this development or not? Obviously, despite qualified favourable statements, the US government is not partial to anything that could diminish the role and unbridled freedom of the dollar. How, then, should we evaluate this statement by A.M. Solomon, undersecretary of the Treasury for monetary affairs in the Carter administration: 'Let me make clear that the United States has no interest in artificially perpetuating a particular international role for the dollar. The dollar's present role is itself the product of an evolutionary process. We would expect the dollar's role to continue to evolve with economic and financial developments in the world economy, and a relative reduction in that role in the future could be a natural consequence. . . . Certainly we would expect Special Drawing Rights to take on a growing role in the system. . . . Another possibility is that certain national currencies will play an increasing role. Indeed, an expansion of the reserve roles of the Deutsche mark and the Japanese yen has occurred over the past decade in both absolute and relative terms. I would note that the authorities of other countries have generally tended to discourage use of their currencies as reserves, largely because of concern about the implications for the domestic money supply and fear that domestic

[71] See Bank of Italy, *Relazione all'Assemblea*, Rome 1979, pp. 36–38 and appendix, p. 147.

financial management will be made more difficult.'[72] Perhaps these words reflect a genuine difference of opinion in the American government. Carter's Treasury Secretary Blumenthal, for example, said: 'A change in the role of the dollar is not a cure for our problems. . . . As the largest economy and provider of the world's vehicle currency, we understand that the burden falls especially heavily on the United States to maintain economic discipline. . . . But we do not look to a revision of the international monetary system, or to a change in the dollar's role in that system, or to other devices such as the introduction of a substitution account to replace dollars with SDRs, as a solution to the difficulties the dollar has faced.'[73] Even if these differences of view are real and not merely window-dressing, in international monetary policy, as in other sectors of US foreign policy, the 'hawks' are usually victorious over the 'doves'. Nearly twenty years ago, at a time when the dollar was encountering difficulties, then secretary of the Treasury R. Roosa maintained that the international monetary system had to evolve toward a multi-currency arrangement.[74]

The American veto can be quite effective in curbing the emergence of new reserve currencies, for Washington can act on either supply, seeking to prevent potential reserve-currency nations from issuing their currency, or demand, discouraging the use of other currencies as reserve assets. Apart from this, the supply of other currencies may be limited by the issuing government's concern that it could lose control of national financial policy. The American money market is still larger than total international liquidity in dollars, both official and private. This ensures that the conditions determined on the American market by US monetary authorities are transmitted to the Eurodollar market, and not vice versa, even though there has been no lack of expressions of concern to the contrary, leading to American proposals to regulate the market.

Nevertheless, there are very powerful impulses encouraging the development of other reserve currencies, on both the supply and the demand sides. In a situation marked by the sort of sweeping shifts in the centre of gravity of world accumulation that prevailed in the

[72] 'The Evolving Monetary System', *Department of the Treasury News*, 12 January 1979.

[73] Blumenthal, p. 7.

[74] 'Multilateralizing International Responsibility', speech delivered May 1962, reprinted in *The Dollar and World Liquidity*, New York, 1967.

seventies and are likely to continue through the eighties, the major capitalist powers compete frantically on the level of trade and direct investments. On the one hand, the revaluation of European currencies relative to the dollar discourages investment in sectors of average technology in Europe and encourages it in the United States. On the other hand, traditional low-technology sectors are being transferred to the more advanced developing countries of South America and Southeast Asia, where new industrial markets are opening up with growth rates double or triple those of the industrialized countries.[75] The growth of American investment in Europe is therefore slackening, while the growth of European and Japanese investment in the United States is accelerating. At the same time, the entire industrialized world—Europe, Japan, and North America—is increasing its direct investment in the most dynamic countries of the Third World. These investments are flowing into manufacturing sectors and financial and insurance services, and no longer mainly to the primary sector. Finally, the growth of the advanced developing countries is occurring through their purchase on credit of capital goods and intermediary products from the industrialized countries. Finance is essential for survival in an ever more competitive world. It is needed to sell on credit enormous quantities of goods to buyers who only gradually will be able to sell enough of their products on foreign markets to pay for what they have bought. It is needed to guarantee the multinational expansion of national companies and banks. The United States has an edge in this competition, for it takes advantage of seigniorage; it is therefore only natural that countries like Germany and Japan should be tempted to imitate the United States, albeit in a limited manner.

At the same time, room for new international currencies does exist. Money is defined by the functions it fulfils: as unit of account, means of exchange, and store of value.

When a currency is employed as unit of account in international transactions, it becomes easier to use it as a means of exchange, and a demand for stocks of this currency thus arises among commercial operators. The existence of a market for this currency impels monetary authorities to constitute stocks so as to deal with fluctuations in supply and demand. Now, the statistics on invoicing in

[75] On the growth of these new markets, see C. Stoffaes, *La grande menace industrielle*, Paris 1978; OECD, *L'incidence des nouveaux pays industriels sur la production et les échanges des produits manufacturés*, Paris 1979.

international trade demonstrate that the major industrialized countries generally invoice in their own currencies. Not many studies have been done on this subject, and the existing efforts do not permit accurate cross-temporal comparisons. Nevertheless, it is known that Germany, France, and Britain invoice between 70% and 80% of their exports in their own currency.[76] Japan invoices a much lower percentage of its exports in yen, between 20% and 30%.[77] The rest of the exports of the industrialized countries are invoiced either in the currency of the importer or in dollars. The exports of the smaller industrialized countries are also invoiced largely in national currency or in the currency of the importer.[78]

The dollar, on the other hand, is generally used by the developing countries to invoice the exports of primary products; moreover, it seems to be the only 'third-party currency'. In other words, if neither the currency of the exporter nor that of the importer is used, rarely will anything but dollars be used. The share of world trade invoiced in dollars is therefore still much higher than the American share of total world trade, but the use of the dollar as invoicing currency is not as prevalent as might be expected. According to Grassman,[79] in 1968 some 25% of world trade was invoiced in dollars, while the American share of total world trade was about 15.5%. It is possible that the share of dollar invoicing has not changed since then, and may even have risen significantly during the seventies, despite the decline of the American share of world trade, which had fallen to 12.1% in 1975. In fact, the share of raw materials in the total value of world trade has risen because of the relative increase in the prices of these products compared with those of manufactures, and there has been a further erosion of the residual role of sterling as a third-party currency. In 1977 the last oil producers invoicing in pounds decided to switch to dollars. Even in the absence of more profound studies to clarify the

[76] The data are taken from S.A. Page, 'Currency of Invoicing in Merchandise Trade', *National Institute Economic Review*, August 1977.

[77] See S. Matsukawa, '"Yen zone" Still a Long Way Off', *Financial Times*, 2 July 1979. Nevertheless, it must be recalled that a large portion of Japanese exports go directly to the United States.

[78] Thus S. Grassman ('Currency Distribution and Forward Cover in Foreign Trade', *Journal of International Economics*, May 1976) found that the portion of Swedish trade invoiced in crowns was 67% in 1973; the same author reports a similar share for Danish exports: 'A Fundamental Symmetry in International Payments Patterns', *Journal of International Economics*, May 1973.

[79] Ibid., 1973.

effect of the variation of exchange rates on the choice of invoicing currency, it seems clear that the trend towards wider roles for many currencies in the settlement of international transactions is solidly rooted in the reality of trade practices.

Table 4

New Issues of International Bonds*
(in millions of $)

	Total, of which:	US$	(%)	DM	SF**	Yen**
1973	7,779	3,407	43.8	1,387	1,526	—
1974	6,857	4,287	62.5	597	911	—
1975	19,913	10,200	51.2	3,367	3,297	67
1976	32,518	19,729	60.7	4,001	5,359	226
1977	33,976	19,055	56.1	6,312	4,970	1,271
1978	34,279	13,085	38.2	9,040	5,698	3,862

*   International bonds include both Euro-bonds and foreign bonds issued on national markets.
** Issues in Swiss francs and Japanese yen are foreign bonds only, since there are no Euro-bonds in these currencies.

Source: Morgan Guaranty Trust, World Financial Markets.

Similar suggestions may be gleaned from consideration of the role of money as a store of value, which in the past decade has been better fulfilled by currencies other than the dollar. There is an active demand for financial assets in German marks, Japanese yen, and Swiss francs. Table 4 shows that international issues of dollars[80] declined relative to those of strong currencies, in spite of the complete opening of the vast American financial market to foreign borrowers during the seventies. The existence of bonds denominated in strong currencies does not mean that these currencies are in active circulation, because the proceeds of the issues made in the financial

[80] International issues include both Euro-issues and foreign issues on the national market. Dollar-denominated Eurobonds can therefore be deposited in the American market ('Yankee bonds') and foreign bonds in dollars on the same market. The same situation occurs in the case of Germany. Not so the cases of Japan and Switzerland, which succeeded in convincing international financial brokers not to launch issues in Euroyen or Eurofrancs. The difference between a foreign issue and a Euro-issue on the currency market of the given denomination consists in the fact that the former is regularly quoted in the official markets, while the Euro-issue is not.

markets of Germany, Japan, and Switzerland must be converted into dollars before they can be exported from the country.[81] The existence of these issues also helps the countries concerned to partially 'deflate' the surplus in their own payments, which was perhaps excessive between 1976 and 1978, partly because of the inflow of speculative capital, which they were unable to control. Nevertheless, financial assets in strong currencies do not suffice to meet foreign demand. Indeed, the greater demand is for monetary assets that, besides maintaining their purchasing power, have the requisite characteristics of liquidity. How can the rest of the world procure marks, francs, and yen? The most direct way would be to acquire bank deposits in the appropriate banking system, but this would lead to short-term capital movements towards countries with strong currencies, giving yet another impulse to the rise in value of these currencies. Indeed, during the seventies both Germany and the other two countries established more or less effective control networks designed precisely to prevent the influx of short-term funds from abroad.[82] In a further effort to avoid revaluation, these controls have in some cases been extended to long-term inflows. The demand for liquid balances in marks, francs, and yen has thus been shunted to the Eurocurrency market.

The Euromark and Eurofranc (Swiss) markets developed rapidly during the seventies. Table 5 illustrates to what extent the share of these currencies grew to the detriment of the dollar. But the growth in these shares was due largely to the revaluations of these currencies relative to the dollar. Correcting the data to compensate for the revaluation of the mark and the franc, we find that their shares were quite similar to those that prevailed in 1968. In other words, the Euromark and Eurofranc markets grew at the same rate as the market as a whole. This is no small thing, considering that the market swelled something like tenfold between 1968 and 1978. At the end of

[81] Even though there are Euro-bonds in marks, the German monetary authorities, in collaboration with the international banking system, seek to restrict these issues to Germany, so that their volume is always under the control of the German authorities.

[82] For a description of the controls of these markets, see B. Brown, *Money Hard and Soft on the International Currency Markets*, London 1978. A more analytical account of the controls in effect in Germany and Switzerland as of the end of 1977 may be found in OECD, *Regulations Affecting International Banking Operations (Of Banks and Non-Banks in France, Germany, the Netherlands, Switzerland, the United Kingdom)*, Paris 1978.

Table 5

Evolution of the Currency Composition of Eurodeposits in European Banks*
(in %)

	US $	DM	SF	Other Currencies
1968	79.7	8.9	6.8	4.6
1969	81.4	8.2	7.1	3.3
1970	77.9	10.7	7.6	3.8
1971	72.4	15.0	7.9	4.7
1972	73.3	14.8	6.7	5.2
1973	68.4	16.7	8.9	6.0
1974	70.8	15.6	8.3	5.3
1975	73.2	15.4	5.9	5.5
1976	74.0	15.2	5.1	5.7
1977**	70.4	17.3	5.7	6.6
1978	68.2	18.2	5.4	8.2

* US dollars, German marks, Swiss francs, and other currencies.
** Including, for the first time, the deposits of Austrian, Danish, and Irish banks.

Source: Bank for International Settlements.

1978 deposits in Euromarks totalled $93 thousand million, those in Swiss francs $28 thousand million.[83] In 1968 the comparable figures were $4 thousand million and $1.8 thousand million.

Since the balance of payments of these two countries were generally in surplus during this decade, the problem arises of locating the channels through which the market was supplied with marks and francs. Initially, between 1969 and 1973, the growth of the Euromarket in these currencies was caused by the very powerful sales interventions by the German and Swiss central banks, which strove to ward off the revaluation of their currencies by buying dollars whenever they were offered. The marks and francs thus created augmented the domestic money supply, but also the number of Euromarks and Eurofrancs, thus making these strong currencies available to those who wanted to diversify their portfolios. Between 1973 and 1975 the exchange rate of the dollar relative to the mark exhibited ups and downs that did not require net intervention of significant scope.

[83] The data refer to the foreign position of the European banks only, published by the Bank for International Settlements, on the assumption that the Euromarks are deposited primarily in Europe.

Finally, at the Western summit of Rambouillet in November 1975, an accord was reached on the basis of which the six major capitalist world economic powers committed their respective 'monetary authorities to act to countervail disordered market conditions or erratic fluctuations of exchange rates'.[84] The prevailing interpretation of this agreement was that the central banks were not obliged to counteract the basic, underlying trend of exchange rates. This interpretation was incorporated into the new Article IV of the IMF, which stipulates that member countries must 'refrain from manipulating exchange rates or the international monetary system with the aim of preventing an effective adjustment of balance of payments or of garnering unfair competitive advantage over other members'. Germany consequently ceased intervening in the dollar-mark exchange rate. More precisely, Germany intervened only when the dollar fell excessively, selling marks; later, barely had the dollar been strengthened, the Germans resold the acquired dollars, buying back the marks that had been placed in circulation. The result has been that the increase in Germany's dollar reserves in recent years has been nearly equal to the evolution of the balance of payments, without being influenced by the management of the Bundesbank's position in marks and currency.[85] The United States acted similarly, either completely refraining from intervention for long periods (following a policy of 'benign neglect') or intervening by taking loans in marks by activating swap agreements with the Bundesbank. Since these are short-term credits, the United States always repurchased the marks used in order to repay the Bundesbank.[86] According to journalistic sources, the same happened with the marks the American government obtained by issuing mark-denominated medium-term bonds on the German market at the end of 1978 ('Carter bonds'): the marks used in interventions to support the dollar in the winter of 1978–1979 were subsequently bought back.

Between 1973 and 1978 interventions in exchange markets were not the principal source of creation of Euromarks, although they did continue to play an important role, partly because of interventions in the 'snake'. German banks, on the other hand, did represent a

---

[84] See the text published in B. Tew, p. 222.

[85] For the analysis of the direction of the Bundesbank's interventions in exchange markets, see Deutsche Bundesbank *Report*, issued annually.

[86] The relevant information is in the *Federal Reserve Bank of New York Quarterly Review*, 'Treasury and Federal Reserve Foreign Exchange Operations'.

significant source of supply, for they were free to extend credit in marks to non-residents. The foreign assets of German banks in marks thus rose from the equivalent of $8 thousand million in 1973 to $40 thousand million in 1978, while their assets in foreign currencies in the latter year amounted to only $20 thousand million. By way of comparison, the foreign assets of French banks in francs in 1978 were equivalent to $18 thousand, while their assets in foreign currency were approaching $80 thousand million.

Swiss banks likewise began lending more and more in Swiss francs. Their foreign assets in francs stood at $19 thousand million in 1978, while their foreign-currency assets amounted to $31 thousand million. Japanese banks have recently begun to move in the same direction, but the Euroyen market is still quite limited.[87] It thus seems clear that the countries with strong currencies have a common method of taking advantage of the international use of their currencies: they guarantee funds to their own banks so as to allow them to expand internationally. The international extension of a country's banking system in turn facilitates the commercial and industrial penetration of national capital into foreign markets.[88] In part this is done by using Eurodollars, but it is an advantage to be able to use the national currency, especially since the banks' customers are then assured that if difficulties arise the bank can always be refinanced by its central bank. Until recently, this privilege had been enjoyed only by American banks, while non-American banks were never sure that they could have access to adequate quantities of the dollar reserves of their own central banks if the need arose.

Apart from bank loans, there are signs that the strong-currency countries are beginning to issue medium- and long-term financial credits in their national currencies. Switzerland often does this, and so did Japan in an important loan to China. Britain has begun to follow suit: its Export Credit Guaranty Department has authorized the financing of long-term export credit in sterling. Nor are instances of the use of national currencies in international operations limited to

[87] For data on the foreign position of credit agencies, see Bank for International Settlements, *Report*, issued annually. On the mounting internationalization of the yen, see 'Business Brief: A Less Arthritic Yen?', *The Economist*, 1 September 1979.

[88] Some data on the international expansion of the European banking system are contained in D.F. Channon, *British Banking Strategy and the International Challenge*, London 1977.

the triad of strong currencies—marks, yen, and Swiss francs. Indeed, we now find such trends, though perhaps somewhat tenuously, for all currencies that evince the slightest degree of stability. When the pound began to be bolstered by North Sea oil income, for example, it began to acquire an international role again, and non-resident deposits in sterling rose significantly. Thus also the French franc, which the French banks are seeking frequently to use and the government wants to employ for international loans and aid. The Saudi Arabian riyal can be added to the list as well, for the Saudi authorities are seeking to establish it as a regional reserve currency.

Nevertheless, great prudence has been in evidence in officially sanctioning the use of these reserve currencies in the international monetary system.

Similar circumspection was apparent in determining the characteristics of the European Currency Unit (ECU). This unit, created by the Brussels Accord of December 1978, represents not an addition to international liquidity, but only a redenomination of a portion of the reserves of the European countries. During discussions on European monetary union it was often asserted that the currency unit ought to have features similar to SDRs: created by the European Fund for Monetary Cooperation (FECOM) and allocated to EEC members in proportion to their economic importance.[89] The unit that was actually established, however, is issued by FECOM in exchange for cessions of gold and dollars by the European central banks.

Despite the circumspection in officially sanctioning the role of currencies alternative to the dollar, the presence of great quantities of these currencies on Euromarkets is leading to some diversification of reserves. Table 6 presents the growth and evolution of the composition of official reserves of world exchange. Alongside some rise of official assets in marks for Germany, which largely compensates for the fall in the scope of sterling assets, we may note a hefty growth of holdings in Eurocurrencies other than Eurodollars, which totalled $12 thousand million by the end of 1977. According to unofficial information reported in the financial press, holdings in other Eurocurrencies may actually be much greater, for they are partially concealed, either in the category labelled 'residual' in table 6, or in a different definition of reserves by some countries. Moreover, the data of table 6 refer only to members of the IMF and therefore exclude the

---

[89] See Bank of Italy, *Relazione all'Assemblea*, Rome 1973, pp. 387–95.

Comecon countries (except Romania), which seem to possess substantial quantities of German marks.[90] But even the official data demonstrate a mounting tendency to use 'other currencies'. It is known that the countries of the Group of Ten, which hold the lion's

Table 6

Official Foreign-Currency Holdings: Size and Composition at Year End (in thousands of millions of SDRs)

	1969	1974	1977
Official assets deposited in the US	16.0	62.8	103.8
Official sterling assets deposited in the UK	5.2	8.3	3.3
Official assets in marks deposited in Germany	0.5	2.4	5.7
Official assets in francs deposited in France	0.4	1.1	0.8
Other official assets deposited in other countries, in holding country's currency	—*	1.5	4.6
Official currency assets originating from swap credits or aid	2.8	1.3**	1.2**
Official holdings of Eurocurrencies, of which:	4.9	38.2	70.3
Eurodollars	4.9	32.4	58.0
Other Eurocurrencies	—	5.8	12.3
Official assets identified by IBRD and AID	0.6	0.9	2.1
Residual***	2.6	10.4	9.4
Total of official holdings in foreign currency	33.0	126.9	201.2

*   This figure was not available before 1970; the 1969 figure is included as 'residual'.

**   Includes the reciprocal double-deposit agreement in gold and dollars between the Bundesbank and the Bank of Italy.

*** Part of this residue exists because some member countries do not specify the nationality of all their currency assets. It also includes asymmetries that arise from the fact that data on the currency debits of the US and UK are more general than the data on official currency holdings given by other countries.

Source: IMF.

[90] See D. Marsh, 'The Move Away From the Dollar', *Financial Times*, 7 March 1979. According to this source, official mark holdings at the end of 1978 amounted to $28 thousand million, Swiss-franc holdings were $6 thousand million, yen holdings $6–7 thousand million. A good part of the official holdings of marks was accounted for by the $3.2 thousand million in marks obtained by the American government by issuing four-year mark-denominated bonds on the German market in November 1978 (so-called Carter bonds). For the first time since the war, the United States created a reserve consisting of a foreign currency. It remains to be seen whether this initiative was merely an emergency measure or whether it is due to become a common practice.

share of reserves, do not possess significant quantities of 'other currencies'. The increment in this category of reserves is therefore due exclusively to the diversification of reserves by the developing non-oil-exporting countries (since OPEC members also apply a rigid 'dollars only' rule when it comes to reserves). It is thus evident that without a decision by the industrialized countries, the diversification of official reserves will not be very significant. And it seems hard to believe that any move to diversify reserves seriously could be taken without the assent of the United States.

In the absence of such a decision, we will continue to see a rise in private liquidity denominated in other currencies. Concern that the existence of extensive Eurocurrency markets will make the exercise of national monetary policy difficult is far from becoming a real threat: Switzerland can easily tolerate a Eurofranc market about one-third the size of the Euromark market, for its national income and money supply are a much lower fraction than Germany's. There is thus plenty of room for expansion of the Euromark, and even more for expansion of the Euroyen. There is, of course, little need to emphasize that this uncontrolled expansion of the reserve role of some currencies potentially poses enormous problems for the future of the international monetary system. The vast quantities of convertible money in the hands of non-residents could boomerang on the issuing countries if doubts about the stability of these currencies begin to arise. In some respects the problem is similar to that of the sterling balances of the post-war period.[91] Looking beyond the immediate conjuncture, then, it seems that a tendency toward the strengthening of the dollar may be in the cards. The rise in the price of energy, if it continues, will inevitably render the United States self-sufficient, and probably even a net exporter, for the country commands extensive reserves of oil, coal, and uranium. In addition, the amount of cultivable land per capita, which is higher in the United States than in the other industrialized countries, will help to preserve the US trade

[91] During the Second World War Britain was unable to cover its imports with export sales. The countries of the sterling area and some others not belonging to the area therefore accumulated sterling balances in London. When the British economy began to become less competitive despite the devaluation of 1949, fears about the stability of the pound triggered conversions of these enormous sums into dollars. The conversions were further stimulated by the need for dollars on the part of those countries whose trade was increasingly shifting outside the sterling area. The problem dragged on through the middle of the seventies, and was one of the major factors in both the stop-go economic policy and the belatedness of British adherence to the EEC.

surplus in agriculture. If the technology and productivity gap that still separates the United States from the other industrialized countries continues to narrow, its vast natural resources will continue to favour the American economy and its currency, in the future as in the past.

2
The Devaluation
of the Dollar

1. The Great Crisis

The analysis presented in chapter 1 emphasized that one of the major factors unbalancing the international economy during the seventies was the strong increase in the price of oil, made possible by the augmented oil imports of the United States. In itself, however, the rise in oil prices would not have been able to plunge the entire industrialized world into a crisis that is now frequently compared to the great slump of the thirties in duration, gravity, and scope. Although unemployment has not reached the level of the thirties in relative terms, the total number out of work in the countries of the Organization for Economic Cooperation and Development (OECD) has not dipped below 15 million since 1974.[1]

The comparison to the great slump may be useful in clarifying some of the underlying reasons for the disorders of the international economy in the seventies. In the thirties two international factors assumed particular importance: the devaluation of the pound and the dollar, and the crisis in international financial relations. The hefty devaluation of the two major currencies of the international economy of the time brought about a restriction of outlets for the other countries, which reacted with competitive devaluations and protectionist measures. The effect of these reactions was to exacerbate the contraction of world trade, making it increasingly difficult for each country to sell on foreign markets a volume of exports sufficient to pay for imports, the demand for which was stimulated by the income generated by the near-full employment of the twenties. This

[1] The OECD includes twenty-four industrialized countries. Only Israel and South Africa are not members.

uncooperative behaviour by the various nations was exacerbated by the shortage of international reserves and the nearly complete lack of official financial channels. Indeed, international financial relations had been undermined by the thorny problem of German war reparations, which was linked in turn to the settlement of the debts incurred by the allies during the First World War.[2] As we know, the story had an unhappy ending, for many countries found that the only way to secure the export outlets through which to earn revenue with which to pay for imports seemed to be to stake out areas of their own exclusive preserve—the Commonwealth for Britain, the central Danube region for Germany, the 'sphere of co-prosperity' in the Far East for Japan, thus creating the conditions for the second world conflict.

Historical comparisons are legitimate and useful, even though the actual course of history may be very different in the two cases. Thus, at the root of the crisis of the seventies we find a heavy devaluation of the dollar, which occurred in three phases: 1971, 1973, and 1977–78. Thus also, the increase in the price of oil alarmingly weakened the international financial position of the developed countries. Because of the simultaneous occurrence of these two phenomena, the complex inter-weaving of financial institutions and channels that had evolved from the structures established by the Bretton Woods agreement to assure adequate stocks of reserves for the various countries encountering balance of payments difficulties became inadequate. But the comparison stops there. Indeed, despite the influence of common factors, the aetiologies of the two international crises seem profoundly diverse. The origin of the crisis in the thirties is usually—and rightly—located in a severe plunge in income in the United States during the first part of the decade, the origins of which must in turn be sought in the characteristics of American development in the twenties and in the economic policies applied by successive American governments, especially in the realm of finance.[3] The American

---

[2] On the economic policies of the major economies during the 1930s, see E. Lundberg, *Instability and Economic Growth*, New Haven 1968. On the evolution of international monetary relations, see L.B. Yeager, *International Monetary Relations*, New York 1966. On the problem of German reparations, see D.H. Aldcroft, *From Versailles to Wall Street 1919–1929*, London 1977, and H. Fleisig, 'War-Related Debts and the Great Depression', *American Economic Review*, May 1976.

[3] On the American crisis, see J.K. Galbraith, *The Great Crash, 1929*, London 1955, and C.P. Kindleberger, *The World in Depression, 1929–1939*, London 1973.

depression was transmitted to the other countries, and its effects on world trade, and therefore on income, were aggravated by the factors mentioned above—competitive devaluations and disorder in financial relations.

We find nothing similar in the economy of the 1970s. The origin of the crisis cannot be located in a decline in income in any particular country (although there is no doubt that recession began in the United States in the first quarter of 1973 and was already well under way before the increase in oil prices, the effects of which began to take hold only in 1974). This, of course, is related to the orientation of economic policy during the post-war period, profoundly different from that of the pre-war period, stamped as it was by the teachings of Keynesianism. The instruments of control of aggregate demand were firmly in the hands of national governments, which strove to use them to stabilize income. Nevertheless, ability to employ these techniques had been reduced somewhat during the second half of the sixties and the beginning of the seventies as a result of accelerating inflation in the Western economies.

It is beyond the scope of this book to assess the degree to which preoccupation with inflation may have determined the orientation of economic policy in the industrialized countries during the 1970s. Our concern is primarily with the way in which the particular factors of international financial relations influenced the stagnation of the international economy during the seventies. Nor will I consider the problem, in any case insoluble, of determining whether inflation alone would have led to the adoption of deflationary policies of the scope that were actually applied during the seventies, under the impact of the collapse of international financial co-operation and the inadequacy of the Bretton Woods system. Therefore, although I would not like to underestimate this order of problem, which is related both to the inflationary propensities of the development of the capitalist economies in the post-war period and to the role the system of fixed exchange rates may have played in spreading and intensifying these propensities, it is nevertheless useful to focus attention on the factors linked specifically to the dysfunction of the international financial system. These factors have been identified, by comparison with the 1930s, as the devaluation of the dollar and the inability of the international financial system to supply an adequate level of reserves. The present chapter will examine the devaluation of the dollar.

2. Us Monetary Policy and the Dollar

There is little doubt that the development of inflation is itself inextricably linked to the sphere of international finance. Indeed, the options of us monetary policy, which brought about the devaluation of the dollar, greatly contributed to the acceleration of inflation. Table 7 shows that the rate of inflation in the United States began accelerating in the second half of the 1960s. The accepted canons of economic policy would have induced the government to adopt restrictive fiscal and monetary policies. Instead, as of 1970 the United States adopted an expansive fiscal and monetary policy, relying on price and wage controls alone in the struggle against inflation. The American reflation of the early seventies is the real cause of the acceleration of inflation, not only in the United States but in the rest of the world as well. In conditions that were *already* inflationary, as was the case in the United States and the world as a whole at the end of the previous decade, a rise in the money supply at a rate several times greater than the increase in nominal income, combined with the

Table 7

Rates of Consumer Price Increases in the Six Major Industrialized Countries, 1960–78 (in %)

	1960–65	1966–9	1970	1971	1972	1973	1974	1975	1976	1977	1978
USA	1.3	3.9	5.9	4.3	3.3	6.2	11.0	9.2	5.8	6.5	6.8
Japan	5.9	5.0	7.2	6.3	4.8	11.8	22.7	12.2	9.3	8.1	4.5
France	3.7	4.0	5.2	5.5	5.9	7.3	13.6	11.8	9.6	9.5	9.3
Germany	2.6	2.3	3.7	5.3	5.5	6.9	7.0	6.9	4.6	3.9	2.6
Italy	4.5	2.4	4.9	4.8	5.7	10.8	19.1	17.2	16.7	16.9	12.1
Britain	3.1	4.1	6.4	9.4	7.1	9.1	15.9	24.2	16.8	15.9	8.5

Source: IMF.

consequent lowering of interest rates, was surely fated to speed inflation. The impetus to productive activity generated by rising prices was further amplified by the reduction in the cost of money and the easy availability of credit. The mounting pressure on productive capacity and availability of labour-power caused a further rise in prices. Once it was firmly expected that prices would continue to rise faster than the low interest rates (especially for some goods for which elasticity of supply is low), speculation mounted, in the form of the production of goods to be hoarded until prices rose above the cost of production plus maintenance. The excessively expansive monetary policy also stimulated financial speculation, which had the effect, at least initially, of swelling corporate liquidity and thus permitting investments that otherwise could not have been undertaken because of the financial constraints to which companies were subject.[4]

In the light of these considerations, the decision of the Federal Reserve System to allow the money supply to rise by more than 10% a year (table 8) for three successive years under conditions of inflation seems difficult to justify merely by concern about the business cycle and the liquidity of financial brokers caused by the recession of 1969.[5] Even if such concern may have been justified in 1970, it was no longer so by 1971, when the recovery was already well under way and the liquidity of the financial system fully re-established. Nor can we accept the theory that the US government was concerned to obtain the maximum expansive effects during the recovery phase. Indeed, even if the government had wanted to force the issue (to achieve full employment by the time of the presidential election campaign, for example), it could have relied more heavily on tax policy, which inevitably has more immediate and less inflationary effects than monetary policy.

We may thus rule out the 'benevolent' interpretation of US monetary policy during the three years 1970–72: the claim that the administration was simply pursuing its own development objectives, creating money without considering the effects this would have on the rest of the world. On the contrary, the US government could have pursued exactly the same aims through a different economic policy— one which, relying more moderately on monetary expansion, would have had less dangerous consequences for the rest of the world.

Of course, the United States created money not because it was

[4] The importance of the money supply in an inflationary situation is demonstrated in M. Kalecki, 'A Model of Hyperinflation'. *The Manchester School*, September 1962.

[5] In 1969, in an effort to bring inflation under control, the United States had adopted a restrictive monetary policy that wreaked much damage to the financial structure of the American economy: there were instances of 'disbrokerage' of the commercial banks, which were hampered in their competition with other brokers not subject to controls on debtor interest rates, and serious difficulties for many companies, some of which went bankrupt, thus endangering the credit-finance institutions. For an analysis of this phenomenon of interaction between financial structure and restrictive policy with reference to the British experience of 1973, see A.T.K. Grant, *Economic Uncertainty and Financial Structure*, London 1977.

impossible to apply any particular tax policy, but rather in order to devalue the dollar relative to other currencies, thus simultaneously protecting its supremacy in the world financial order.

An analysis of the process of the devaluation of the dollar will enable us to grasp how the expansion of the US money supply was generalized throughout the capitalist world. Since the expansion of the money supply in the United States caused a lowering of US interest rates relative to those prevailing in other countries, funds were shifted from the United States to the rest of the world. The countries subjected to the influx of US capital (all the other countries of the OECD, but especially Germany, Switzerland, the Netherlands, and Austria) were compelled to create national money in exchange for the dollars flowing into their reserves. The shift of funds assumed truly

Table 8

Rates of Growth of Some Monetary Aggregates, 1968–73
(in %)

	(1)	(2)	(3)	(4)
1968	9.83	1.7	10.29	12.78
1969	− 0.69	2.1	9.06	5.87
1970	12.63	22.0	12.37	16.40
1971	12.05	32.5	18.69	25.44
1972	11.47	19.5	16.96	20.50
1973	12.09	4.7	19.04	22.54

(1) Us money supply.
(2) International reserves, worldwide.
(3) Eurodollar market.
(4) World money supply.

Source: IMF.

enormous proportions. Germany alone had to absorb more than $4 thousand million during the first five months of 1971, before its decision to let the mark float, and it had already absorbed $9 thousand million during 1970. Any attempt to 'sterilize' the inflow of foreign funds was automatically transformed into the maintenance of differential interest rates in favour of national currency, thereby encouraging even greater influxes from the United States. This wave of incoming dollars during 1970 and the first five months of 1971 swelled European and Japanese reserves; the countries subjected to the flood of dollars in turn sought to invest them profitably in the Eurodollar market, thus stimulating its growth (table 8). Since the continuous influx of dollars into countries with strong balances of payments (like those named above) gave rise to expectations that these countries would revalue their currency relative to the dollar, the influx of funds motivated by the differential interest rates was compounded by transfers by speculators hoping to profit from the revaluation. These speculative shifts were fuelled by funds borrowed from the Eurodollar market (which had been deposited by the central banks), itself a target of speculative attack. In March 1971 the major central banks decided to freeze the deposit of reserves on the Euromarket.

By now, however, expectations that European currencies would be revalued relative to the dollar were so strong that they provoked an increment in the demand for loans (for speculation) on the Eurodollar market, such that the level of rates on Eurodollars rose well above the usual spread of $\frac{1}{2}\%$ on the us rate.[6] The stream of funds from the United States to the Euromarket thus continued, supplanting the deposits of the European central banks and fuelling speculation on strong currencies. In view of this avalanche of dollars, it was inevitable that the currencies of the European countries and Japan would have to be revalued, although to varying extents.

3. The Currency Crises of 1971 and 1973

Briefly, the developments of the currency crisis were as follows.[7] The impossibility of maintaining the previous par value relative to the dollar impelled the strong currencies to revalue or float in May 1971. The persistence of speculative expectations on the market because of the us balance of payments deficit created by the American recovery provoked a new wave of speculation against the dollar, which resulted in August 1971 in the declaration that the dollar was no longer convertible for gold and in the subsequent fluctuation of the

---

[6] The relation between rates on the Eurodollar market and rates on the us market is explained in G. Dufey and I.H. Giddy, *The International Money Market*, Englewood Cliffs, New Jersey 1978, chapter 11.

[7] An excellent review of the events of the period is contained in the annual *Report* of the Bank for International Settlements of the appropriate years.

other currencies relative to the dollar until the establishment of new par values in December of the same year.[8] Because of the strong opposition of competing countries, the new par values did not satisfy the US demand for an adequate devaluation of the dollar: it had depreciated by only 9% relative to the other currencies.[9] The reestablishment of currency normality was followed by a period of rigidification of US monetary policy, which froze the outflow of dollars. Nevertheless, while the United States expressed dissatisfaction with the inadequate scope of the devaluation, policy became permissive again, even though the US business cycle was peaking once more and therefore should have elicited a restrictive policy.

Outflows of the dollar began again during the second half of 1972, and the central banks of the competing countries were plunged into difficulty once again, for they were committed to controlling an ever rising inflation. In the meantime, Britain engaged in an operation similar to that of the United States, although on a smaller scale: strong monetary expansion was accompanied by the fluctuation of sterling in June 1972. The pound consequently fell in value rapidly, while inflation in Britain accelerated under the dual impact of monetary expansion and increases in the price of imports. The British experience is of interest, for it was repeated in 1973 by Italy, which detached the lira from the other European currencies and pursued an extremely expansive monetary policy. Obviously, under these conditions the float of the lira brought about a significant devaluation, which fuelled a galloping inflation that managed, in the space of just a few quarters, to readjust the distribution of income in favour of profits and rents, a distribution that had previously been shifted in the opposite direction by the wage struggles of the workers.

In the first half of 1972, in face of the outflows of dollars caused by the slackening of US monetary restrictions (which were, in any event, more limited than those imposed in 1971) and under pressure from the other industrialized countries, the United States began intervening to support the dollar again, scotching the speculative expectations that were once more on the rise. Nevertheless, the increase in the US trade deficit, brought about by the rise in imports (caused in turn by the strong recovery of the economy, and in part by the devaluation

[8] The so-called Smithsonian par values.
[9] In part this was a modest devaluation relative to gold, the price of which rose from $35 to $38 an ounce; in part it was a direct devaluation relative to the other currencies.

itself, with the consequent relative rise in the cost of imports), gave rise to a fresh wave of speculation against the dollar at the beginning of 1973. In February the dollar was devalued by 10%.[10] In order to keep control of their national money supplies, the other countries decided to let their own currencies float. Some of the European currencies floated together, the lira and pound independently.[11]

But the devaluation of the dollar did not convince the market. In March 1973 it was officially decided to abandon the system of fixed exchange rates and to inaugurate the generalized floating of currencies. Not all currencies floated freely. Many preferred to hitch themselves to the currency of the country with which they maintained the most intense trade relations. The European countries had agreed in the spring of 1972 to jointly float their own currencies within the enlarged band around the central rate of the dollar established by the Smithsonian agreement of December 1971. This joint float, known as the 'snake', remained in operation (though without the lira and pound) even after the shift of world currencies to generalized floating.[12]

The essential characteristic of the system of floating exchange rates is that it enables the dollar to depreciate without serious inflationary consequences, whereas the depreciation of other currencies provokes an acceleration of inflation in their respective national economies. The dollar continued to depreciate throughout 1973, especially relative to the stronger currencies. This completed the first two phases of devaluation. Once this second phase was over, the dollar generally entered a period of strength, despite the wild gyrations in its value relative to various particular currencies. By the beginning of 1977 its average rate of depreciation, corrected for differential inflation rates (this is called 'average real depreciation'), had returned it more or less to the level of December 1971. In other words, the advantages won in 1973 had been almost completely eroded. In the summer of 1977 the era of 'benign neglect', during which US monetary authorities had abandoned the dollar's exchange rate to the market and had formulated economic policy on the basis of internal objectives alone, came to an end. It was succeeded by a period of repeated fiery

[10] Once again, through a slight devaluation relative both to gold, the price of which rose from $38 to $42 an ounce, and to the other currencies.

[11] See chapter 1.

[12] Chapter 5 will discuss the evolution of the snake up to the establishment of the European Monetary System.

declarations by Treasury Secretary Michael Blumenthal about the alleged over-valuation of the dollar, in what came to be called the 'open mouth policy'.

This rapid sketch of the major monetary events of the first part of the seventies makes it clear that during the initial phase of dollar devaluation there was a close connection between US monetary policy and the international position of the dollar. This link caused an enormous expansion of international liquidity. The expansion of liquidity in turn brought about a leap in the rate of price increases in various countries throughout the world.[13] Increases in the money supply were propagated to prices through many channels, thus accelerating inflation. In particular, raw materials, both reproducible and otherwise, became targets of speculation. Raw materials prices consequently soared to unprecedented heights, temporarily altering the terms of trade in favour of the producing countries and facilitating the establishment of accords to maintain or increase already high prices.[14] The most successful manoeuvre by producers was the decision to raise the price of oil, the effect of which in the context of US strategy will be examined later. Nevertheless, the rise in inflation was a by-product of US monetary moves, the true aim of which was to devalue the dollar. At this point we must ask why the United States could not have attained the same result simply by devaluing the dollar relative to gold, in accordance with the terms of the Bretton Woods agreement under which the IMF had been constituted.

[13] Of course, floating exchange rates also accelerate inflation, as pointed out in chapter 1, because the rise in the price of imports consequent to downward fluctuations of the exchange rate is transmitted through the entire system of national costs. Nevertheless, in the years we are considering here, from 1971 to 1973, the effects of the rise in raw materials prices was the major influence on inflation. For a deeper examination of the relationship between floating exchange rates and inflation, see H.G. Johnson and A. Swoboda (eds.), *The Economics of Common Currencies*, London 1973. See also the accurate and careful scrutiny of the thesis that floating exchange rates generate inflation in M. von Neumann Whitman, 'Global Monetarism and the Monetary Approach to the Balance of Payments', *Brookings Papers on Economic Activity*, no. 3, 1975. For an overall view of the influences on the international inflation rate, see A. Crockett, *International Money—Issues and Analysis*, Middlesex 1977, chapter 11.

[14] The link between the increase in international liquidity and inflation is accepted without reserve by the economists of the monetarist school. For the most consistent expositions of this point of view, see A.K. Swoboda, 'Monetary Approaches to Worldwide Inflation', in L.B. Krause and W.S. Salant (eds.); H.R. Heller, 'International Reserves and Worldwide Inflation', *IMF Staff Papers*, March 1976; and G.

4. Devaluation and the International
Position of the Dollar

In this interpretation, then, the international acceleration of inflation is a by-product of the continual devaluation of the dollar. It is indeed doubtful whether the boom in raw materials prices during 1972–74 could have occurred without the increase in liquidity produced by the flow of American payments, even given the high level of demand. [15] On two occasions, in 1971 and 1973, the United States was compelled to force a market crisis of the dollar through an excessive expansion of the money supply, because this was the only way to effect a devaluation of the dollar sufficient to redress the American balance of payments while simultaneously protecting the international role of the dollar. In chapter 1 I sought to demonstrate that the United States draws substantial advantages from the dollar's function as a reserve currency and that there was little chance that the American government would accept a significant reduction of this role. Now, the more damaging collateral effects of the devaluation of the dollar—excessive creation of international liquidity, abandonment of the system of fixed in favour of floating exchange rates—could have been averted if the dollar had been devalued in accordance with the rules established under the Bretton Woods system. This could have happened in two ways: either revaluation of the other currencies relative to the dollar, the gold-value of the dollar remaining

---

Zis, 'Political Origins of the International Monetary Crisis', *National Westminster Bank Quarterly Review*, August 1975. Nevertheless, it is not necessary to accept the monetarist paradigm to recognize that there is a causal relation between international liquidity and inflation, provided one agrees—as do the overwhelming majority of economists concerned with the problem—that the increase in raw materials prices generated by the high demand brought about by the synchronization of the economic recovery of the various industrialized countries was inflated out of all proportion because of the high liquidity available to speculators. See T. Balogh, *Fact and Fancy in International Economic Relations*, Oxford 1973; R.N. Cooper and R.Z. Lawrence, 'The 1972–75 Commodity Boom', *Brookings Papers on Economic Activity*, no. 3, 1975. And on the general aspects, see C.F. Bergsten, 'The New Era in Commodity Markets', *Challenge*, September–October 1974.

[15] Let us note once again that the increase in liquidity, according to this interpretation, only permits but does not cause the explosion of prices. Indeed, in the period 1974–79 the American deficits and the expansion of international liquidity (both private and official, although private to a much greater extent) continued to occur at an order of magnitude relatively comparable to that of the early years of the seventies. And yet there was no new raw materials boom, because the conditions of international demand did not favour the stimulation of speculation.

unchanged, or devaluation of the dollar relative to gold, and consequently relative to the other currencies, these maintaining the same gold value.[16] In the event, the other industrialized countries were not inclined to revalue their own currencies relative to the dollar while leaving the gold-value of the dollar unchanged. In December 1971 and February 1973, under the pressure of the crisis of the dollar triggered by the withdrawal of funds for speculation, the industrialized countries had accepted a compromise: the devaluation of the dollar was effected partly through a revaluation of their own currencies and partly through a diminution of the gold-value of the dollar. But this solution was not congenial to the United States, because it tended to raise the importance of gold in the international monetary system, despite the declaration of inconvertibility in August 1971. Indeed, the devaluation the United States was seeking for its currency was so great that, had it been effected relative to gold even in part, it would have seriously endangered the survival of the international role of the dollar.

To clarify this relationship, let us examine the particular problems of the settlement of the American balance of payments. To begin with, it should be noted that for the United States, settlement does not mean bringing the current account into balance, but obtaining a high current-account surplus with which to finance the outflows of funds that are part and parcel of the role of a country that stands at the economic, financial, political, and military centre of the world.[17] Indeed, during the sixties, when the dollar was already encountering serious problems, the American deficits were made up of capital movements; the current-account remained generally in surplus, partially contributing to financing the capital movements. Therefore, for the United States at the beginning of the seventies, settling the balance of payments meant attempting to achieve a consistent current-account surplus (during the negotiations preceding the

---

[16] It should be recalled that under the Bretton Woods system only the value of the dollar was expressly fixed in terms of gold, at a price of $35 per ounce of refined gold. The gold value of the other currencies was derived from their exchange rate with the dollar at the official par value.

[17] The analysis here is somewhat simplified, for it ignores the not insignificant effects devaluation can have on capital flows, for both direct and portfolio investments. For an examination of these effects in the case of the United States, see the essays contained in section II of P.B. Clark, D.E. Logue, and R.J. Sweeney (eds.), *The Effects of Exchange Rate Adjustments*, OASIA Research, Department of the Treasury, Washington DC, 1974.

Smithsonian agreement there was talk that the United States was aiming at a $15 thousand million surplus) with which to finance capital movements, traditionally negative for the United States (although a portion of the capital-account deficit had been eliminated in the 1960s by the imposition of various forms of administrative controls on capital flows).[18]

To achieve a current-account surplus of this magnitude would have meant a considerable devaluation, well above those realized by the modifications of par value in December 1971 and February 1973. If all, or at least a large portion, of such a devaluation had been effected through an increase in the official gold price, the trend toward the restoration of a greater monetary role for gold would have become irresistible.[19] A 'return to gold' would have been even more likely in view of the difficulties in settling the US balance of payments, even after a hefty devaluation. Indeed, the American economy is so large and represents such a vast market for the rest of the world that any diminution of its imports and rise in its exports tends to result in a surge of balance of payments problems for the other countries, which are compelled to enact restrictive policies or to devalue in turn, however painful the inflationary cost. If income in the rest of the world contracts, American exports decline and settlement tends to be postponed, thus perpetuating the weakness of the dollar in the intervening period. After a big devaluation relative to gold, then, the dollar would have been at the mercy of European economic policy, which could have weakened it further by unleashing a recession under the constraint of balance of payments difficulties;[20] in that event the drive of the market toward gold would have become irrepressible. For the first time Europe would have commanded an effective weapon against the United States. The only way to square the circle would have been to finance a European recovery, despite the

[18] On the control of portfolio capital movements, see W.H. Branson, 'Monetary Policy and the New View of International Capital Movements', *Brookings Papers on Economic Activity*, 2, 1970. On the control of direct investments, see H. David Wiley, 'Direct Investment Controls and the Balance of Payments', in C.P. Kindleberger (ed.), *The International Corporation*, Cambridge, Mass. 1970.

[19] The hope that gold could play a greater role as a means of payment has never really died among a large group of European countries, which constitute the so-called gold bloc. This is demonstrated by the care with which these countries reconstituted significant gold stocks during the sixties, even higher than those of the pre-war period.

[20] In practice, a decision by Germany alone to deflate would suffice to trigger European deflation, given the importance of the German economy.

emergence of payments deficits. But since the financing would not have been in dollars, for that would have compromised the stability of American currency even further, alternative means of international finance would have had to be used: SDRs or the European currencies themselves, which thereby would have assumed the status of reserve currencies.

Once it was decided to devalue the dollar, the only way to do so effectively,[21] in a manner not dangerous to the role of the dollar, was to jettison even the indirect reference to gold expressed in the par values of the Bretton Woods system. It was therefore necessary to effect devaluation not through constant tinkering with par values but through a continuing series of depreciations under a system of floating exchange rates, which is just what began in March 1973. The system of floating exchange rates also eliminated any need for the United States to control its own balance of payments deficit, no matter what its source, because it was now possible to release unlimited quantities of non-convertible dollars into international circulation. Therefore, while continuing to depreciate the dollar in an attempt to recover competitivity in the production of goods, the United States was no longer saddled with the problem of generating a

[21] It is known that the dollar can be devalued without serious inflationary consequences, but the effect of devaluation on trade flows is difficult to measure, partly because American exporters facing stagnating markets are unable to take advantage of the full competitive scope offered them by devaluation; they generally continue to orient productive investment toward the national market. In other words, the 'income effect' acts against the 'price effect' in the process of settlement of the US balance of payments. In effect, as I will argue later in this chapter, the United States applied an expansive policy in the seventies, but the income of the European countries was restricted by the oil deficits, and that created unfavourable conditions for the growth of American exports and simultaneously impelled European and Japanese producers to seek outlets in the American market (which was then expanding rapidly), thus increasing American imports. Some data on American trade after the devaluation may be found in R. Brusca, 'United States Export Performance'. Indeed, it appears that the manufactured exports of the United States are made up almost entirely of capital and intermediary goods, the demand for which is highly sensitive to the business cycle in the rest of the world. It is well known that the investment cycle has higher peaks and lower troughs than the income cycle. The composition of American exports accounts for their particularly elastic dependence on the income of the rest of the world. In part these inter-reactions explain why variations in *real* exchange rates (in other words, variations adjusted for the differential in inflation rates) have failed to modify the share of world trade made up of the manufactures of the major capitalist countries—a failure that has generated a wave of 'devaluation pessimism' similar to the 'elasticity pessimism' of the 1950s. A radical expression of devaluation pessimism may be found in N. Kaldor, 'The Effects of Devaluation on Trade in Manufactures', in *Further Essays on Applied Economics*, London 1978.

current account surplus with which to finance its capital-account deficit.

This new situation was reflected on the one hand in the energy policy discussed in chapter 1, which increased oil imports and thus sent the trade balance into irremediable deficit. On the other hand, in January 1974 controls on foreign capital movements were completely abolished, which facilitated the emergence of hefty deficits in both the long-term capital account and the banking account (see table 2). In practical terms, the problem of the settlement of the American balance of payments simply disappeared. The administration duly drew the conclusion and, in 1976, ceased calculating the statistics previously used to determine the overall state of the US balance of payments (the balance as calculated on the basis of official settlements, on the basis of the balance of payments model of the IMF, and on the basis of net liquidity),[22] furnishing only partial balances of current items and some varieties of capital movements. These statistics are difficult to compare with the previous series, because items are constantly shifted from one account to another.[23]

The rise in American oil imports facilitated the price increases ordered by OPEC in the fourth quarter of 1973. The rise in oil prices had a terrible depressive effect on the economies of the industrialized countries, saddling them with current-account deficits and consequent problems of financing;[24] at the same time, it gave powerful impetus to inflation, which in turn made deflationary policies necessary. The United States, however, did not have to bother about foreign financial constraints. Its deflation was therefore of short duration, and by 1975 a recovery had already begun that produced US growth rates among the highest of the post-war period. The recovery lasted until the beginning of 1979, reabsorbing a good part of the high unemployment. The other industrialized countries, on the other hand, were throttled by the financial constraint, partly because of the perverse functioning of international financial mechanisms (see

[22] See 'The Presentation of the US Balance of Payments: A Symposium', *Essays in International Finance*, no. 123, Princeton University, August 1977. See especially the critique by R. Triffin, pp. 24–34.

[23] Other modifications have been made as well, such as listing the profits of multinational corporations reinvested abroad as a credit in the current account, thus counting these profits simultaneously as a current entry and a long-term capital outgo in the form of direct investments.

[24] For an analysis of these problems, see L. Izzo and L. Spaventa, 'Alcuni effetti interni ed esterni dell'aumento del prezzo del petrolio', *Moneta e credito*, March 1974.

chapter 3), and sank into a recession that lasted through the remainder of the decade, halving their growth rates compared with the preceding period.[25]

The Euro-Japanese recession resulted in a stagnation of American manufactured exports, save the occasional uptick, and simultaneously encouraged foreign producers to orient to an American market undergoing a vigorous expansion—especially Japanese producers frozen out of a European market mired in crisis. This was accompanied by a series of competitive devaluations on the part of countries like Italy, Spain, Mexico, Canada, Brazil, and others, which succeeded, despite the inflationary cost, in restoring competitivity to these economies, nearly annulling, by the end of 1976, the average gains in US competitivity. The United States then modified its currency policy, which from the end of 1973 to the second quarter of 1977 had been guided by benign neglect of the dollar's exchange rate, and began an aggressive drive toward devaluation, in an attempt to recover competitivity not so much relative to the countries with which it was trading, but relative to its most threatening competitors, Germany and Japan. The financial press called the new line the 'open mouth policy', for it was characterized by constant claims by Treasury Secretary Michael Blumenthal that the dollar was overvalued. The devaluation campaign was opened by a Blumenthal speech in Tokyo in June 1977 in which he insisted that the yen had to be revalued relative to the dollar. These statements continued in subsequent months, until the market became convinced that the dollar would soon depreciate. Thus began the third phase of the devaluation, which lasted until the Carter measures of 1 November 1978.[26] In 1979 the dollar's exchange rate stabilized, but the attitude of the market was profoundly altered and apprehensive: never again would American currency, debased by the American Secretary of the Treasury himself, be able to assume in the eyes of the world the role of guarantor of stability and secure bastion of purchasing power.

At the same time, the focal point of competitive conflict between the industrialized economies shifted from the markets of the industrial countries themselves toward new markets, both in the oil-

[25] Some of these countries, Germany in particular, made a virtue of necessity, applying a deflationary policy in order to strengthen the international position of its economy. I will return to this point in chapter 4.

[26] On the Carter measures, see chapter 1. For an overall assessment of the new devaluation of the dollar, with special reference to German policy, see chapter 4.

producing countries (the annual value of which amounted to about $100 thousand million over the decade), and in those of the newly industrializing countries, which were supplied with financing through private channels; the industrialized countries, however, have been unable to tap official financial channels sufficiently. Before analysing the perverse functioning of international financial mechanisms, it may be opportune to indicate why the United States finds it necessary to recover competitivity.

5. The Relative Decline of the American Economy

The idea that the US government desires to maintain the competitivity of its own economy was an underlying element of the preceding discussion. Maintenance of competitivity is indeed essential if the relative decline of the United States is to be halted. The scope of this decline is easily gleaned from the evolution of the comparative growth rates of the major OECD countries, illustrated in table 9. The post-war period has seen the economies of Japan, Germany, and France rise to the forefront. The performance of these economies has been superior to that of the United States in every respect: gross and net rate of accumulation, rate of expansion of exports, rate of development of share of world trade, rate of growth of per capita income, rate of growth of industrial productivity (see tables 10, 11, and 12).

Table 9

Rate of Growth of Gross National/Domestic Product of the Six Major Industrialized Countries, 1953–78
(in %)

	1953–60	1961–71	1972	1973	1974	1975	1976	1977	1978
USA	2.4	4.2	5.8	5.4	−1.6	−1.3	5.7	4.8	4.9
Japan	9.4	10.2	8.9	9.8	−1.1	2.4	6.4	5.4	5.6
Germany	7.0	4.6	3.4	5.1	0.7	−2.5	4.8	2.7	3.3
France	4.9	5.8	5.8	5.3	2.9	−1.0	4.5	2.3	3.4
Italy	5.8	4.2	3.1	6.8	3.4	−3.7	5.7	1.7	2.6
Britain	3.0	2.6	2.6	6.0	0.3	−1.6	2.2	2.4	3.2

Source: OECD.

Table 10

Annual Growth Rates of Industrial Productivity* in the Six Major Industrialized Countries, 1950–76
(in %)

USA	2.8
Japan	8.3
France	5.0
Germany	5.4
Italy	4.3
Britain	2.6

* Output per employee.

Source: A. Maddison, 'La dinamica della produttività nel lungo periodo', *Moneta e credito*, March 1979.

Table 11

Annual Growth Rate of Total Fixed Capital Stock (Excluding Housing) in the Six Major Industrialized Countries, 1950–77
(average of stocks, net and gross) (in %)

	1950–70	1971–77
USA	3.8	3.0
Japan	8.8	7.9
France	5.4	6.3
Germany	6.2	4.8
Italy	5.1*	5.0*
Britain	3.9	3.7

* Net stock only.

Source: See table 10.

Table 12

Evolution of Shares of World Exports in Manufactures of the Six Major Industrialized Countries
(in %)

	1956	1970	1976
USA	25.5	18.5	17.3
France	7.9	8.7	9.8
Germany	16.5	19.8	20.6
Japan	5.7	11.7	14.6
Italy	3.6	7.2	7.1
Britain	18.7	10.8	8.7

Source: UN.

Despite the improvement of the American economy in the sixties, the gap between the growth rates of the United States on the one hand and its competitors on the other, if it continued at the level of the seventies, would lead to dramatic results by the middle of the eighties: Japanese per capita income would equal that of the United States, and Germany and France would come close to achieving that same result. At the end of the sixties the United States faced a future of gradual loss of economic influence, and consequently of political power, over the rest of the capitalist world.

The causes of the low rate of development of the us economy are not very clear, particularly in view of the lamentable state of economic theory on the question of growth. Nevertheless, it seems clear that the over-valuation of the dollar during the post-war period[27] definitely aggravated the other contributing factors, even though it was not the sole cause.[28] Indeed, the rate of growth of a capitalist economy is a function of the rate of accumulation, and the dollar's high exchange rate reduced accumulation, in two ways. First, the need to maintain a trade surplus led the United States, particularly after the war, to adopt demand policies that held income below its potential; the low level of demand in turn reduced the rate of investment. Second, the over-valuation of the dollar made investment abroad more attractive.[29]

The relative improvement of the American growth rate in the sixties was due to the relaxation of the balance of payments

[27] This over-valuation probably dates from the wave of devaluation of European currencies relative to the dollar in 1949, followed by that of many non-European currencies.

[28] For a discussion of the relative weakening of the us economy and its connection with the international position of the dollar, see Bergsten, *The Dilemmas of the Dollar*; M. von Neumann, 'The Current and Future Role of the Dollar: How Much Symmetry?', *Brookings Papers on Economic Activity*, no. 3, 1974; 'International Interdependence and the Us Economy', in W. Fellner (ed.), *Contemporary Economic Problems*, Washington 1976. As regards the commercial performance of the United States compared with that of Germany and Japan, see N. Kaldor, 'The Effects of Devaluation on Trade in Manufactures'.

[29] In the fifties and sixties the differential in the cost of labour was so unfavourable to the United States that American companies were driven to transfer abroad all production that, having reached the stage of 'maturity', could easily be completed in countries whose average technological level and labour skills were lower than those of the United States. (On the theory of product cycles as a motivation for direct investment abroad as an alternative to exports, see R. Vernon, *Sovereignty at Bay: The Multinational Spread of Us Enterprises*, New York 1971.) Through this process, the ratio between production abroad by American enterprises and exports became ever greater, reaching 3.96 in 1971; the equivalent ratios for Germany and Japan at the same

constraint, made possible by an improvement in the US performance on inflation compared with its competitors in the early years of that decade. This permitted the adoption of more expansive demand policies. Nevertheless, the worsening of US inflation as of the middle sixties imposed balance of payments constraints once again. Hence the American decision to recover competitivity, devaluing the dollar once the inflationary pressure generated by the Vietnam war had run its course.

In fact, the devaluation of the dollar did lead to a considerable improvement in American competitivity, as is shown by the evolution of hourly wage costs. By the end of 1977 these were about 20% lower in the United States than in Germany and the other more advanced countries of Europe.[30] Nevertheless, because of problems we have already discussed, the improvement in competitivity was not reflected in an increase in the US share of world exports or in a consistent reduction in US imports,[31] but rather in a very strong increment of direct foreign investment in the United States, the scope of which more than tripled during the 1970s. In part there seems also to have been a dampening of US investment in the industrialized countries, but this was compensated for by a rise in investment in the newly industrializing countries.

The United States thus seemed to have averted the spectre of de-industrialization, of reduction to a service economy lacking any consistent industrial base, a spectre that had seemed especially threatening at the end of the 1960s.[32]

---

date were 0.37 and 0.38 respectively. See United Nations, *Multinational Corporations in World Development*, New York 1973. This process, which caused a gradual de-industrialization of the United States, began to trigger strong reactions among US public opinion, especially in the trade unions, during the seventies. On these subjects, see D.J.B. Mitchell, *Labor Issues of American International Trade and Investment*. Baltimore, Maryland 1976. For a complete review of the theoretical and applied literature on direct investment, see G.C. Hufbauer, 'The Multinational Corporation and Direct Investment', in P.B. Kenen (ed.), *International Trade and Finance: Frontiers for Research*, Cambridge 1975.

[30] For a deeper discussion of this point, see chapter 4.

[31] In part this may depend on the particular features of Japanese competition, concentrated in a few sectors in which the rates of investment and of increase in productivity are so high that the differentiation is nearly insurmountable by any devaluation.

[32] It is well known that the share of industrial production in gross national product is much lower in the United States than in the other industrialized countries, especially Germany.

But it does not seem that the United States has yet succeeded in raising the growth rate of its industrial productivity.[33] In other words, the potential growth rate of national income remained unchanged. During the seventies the United States was able fully to exploit this growth potential; but success in preventing the further deterioration of US economic strength (measured by share of total income of all OECD members) was achieved only because competing countries performed below their potential, fundamentally because of the financial problems created by the oil crisis and by a trend toward the modification of the international division of labour, which will be examined in chapter 6. That such a trend toward loss of economic supremacy is of great concern, since it leads ultimately to a loss of political supremacy, is demonstrated by the British precedent.

6. The Precedent of Britain

Us efforts to reorder its growth rates relative to those of the capitalist world as a whole must be viewed within a broader historical perspective. Indeed, it is well known—and the precedent certainly did not escape American policy-makers—that during the nineteenth century Britain suffered a decline similar to that which the United States has begun to experience during the past two decades.

In the British case, too, the international role of the pound was a fundamental factor. The British economy, which reached its apogee after the first quarter of the nineteenth century, maintained its lead through the 1880s, when it became clear that the gradual industrialization of the United States and of many continental countries, with the associated protectionist policies, was beginning to deprive British goods of outlets. It quickly became evident that some competitors were enjoying a rate of development superior to that of Britain—in particular the United States and Germany. The differential in growth rates, however, was never as striking as that between the United States and its competitors during the period after the Second World War. Indeed, it hovered around 0.5%. This is the reason for the

---

[33] On the post-war evolution of productivity in the United States see J. W. Kendrick, *Postwar Productivity Trends in the United States*, New York 1973. The concern of the US authorities about the low growth of productivity is demonstrated by the rich collection of essays published under the auspices of the National Centre for Productivity and the Quality of Working Life: *The Future of Productivity*, Washington 1977.

slowness of the historical process that reduced the United Kingdom from the world's leading political and economic power to its present position in the lower ranks of the hierarchy of industrialized countries, alongside Italy.[34]

One of the reasons the British bourgeoisie was slow to become aware of this decline was that it had, at least for a long initial period, scant effect on the position of the pound. In the final analysis, the British commercial decline, which was contemporaneous with a deeper industrial decline, was the fruit of an over-valuation of the pound. The currency was over-valued because the trade balance was artificially kept in surplus by the *de facto* protection enjoyed by British commodities in the colonies. Moreover, the income Britain derived from its enormous foreign investments during the nineteenth century effectively contributed to maintaining the gold value of the pound. Consequently, the loss of competitivity of British products, which became ever dearer compared with those of competitors because of Britain's meagre national industrial dynamism, was concealed: it never showed up in a payments deficit.

The fact that the pound remained linked to a gold parity, and especially that the pound was restored to its old parity long after the First World War (in 1925), undoubtedly facilitated the relative decline of the British economy.[35] In reality, the entire past fifty years may be viewed as a period in which Britain has sought to escape from this decline by recovering competitivity through successive devaluations. The first, in 1931, was brought about by the fluctuation of sterling after the gold standard was abandoned, but it was not very effective, because of the subsequent devaluation of the dollar in 1933 and the competitive devaluations of many competing currencies.[36] The 1949 devaluation was also largely wiped out by devaluations of the currencies of nearly all Britain's trading partners except the United States, and probably was not backed by the requisite economic policy of national deflation, nor by adequate support to

[34] The literature on the decline of the British economy is quite vast. A good presentation of the problem may be found in W. Beckermann *et al.*, *The British Economy in 1975*, Cambridge 1965. For more detailed information, refer to the various essays devoted to analysis of this problem in N. Kaldor, *Further Essays on Economic Theory*, London 1978, and N. Kaldor, *Further Essays on Applied Economics*.

[35] On British policy in the twenties, see D.E. Moggridge, *British Monetary Policy 1924—1931*, Cambridge 1972.

[36] On the situation during the thirties, see B.M. Rowland (ed.), *Balance of Power or Hegemony: The Interwar Monetary System*, New York 1976.

export sectors. The later devaluation of 1967 and the one that occurred after the 1972 float were accompanied by such accelerations of inflation as to be virtually nullified.

As we have already seen, the United States is much better placed than Britain to effect a successful devaluation of its currency. To begin with, the inflationary effects of devaluation are negligible in the US case. Moreover, because of the greater relative weight of its economy and its nearly complete financial, political, and military control of the capitalist world, the United States is in a position to resort to various weapons in its efforts to restore competitivity. These have been used both to make the devaluation of the dollar effective and to bring about consequences that would further enhance American advantages. It is not inappropriate to define the 1970s as an extended period of economic warfare between the United States and the other capitalist powers.

Uneven development is an intrinsic feature of capitalism, and lies at the origin of imperialism. Until recently, imperialist contradictions were resolved primarily through war and other forms of direct political control. These sorts of actions, however, have not always been sufficient to maintain domination, as is demonstrated by the experience of Britain, which won all the wars but lost the economic contest. The United States, taking advantage of the political and military predominance over the capitalist world that it won after the defeat of German and Japanese imperialism, and cleverly exploiting fear of socialism, is now attempting an unprecedented initiative: to establish control, through the mechanisms of the market itself, over the variables (cost and dynamic of exports, rate of inflation, and so on) that inflect the fundamental magnitudes of capitalist development: productivity and accumulation.

3
Crisis and Inflation in the World Economy

1. The Effects of the Dollar Devaluation

The devaluation of the dollar has markedly deflationary long-term effects on the European economy. The reestablishment of American competitivity will inevitably reduce the powerful impulses previously imparted to other economies by the continual rise of American imports as a share of national income and the continual reduction of American exports as a share of world exports. Demand impulses from the United States were the real motor force of world economic expansion through the post-war period, with the exception of a few isolated instances of regression. The impact of these impulses has always been especially great, since every successive wave of expansion of the American economy (and the sixties were a period of uninterrupted growth in the United States) was accompanied both by an increment of the US tendency to import and by a reduction in its ability to take advantage of the reflexive expansion of the other economies to maintain its own share of world exports. Besides benefiting from this demand impulse, the European countries managed, by gradually achieving balance of trade surpluses with the United States, to accumulate the reserves with which to finance the expansion of both inter-European trade and trade with other areas. A conjunction of material and financial factors thus permitted the great cycle of expansion that ended with the recession of the middle seventies.[1]

[1] The literature on the features of world development after the Second World War and on the growth of world trade is vast. For a general view that remains valid, see A. Maddison, *Economic Growth in the West: Comparative Experience in Europe and North America*, New York 1964. For an analysis of the growth factors of post-war capitalism, see the theoretical work of J. Cornwall, *Modern Capitalism: Its Growth and Transformation*, New York 1977.

During this great wave of growth, the income of the capitalist countries rose faster than ever before in the history of capitalism. Not all countries grew at the same pace. Some were unable to take full advantage of the favourable demand conditions created by the expansion of world trade; some suffered from bottlenecks on the supply side—in other words, they were unable to lift the volume and composition of their manufacturing industries in a manner adequate to the changed conditions of world demand, and therefore developed at a slower rate than the others. Britain in particular, although it did enjoy an expansion greater even than that achieved in the days of its industrial splendour, failed to keep pace with the more dynamic Japanese, German, and French economies. The reason for this must be sought in the dynamic of British industrial productivity, which was particularly low. In general, however, the European countries and Japan enjoyed higher growth rates than the United States.

After the devaluation of the dollar, this conjunction of favourable conditions of demand and finance no longer pertained. On the demand side, the United States exercised less attraction on the world economy than it had in the past.[2] The devaluation of the dollar, moreover, was not a discrete event, but a developing process. If the present extent of devaluation is not sufficient to eliminate the US trade deficit, the system of floating exchange rates permits further devaluations relative to the currencies of the countries with which the trade deficit is concentrated. On the other hand, no other country would be strong enough to supplant the United States in the role of propagator of development impulses unless it commanded the guarantee of a reserve currency that would enable it to overcome possible payments deficits painlessly. It is even difficult to see how a decentralized—or better, *polycentric*—mechanism of development of world trade could be established, because of the deficiencies of the international financial system.

[2] Because if we exclude the abnormal rise of oil imports, devaluation tends inevitably to reduce the propensity to import and to facilitate the recovery of the US share of world exports. Thus, eight years after the devaluation of the dollar began, the US share of world exports had stabilized, whereas it had been almost halved over the previous twenty years.

2. The Effects of the Oil Crisis

The increase in the price of oil, which rose from an average of $3 a barrel at the beginning of the seventies to an average of $20 a barrel at their end and has since climbed past $30, makes it quite difficult for other countries to replace the declining impulses from the American economy.[3] In fact, the rise in oil prices has introduced a permanent deflationary element into the world economy, which could be overcome only through a radical and courageous restructuring of the entire international financial system.

The deflationary element, of course, is the existence of a total balance of payments surplus of OPEC members that ran at an annual average of $40 thousand million between 1974 and 1978. This surplus, which is an expression of the inability of the producing countries to spend their entire oil income in the short run, did decline from a little less than $70 thousand million in 1974 to about $15 thousand million in 1978. But the particular features of the OPEC cartel,[4] combined with the continuing high level of US oil imports, has enabled the producing countries to take advantage of every tension in the market (such as that caused by the temporary interruption of the supply of Iranian crude in 1978) to impose fresh price increases that at least preserve the more favourable relationship between the price of crude and the price of the manufactures of the industrialized countries brought about by the first price increase, in 1973. The oil surplus can confidently be considered a characteristic of the world economy not only in the seventies but in the eighties as well; it will persist until the industrialized countries achieve considerable energy savings or develop methods to produce energy from different sources.[5]

[3] The reference is to the tendency toward expansion as a result of the gradual loss of American competitivity; in the short run a powerful American upturn can equally impart expansive incentives to the world economy.

[4] The cartel is built around Saudi Arabia, whose share of the cartel's total production is nearly 50% and which enjoys far the greatest productive capacity (wells already producing) and reserves. Thus, if some producers are inclined to lower prices so as to obtain marginal gains over the others, Saudi Arabia can counter the manoeuvre by reducing supplies in order to raise prices. But it can also bring its power to bear in the opposite direction, moderating the efforts of the more aggressive countries to drive prices up.

[5] The brunt of these efforts is completely borne by the European countries and Japan, since the United States is committed only to holding net oil imports within 8.5 million barrels a day by 1985.

The existence of the oil surplus is deflationary not so much because of its direct effects on demand as because of the financial problems it entails. The industrialized countries, unable to increase their exports to the oil-producing countries sufficiently to compensate for their more expensive imports, are driven to diminish overall imports in order to economize reserves. It is thus clear that the industrialized countries cannot be the motor force of a fresh expansion of the world economy, unless they can acquire the abundant international finance that would enable them confidently to overcome their deficit with the oil-producing countries. The real crux of the crisis, then, is not the increase in the cost of oil in and of itself, but the lack of adequate financing with which to cope with it. If we understand this aspect of the present slump, then we can determine the particular features of the international crisis of the seventies that render it profoundly different from that of the thirties.

3. Alternative Explanations of the Crisis

In point of fact, the crisis is not really a *world* crisis, for it afflicts only the countries and areas that lack adequate finance: Europe, Japan, and those non-oil-producing developing countries that are excluded from the channels of private international credit.[6] The United States, the OPEC members, and those developing countries that enjoy special access to credit are developing at extremely high, even historically unprecedented, rates. In the second half of the seventies the United States achieved growth rates equal to those of the period of Johnson's 'Great Society', which were the highest in its history. The OPEC members and the newly industrializing countries grew at rates double and triple those of the developed countries in the seventies.[7]

Only the West European countries suffered drastic reductions in their rates of development during the second half of the 1970s. The demand for labour associated with these low growth rates was insufficient to absorb the additional labour supply, and was still less

---

[6] For an analysis of the divisions among the developing countries, see chapter 6.

[7] The socialist countries also continued to develop more or less in accordance with the high rates called for in their development plans, either by maximizing the coordination of their own economies or by resorting abundantly, like the under-developed countries, to international finance, accumulating debts conservatively estimated at $55 thousand million by the middle of 1979.

able to reabsorb the unemployment that had mounted during the earlier acute phase of recession. Even Japan, which enjoyed an enviable growth rate by international standards (about 6% a year), was marking time in comparison with the rates it had achieved in the past (in excess of 10% annually).

A note of caution is required in assessing these data as they concern the United States: that the United States enjoyed an upturn in the business cycle does not mean that it halted or reversed the process of the relative weakening of its economy. This decline is reflected fundamentally in the low level of manufacturing investment relative to national income (the lowest of the industrialized countries), in the low rate of growth of productivity in manufacturing (also the lowest of the industrialized countries), in the loss of technological leadership, at least with respect to Germany, and in the existence of many industrial sectors (including important ones, like steel) incapable of resisting international competition without the depreciation of the dollar brought about by essentially protectionist-motivated government interventions in foreign-exchange markets. Nevertheless, the ability to maintain a high rate of increase of the gross national product could favourably affect the relative scope of manufacturing investment, and that could have beneficial effects on productivity and the introduction of technical progress as well.

The Euro-Japanese (and not worldwide) character of the crisis suggests that its cause and persistence should be interpreted in a manner thoroughly different from the more common explanations. It may therefore be useful briefly to review some of the hypotheses that have been advanced to explain the crisis, in order to show just how widely at variance with the facts they are.

The first explanation is that the crisis is the result of the effects of the rise in the price of oil on aggregate demand. On this view the increase in oil prices brought about an increment in worldwide saving propensity, thus causing stagnation. The argument is that for the oil-consuming countries the price increase amounts to a transfer of demand out of the circuit of income to the producing countries. These countries are in turn unable to spend all the earnings generated by their exports and therefore fail to compensate for the loss of demand suffered by the consuming countries. The emergence of current-account surpluses on the part of OPEC members thus amounts to a rise in the savings propensity of world income exactly equal to the total OPEC surplus.

Now, although unobjectionable in theory, this explanation does not accord with the statistical evidence. According to IMF economists, the sum of financial surpluses for broad geographical groups in the middle of the seventies was equal to that in the sixties, if reproportioned to account for the increase in nominal income. What had changed was the distribution of the surpluses and deficits. In the 1960s the surpluses were concentrated in the industrialized countries and the deficits in the non-oil-producing underdeveloped countries; OPEC members and the socialist countries were roughly in balance. In the 1970s, after the oil crisis, the surpluses were concentrated among the OPEC members (an average annual value of $40 thousand million from 1974 to 1978) and the deficits divided in fluctuating proportions between industrialized and non-oil-producing underdeveloped countries.[8] It is worth noting that the oil surplus would have been even greater had a recovery occurred in the European countries. A 3% per year acceleration of growth in Japan and the European countries (which constitute 50% of the OECD) would have entailed a roughly similar increase in oil consumption. Since domestic oil production in these countries is negligible, this rising consumption would have been reflected in a corresponding increase in imports from OPEC. Euro-Japanese oil imports totalled about $65 thousand million in 1979; the increase in the oil deficit would thus have been something like $3–3.5 thousand million, if we also take account of the effects on the developing countries.[9] The cause of the crisis therefore cannot be sought in an alleged increase in savings propensity worldwide.

A second interpretation asserts that the crisis is due to disproportions between the price of products and the price of the inputs utilized. If the previous hypothesis can be characterized as Keynesian, this one may be termed neo-classical. It has been formulated in several versions, emphasizing either the disproportion

[8] See the IMF *Annual Report*, 1977, pp. 12–13.

[9] The increase in worldwide saving propensity would not alone be sufficient to trigger a recessive trend, because it is minimal relative to a world income now equivalent to more than $7,000 thousand million. It is otherwise, of course, with an unexpected leap in the price of oil, such as that which occurred in 1979. Then the surplus rises significantly within the first year after the increase, before the oil-producing countries have augmented their spending capacity. But this effect, although significant, is temporary.

between the prices of finished products and raw materials, or between finished-product prices and labour costs. Quite apart from misgivings about the theoretical foundations of this interpretation, it must be pointed out that raw materials prices have fallen significantly from the levels of the 1972–73 boom, and that in any case increases in the prices of raw materials (except oil) automatically become increases in world demand, because the countries that produce raw materials, primarily underdeveloped, 'spend what they earn'. Therefore, the more their earnings rise, the more demand for the manufactured products of the industrialized countries rises. To the claim that labour costs are to blame, we need only respond that in most industrialized countries the cost of labour in real terms diminished between 1973 and 1976—often by a not negligible percentage. Even in Italy, where real wages did not decline, there was a fall in the real compensation paid to non-worker dependents; and most important, productivity rose considerably, such that an examination of company balance-sheets clearly shows that by 1976 labour costs as a percentage of turnover had fallen back to levels close to those of 1968, before the wage explosion. And yet the diminution of wages in the major capitalist countries does not seem to have been accompanied by an upturn of investment in any country.

The third interpretation, which does not aspire to the universality of the first two, does contain useful elements of truth. It emphasizes the fall in the private components of national demand, consumption, and private investment. The tendencies to consume and to invest have both exhibited serious declines in recent years, mainly because of inflation and the establishment of floating exchange rates. Schematically, we may say that inflation, by destroying the *real* value of accumulated household financial wealth, encourages consumers to increase the share of current income that is saved, in an attempt to reconstitute a more balanced relation between financial wealth and income. Fear of the future caused by rising unemployment, which accompanies the measures taken to contain inflation, also acts in the same direction: to increase the propensity to save. Inflation thus also inflects propensity to invest, causing a deterioration in the financial structure of companies. This phenomenon, widely noted in the case of Italian corporations, has also occurred in other countries suffering high inflation. Floating exchange rates, which add uncertainty to the climate in which the entrepreneur operates, are held by many to be a factor that, as much as the others, affects investment adversely. [10]

Finally, it may be added that the emergence of ecological concerns may also have contributed to discouraging the propensity to invest, both directly by preventing the execution of some grandiose projects already decided by companies in the nuclear industry, and indirectly, because of the increase in investment costs generated by the adoption of environmental controls, purification systems, and so on.

These factors, while they are undoubtedly important, cannot alone account for the crisis, for the strong and persistent fall in the level of activity below average tendential levels. Indeed, in all the industrialized countries, the unsatisfactory evolution of the private component of internal demand has been counter-balanced by increases in the public component. We have thus seen the emergence of a hefty deficit in the public sector, averaging about 4–5% of national income, both automatically through the reduction of tax revenue and the increase in payment of subsidies, and deliberately through increases in public spending or reductions in tax rates. On the whole, no particular difficulties have been encountered in financing these enormous deficits (in comparison with previous experience), [11] and in the opinion of the OECD, they seem not to have contributed substantially to the persistence of inflation. Nothing would have prevented—and in particular, nothing would prevent—the deficits from rising even higher, so as to lend vigorous support to demand and to lift the capitalist economies out of recession.

To explain the persistence and aggravation of the crisis, then, we must turn to the fourth explanation mentioned above, which hinges on the difficulties some countries have encountered in financing balance of payments deficits. In discussing the first interpretation I mentioned that the sum of current-account surpluses (and correspondingly of the deficits) relative to world income had not changed very much, even after the oil crisis, since the 1960s. There

[10] For the effects of inflation on the tendency to consume, see W.E. Weber, 'Interest Rates, Inflation, and Consumer Expenditure', *American Economic Review*, December 1975. For its effects on investment, see McCracken *et al.*, *Towards Full Employment and Stability*, Paris 1977. For the effects of floating exchange rates on investment, see F. Machlup, 'Is Greater Flexibility of Exchange Rates a Handicap to Foreign Trade and Investment?', *Note economiche*, November–December 1971.

[11] Except perhaps in the case of Italy, where the deficit hovered at levels in excess of 10% of national income throughout most of the decade, a result of the meagre expansive value of public spending. On budget policies in the industrialized countries, see OECD, *Economic Outlook*, December 1977.

was merely a shift in the distribution of the surpluses and deficits. The deficits that had to be financed in the world economy, however, did increase in nominal terms (since they are calculated as a share of world income, which rose very considerably in nominal terms because of inflation), and their geographical distribution changed. In particular, the industrial countries as a whole oscillated between positions of deficit and equilibrium, while the non-oil-producing developing countries were gradually saddled with deficits corresponding to the surpluses of the oil producers. Among the industrialized countries, however, the deficit was not distributed uniformly, but was concentrated in the United States and those countries that may be called weak. The existence of high foreign deficits encouraged those countries sustaining them to attempt to prevent any further rises, and therefore to reduce income in an effort to reduce imports. Since many countries acted in this way, the result was a diminution both in world income and in export possibilities for all countries.[12] This is the situation that arose in the 1930s, and it is the situation that, albeit in a less dramatic and sweeping form, is taking shape again today, despite the existence of the financial apparatus created at Bretton Woods.

The problem is less general than it was in the thirties, because some countries still command adequate financial resources: primarily the United States, which finances its own imports in dollars and sustained a powerful economic expansion in the second half of the seventies,[13] but some non-oil-producing developing countries too, which have resorted copiously to private financial markets (as we shall see in chapter 6). The financial constraint has thus been concentrated in Europe, and was rendered more stringent by the deflationary practices of Germany, which gave rise to the problem of the German surplus (about which more in chapter 4). The constraint also struck more seriously at the overwhelming majority of the non-oil-producing developing countries.

[12] The method used to analyse the contribution (expansive or deflationary) of the various areas to the determination of world income is the same as that used to analyse the 'flow of funds' between sectors of the national economy. On the 'flow of funds' analysis, see L.S. Ritter and W.L. Silber, *Principles of Money, Banking, and Financial Markets*, New York 1974, chapter 20.

[13] The American deficit, of course, is largely responsible for world deflation, because it is caused predominantly by the oil imports that are in turn responsible for the oil surplus.

But since the economic weight of these countries is quite limited, their financial difficulties and the discrimination they suffer in access to credit are not of great importance in determining the level of world economic activity,[14] although they have a good deal to do with understanding the international division of labour and therefore the future characteristics of world capitalist growth. The analysis must therefore focus on the financial problems of the developed economies.

4. The Inadequacy of International Liquidity

The sluggishness of world demand could be remedied only through a substantial increase in international liquidity. The deficit countries would have to be rendered able to augment their international reserves so as to come through the long phase of structural adjustment required to reabsorb the oil surplus without being compelled to apply excessively restrictive economic policies. Now, the sources of creation of international liquidity are all controlled by the United States, and existing financial mechanisms, better adapted to respond to long-term requirements, are geared to extend financial assistance to developing, and not developed, countries.

The real obstacle that has been impeding the recovery of a satisfactory level of world economic activity since 1974 is that the industrialized countries have been unable to acquire, one way or another, the quantity of finance required to enable them to increase

[14] In recent years there has been no lack of proposals, largely utopian, to make the developing countries the locomotive of world recovery, exceptionally increasing their capacity to import by applying a grandiose aid programme equivalent to the post-war Marshall Plan. The actual import capacity of these countries is dubious, however, even if there were no financial constraints. In essence, these proposals are a reprise of old Keynesian schemes that cropped up several times shortly after the Second World War. The prototype is contained in the essay by M. Kalecki and E.F. Schumacher, 'New Plans for International Trade', *Supplement to the Bulletin of the Oxford Institute of Statistics*, 1943. The same idea lies behind the 'link', the demand advanced several times during discussions on reform of the international monetary system that newly issued SDRs be allocated only to developing countries. It has been developed most consistently by N. Kaldor, *Strategic Factors in Economic Development*, Ithaca, New York 1967. The real problem lies in the fact that the industrialized countries have no intention of supplying financing 'no strings attached', of freely allowing the developing countries to determine their own growth models. As we shall see in chapter 6, through the selective concession of financing, they seek to influence the subordinate integration of some developing countries into the world capitalist market.

their imports in spite of the distortion of their balance of payments caused by their oil deficits. Finance could be raised either by increasing the quantity of reserves, for example through the massive creation of SDRs, or by increasing the speed of circulation of funds through official channels, without imposing interest burdens or conditions on the conduct of economic policy or even on political life itself, of which there has been no lack both through private channels and through the IMF, which is itself run much like a private institution.

Despite repeated entreaties (especially from Britain, in successive meetings of the IMF since 1974), no agreement to expand official international liquidity has been reached. Between 1976 and 1979 increases were granted in IMF shares and in endowments of capital by the World Bank and regional development banks,[15] and there has been a new issue of SDRs. Some emergency financial measures were also enacted, such as the formation of an IMF 'oil facility' of some $6 thousand million in 1974[16] and a new enlarged oil facility (the 'Witteween facility') in 1978 of more than $10 thousand million. Finally, some efforts have been made to improve reciprocal financial assistance both at the level of the developed countries as a whole (through successive enlargements of the scope of the credit network in swaps among central banks) and at the regional level (especially through the EEC, with the improvement of the network of financial accords). On the whole, however, these measures have been insufficient to increase the weight of official relative to private finance within international finance as a whole. The greater part of the effort to finance countries encountering payments difficulties has been consigned to the international financial market, composed primarily of Eurobanks.

Sabotage of proposals designed to raise official international liquidity is primarily the result of tenacious American opposition, which has been motivated by referring to the inflationary dangers that would allegedly arise from an increase in international liquidity. But there are grounds to doubt the validity of the American claim,

---

[15] These last measures concern the developing countries.

[16] The oil facility is a fund established by the IMF with loans from currency-rich countries (initially only oil-producers, later industrialized countries as well). The fund issues unconditional loans to countries facing balance of payments difficulties because of the increases in oil prices. The oil facility is of limited duration. When the debtor repays the loans, the funds are restored to the countries that had placed them at the disposal of the facility.

which is that an increase in *official* liquidity would have inflationary consequences so great as to permit the perpetuation of the rapid inflation that took root in the international economy in the seventies.[17]

Now, as we have already had occasion to argue, the roots of the present inflation stretch all the way back to the achievement of full employment in the majority of industrialized countries at the beginning of the sixties. Inflation was considerably accelerated in the early seventies largely by two factors: the adoption of flexible exchange rates and the rise in the prices of raw materials. Floating exchange rates fostered inflation in the countries whose currencies were suffering downward fluctuations, since the depreciation of the exchange rate was reflected in an increase in domestic prices caused by a rise in the price of imports, with variable coefficients and lead-times depending on the country concerned. The rise in raw materials prices powerfully accelerated the more general price increases, since raw materials are an important component in the formation of prices. These price increases did not affect oil alone. Indeed, between 1970 and 1973 there was a 300% increase in the composite index of all raw materials prices. The exceptional rise in the cost of primary products was principally due to excess demand that arose at the beginning of the decade because of the peaking of the business cycle in the major capitalist countries. This excess demand stimulated a wave of speculation that was financed by the abundant liquidity available in international private markets as a consequence of the outflows of dollars provoked by the expansive monetary policy of the United States. In the first three years of the decade, the US government applied an expansive policy that, by encouraging foreign capital movements, resulted in the devaluation of the dollar and an increment in international liquidity, both private and official. Us monetary policy became restrictive again in the years following 1973; at the same time, inflation, swelling the nominal value of transactions, reabsorbed the excess liquidity. In other words, the quantity of money, deflated by price variations, returned to its previous levels. At this point, as I have already pointed out, a shortage of liquidity developed because of the altered distribution of trade balances. The

[17] On the development of international inflation, see S. Biasco, *Inflazione nei paesi capitalistici industrializzati*, which analyses the role of international liquidity in particular. See also the sources listed in note 57, chapter 1.

US authorities maintain that to increase liquidity would be once again to foster the explosion of inflation, which in any event has not yet been quelled.

A further spurt of inflation, however, would be possible only if international liquidity were created under the system that prevailed in the past, through outflows of funds from the United States to the Eurodollar market, where the great multinational corporations and brokers could acquire capital to loan out for fresh speculation on a rise in raw materials prices.[18] An increase of international liquidity in official hands—in other words, an increase in reserves—would not permit a rise in speculation.[19] The US argument against the creation of liquidity is therefore unfounded. In fact, it may well be argued that the shortage of liquidity is itself inflationary, because it makes it impossible for various states to defend their own currencies and compels them to resort to devaluations. And devaluation in turn accelerates inflation, as is clearly shown, for example, by the Italian experience.[20]

There is, nevertheless, a kernel of truth in the US concerns. If the balance of payments constraint was eliminated, or at least attenuated, then all the OECD countries would be able to apply expansive policies. The resulting excess demand in the raw materials market could once again rekindle the trend towards price increases, even in the absence of overt spurts of speculation. The United States, arrogating to itself responsibility for the overall control of the world economy, thus opposes an expansion of reserves, which would facilitate the adoption of inflationary policies. This argument too,

[18] There have not been many scientific studies of speculation. Journalistic sources, however, suggest that its effects have been immense. It is sufficient to cite two episodes by way of example: the cornering of 50% of the Australian wool market by large Japanese groups and the gigantic losses (sometimes speculation comes a cropper) suffered by a food-products multinational—50 thousand million lire—in an attempt to drive up the price of cocoa in 1973. For an attempt to analyse the role of speculation in the raw materials boom, see R.N. Cooper and R.Z. Lawrence, 'The 1972–75 Commodity Boom'.

[19] It would, of course, be necessary to extend the commitment, now limited to the Group of Ten, not to place reserves on the Eurodollar market. This would prevent the growth of international liquidity from leading to a growth in private liquidity. It would probably also be necessary to consider ways to control the activity of the Euromarket.

[20] On the interaction between floating exchange rates and inflation, see, in addition to the sources cited in notes 8 and 10 of chapter 1, R.E. Baldwin, 'The International Transmission of Inflation', Federal Reserve Bank of Boston, Conference Series, no. 20, *Managed Exchange Rate Flexibility: The Recent Experience*, October 1978.

Table 13

Official Reserves and International Private Liquidity
(in thousands of millions of $)

	(1)	(2)
1960	59.8	7.8
1965	72.4	24.0
1970	92.3	69.8
1971	124.5	90.6
1972	158.7	115.7
1973	184.3	156.1
1974	222.2	213.7
1975	236.3	249.0
1976	258.6	295.0
1977	317.7	356.0

(1) Official reserves (including gold, SDRs, reserve position in the IMF, dollars, and other currencies).

(2) Private international liquidity, defined as the sum of the net dimension of the Eurocurrency market as determined by the Bank for International Settlements plus liabilities to private non-residents of the US and UK.

Sources: Bank for International Settlements, IMF.

however, is not quite compelling, because the United States also rejects the adoption of any policy that would stabilize raw materials prices—and that, if it succeeded, could permit expansion without inflation. In particular, for many years economists and representatives of the developing countries have been discussing what has been called a link between the issue of SDRs and aid policies. Instead of being distributed indiscriminately in proportion to shares of participation in the IMF, SDRs would be allocated only to developing countries, which would thus enjoy an increase in their buying power that would make it possible for them to increase imports of capital goods, which would in turn facilitate expansion in these countries. Many today are wondering whether this link could not be granted in exchange for the participation of countries that produce raw materials in price-stabilization agreements.[21]

[21] The recompense of price stabilization is part of the utopianism of this scheme. For an elaboration of this proposal, see N. Kaldor, 'Inflation and Recession in the World Economy', *Economic Journal*, December 1976.

5. The Perverse Functioning of International Financial Institutions

In the end, American justifications of us international monetary policy do not seem entirely reasonable. They become comprehensible only when seen as part of an approach in which the fundamental concern is to guarantee the centrality and power of the American economy. The United States benefits directly from the maintenance of a low level of development of the capitalist economy as a whole. Since the American economy is relatively unconstrained by balance of payments problems, the United States can strive for maximum growth while the rest of the world has to adopt less than optimal development policies. The narrowing of the gap in growth rates between the United States and the rest of the world adds to the weight of the us economy. By the end of the seventies, it was already stronger than it had been at the start of the decade. It is, of course, impossible to predict whether this reinforcement will continue or whether it will prove ephemeral. For it to stabilize, forces on the supply side, which acted to the detriment of the United States during the post-war period, would have to change. The development of the productivity of us manufacturing industry has been the lowest of all industrialized countries, and continued to be so even after the devaluation of the dollar. Without a reduction of the differential in the rise of productivity, it would be impossible to sustain a reduction in the differential of development rates solely through aggregate demand policies.

The conclusions that follow from this analysis suggest that the slackening of the rate of development of the capitalist economy as a whole is the result fundamentally of the impossibility of shifting from a pattern centred on the locomotive power of the American economy to a polycentric pattern. The difficulties in effecting such a transition are exacerbated by the inflexibility of the present international financial system. This inflexibility is in turn the direct responsibility of the United States. The reasons for the us attitude cannot be unambiguously reduced to a single factor. It is possible that the us government is genuinely concerned about the danger of inflation and considers impractical and utopian the alternative suggestions on inflation control. It is equally possible that the prime motivation is the fundamental exigency of preserving the predominant position of the United States in the world economy, on the level of both finance and productivity. Somehow the second possibility seems more likely in reality.

The price paid for the preservation of American financial supremacy has been the virtual dismantling of the institutional apparatus born at Bretton Woods. The IMF and the World Bank have been reduced to lilliputian dimensions compared to private international financial markets. Those European countries encountering balance of payments difficulties are thus compelled to resort copiously to credit from private institutions, paying high interest rates that burden their balance of payments even further.

The greater initial ease in resorting to private credit markets instead of the IMF has proven to be a trap. When the debt levels of some of these countries rose too high, the private markets closed to them and the countries in question (particularly Italy and Britain) had to negotiate with the Fund from a position of weakness. They were thus compelled to accept onerous and painful deflationary conditions not unrelated to the structural deterioration of their balance of payments brought about by the oil crisis.[22] Other countries (like France) deliberately avoided the critical debt level on the private market so as not to have to resort to the Fund, which surely would have been far more traumatic for French national politics than it was for Britain or Italy.

With the accentuation of the role of private financing, the capacity of minor countries to influence the evolution of international finance, scant enough previously because of the voting system in international financial bodies, has been further reduced.[23] This is now leading to a complete distortion of the aims of the international institutions. The IMF and the World Bank were conceived as instruments designed to assist countries facing balance of payments difficulties, in the awareness that this would help to limit cumulative recessionary pressures in the international economy.[24] Although the Americans and the British disagreed at Bretton Woods about the autonomy of the Fund and the Bank and about the criteria that should govern the

[22] For Britain only temporarily, because of the start of North Sea production.

[23] The financial organisms, although part of the United Nations system, do not follow the voting procedures of the other bodies (one country, one vote); instead, voting power is proportional to financial participation in the institution concerned.

[24] The conceptual framework that underlay the Bretton Woods institutions is outlined in T. Balogh, 'International Aspects of Full Employment', in *The Economics of Full Employment*, Oxford 1944.

allocation of assistance, both were aware that it was essential to avert any repetition of the errors of the thirties. Today, on the contrary, the financing of countries in difficulty is being consigned to the private market, and the IMF intervenes to defend the interests of the international banking community instead of striving for full employment and world economic growth.

Every country encountering difficulties must be in a position to continue to service its foreign debt—contracted at exorbitant rates because of the lack of an adequate supply of international liquidity— regardless of the cost in sacrifices of income and employment. The Fund's 'recipe' for the unfortunate countries that call upon its aid is indeed draconian: currency devaluation, public-spending cuts, abolition of price subsidies for goods of daily necessity regardless of the inflationary consequences, fresh devaluations to compensate for the effects of the resulting acceleration of inflation, monetary and credit restrictions, increases in interest rates, and so on—a recessionary spiral that has had catastrophic consequences for European employment and growth.[25] Europe has come in for the sort of treatment the Fund used to reserve for Central American nations.[26]

The system of financial assistance established at Bretton Woods was designed to minimize the loss of production and employment consequent to the adjustment of imbalances in international payments. The current behaviour of international financial institutions, overtaken by (and completely subservient to) private international finance, on the contrary exalts losses of production and employment, thus contributing to inflicting on the world one of the most serious recessions in the history of capitalism. In other words, the founders of Bretton Woods held that financial institutions should issue loans to countries in difficulty in order to prevent them from devaluing, from

---

[25] T. Balogh has levelled severe criticism against this denaturing of the international financial institutions. See 'Monetarism and the Oil Price Crisis', *Journal of Post-Keynesian Economics*, winter 1978–79, which clearly exposes the role of monetarist doctrine in providing a cover for these aberrant policies.

[26] On the policy of international institutions toward these countries, see T. Hayter, *Aid as Imperialism*, Harmondsworth 1971. In reality, it has always been accepted that the Fund acts as a watchdog for the interests of the multinationals and big banks against these small countries, because their weight in the world economy is limited. If very severe deflationary policies are adopted by these countries, the reverberations on the rest of the world are scant. It is otherwise if the same treatment is accorded a country of the Group of Ten, for then recession is exported to other countries, which are in turn driven to deflationary policies that react with fresh intensity on the country that has had to deflate.

limiting their imports through administrative measures, or from being forced to reduce income and employment in an effort to cut imports. Today, on the other hand, the IMF deliberately imposes devaluations and reductions in income in order as rapidly as possible to generate a surplus with which to repay both the interest on accumulated debt and a portion of the debts themselves—and let it be noted that for the most part these debts were contracted to cope with the rise in oil prices, an event completely beyond the control of the debtor countries, and one that cannot be remedied by internal measures, except perhaps in the very long term through the adoption of energy-saving policies.

6. Blackmailing the Weak Countries

A surprising aspect of present developments in the world economy is the inability of the other capitalist countries to propose alternatives to devaluation. The fundamental reason for this is the conflict of interests between strong and weak countries.

In the absence of an increase in the stock of world reserves, the countries facing balance of payments difficulties have stepped up the rate of circulation of the existing stock. They have thereby gone into debt, through both private and official channels. In doing so they have exposed themselves to foreign interference in their economies. It is in the fundamental interest of the United States that it should not be easy for these countries to continue an accelerated process of economic growth and commercial and financial penetration of the newly industrializing countries. On the whole, the United States does not look unfavourably on the slowdown of economic growth in Japan and Europe, because this makes it easier to tilt differential economic strength in favour of the American economy again. The slow growth of Japan and Europe, although it may retard or even eliminate the danger of the US economy's being overtaken by other capitalist economies, reduces the growth of American exports in the short run and therefore conflicts with the need to stabilize the exchange rate of the dollar, an exigency the US government considered increasingly urgent during 1979. This obvious contradiction between objectives in the long-term (strengthening the American economy at the expense of its competitors) and short-term (stabilizing the now devalued dollar in order to avert the outbreak of a crisis of confidence that could be catastrophic in a market completely disoriented by years of 'benign neglect' and 'open mouth') has not been seized upon by the European countries as an opportunity to seek a fresh recovery of the world economy.

In reality, the strong countries, endowed with adequate reserves, have understood the advantage they enjoy because of the shortage of means of payment supplied through official channels. In this situation they are able to assert their predominance over the weaker, financially dependent countries. The strong countries are consequently in no hurry to reflate their economies. As I will show in the next chapter, they have opted for a period of slow growth in order to restructure and fortify their own economies. A by-product of this policy option is the evident short-term difficulty in which the dollar has been placed, which could, in the event of repeated crises, compel the Americans to come to terms on the question of hegemony in the international monetary system, either through a remonetarization of gold or through a multilateralization of seigniorage, with SDRs or other currencies serving as means of reserve.

Now, the availability of reserves enables the strong countries, Germany in particular, to inflect economic developments in the weak countries to their own advantage, thus easing the pressure brought to bear on their economies by the enhancement of US competitivity. The devaluation of the dollar has narrowed the development margins of the strongest partners of the United States, especially Germany. The decline of foreign demand has plunged the mechanism of German development into crisis, as is demonstrated by the stagnation of investment over the past five years. Germany therefore needs to broaden its scope on European markets. The influence it commands because of its financial power is a useful instrument in the pursuit of this objective.

4
The Conflict Between the United States and Germany

1. Strong and Weak Countries

The analysis of the previous chapter showed that for reasons having to do with the operation of international finance, the hub of the international recession lies in Europe and Japan. This exceptionally grave crisis seems destined to persist for some time yet. The facile optimism of those who greeted the presentation of every new set of statistics detailing the rise of unemployment and stagnation of production and world trade with announcements that these negative figures would be the last and that recovery was at hand had been thoroughly discredited by the end of the seventies. It is now universally accepted that unemployment in Europe will continue to rise until 1985—partly for purely demographic reasons—climbing from more than 6 million at the beginning of the new decade to approximately 10 million in the EEC countries alone. Similarly, medium-term projections on world trade agree that the rate of development of recent years, about 5% annually, is a more realistic approximation of likely future performance than the 10% that prevailed through the sixties. As awareness of the durability of the crisis has spread, a breach has been opening in the mystifications peddled by official and academic sources. The stark truth is now seeping through: the crisis is not the result of so-called objective factors, but is fundamentally the fruit of a grand inter-imperialist conflict the stakes of which is the global redivision of economic and political power between the United States on the one hand and the major powers of the second world—Germany and Japan—on the other. The majority of the weak industrialized countries, caught in the Us-German crossfire, are threatened with having to bear most of the costs of this conflict. It is therefore opportune to rigorously define what is meant by the adjectives 'weak' and 'strong' in the present international context.

To facilitate the analysis, the industrialized countries may be divided into three groups: those that face no balance of payments difficulties because their current-account is in surplus (or at least only modest deficit) even when there is full employment; those that have balance of payments difficulties but have no serious problem financing the deficit; those that are 'financially strapped', in which full employment would entail high balance of payments deficits and which are already significantly in debt, such that an increase in indebtedness would be inadvisable because of the political and economic consequences. (The political consequences consist in interference by foreign countries in the conduct of their affairs, either directly or through the IMF; quite apart from this, however, there is an economic limit to indebtedness, which is reached when the servicing of the international debt requires ever new and greater loans to raise money to pay interest on previous debts.)[1] The position of the financially strapped industrialized countries, however, cannot be assimilated to that of the developing countries: the latter have gone into debt and continue to do so (without, however, requesting any IMF loans in excess of the amount automatically conceded, so as to avoid being subject to the discipline of the Fund) under the presumption, sometimes not even tacit, that some of these debts will not be repaid or that the interest on them will be reduced or annulled whenever it becomes impossible to service the debts.[2] For the developed countries this sort of behaviour is impossible, because they are indeed in a position to repay their debts, albeit through severe sacrifices, and not to do so would entail their expulsion from a system of co-operation that is political and military more than economic and financial.

The first (strong) group of countries includes Germany, Japan, the Netherlands, Switzerland, Norway, and perhaps Britain in the

---

[1] For a formal analysis of the problem, see D. Avramovic *et al.*, *Economic Growth and External Debt*, New York 1964, and W.T. Newlyn *et al.*, *The Financing of Economic Development*, Oxford 1977, chapter 4.

[2] In this regard we may note the requests for rescheduling of debts advanced by the Group of 77 in the course of negotiations over the New International Economic Order and the annulment of official credit to the developing countries on the part of Holland, Sweden, and Canada in 1978. As I shall seek to explain in chapter 6, the problem is quite complex, and the attitude of financial institutions differs depending on the behaviour of the debtor country as regards direct investment and trade, and more generally its political behaviour.

future, at least as long as North Sea oil production lasts. The second includes but a single country: the United States, which has no problem financing payments deficits since its money is both the reserve currency and the major means of payment in international transactions. In addition, through its great political influence it is able to attract to its market the lion's share of oil surpluses, generating capital movements in its favour that reduce the scope of the deficit that has to be financed. The third group is composed fundamentally of the other European countries.

This division of the capitalist world into three parts according to balance of payments conditions lies at the root of my interpretation of the development of the crisis. The financially strapped countries are unable to take any independent initiative aimed at economic recovery—through an increase in public spending, for example—because to do so would automatically run the risk of accumulating a foreign deficit that these countries either cannot or will not finance. They therefore have to await recovery initiatives from the strong countries, which have no fundamental balance of payments problems. The impasse of the crisis is therefore an impasse in the co-ordination of national economic policies. So long as Germany and Japan refrain from reflating their economies, the rest of the capitalist world, with the exception of the United States, can only continue to stagnate.

2. The German Economic Zone

Before proceeding to an analysis of the reasons for the lack of recovery in Germany, it is well to consider one important change that has occurred in trade relations between the major industrialized areas, for it explains one of the enigmas of the present crisis. The enigma is the failure of the American recovery to be transmitted to Europe. This is a result fundamentally of the decline in the relative importance of economic ties between Europe and America. The exports of the EEC to the United States in 1975 amounted to only $17 thousand million, about 1.2% of total Community income for that year. Inter-Community exports, on the other hand, totalled $145 thousand million, or 11% of income.[3] Looking back, we find that

[3] The data are from the GATT, *International Trade 1975–76.*

while EEC exports to the United States rose at the same rate as Community income between 1960 and 1975, quintupling in nominal terms, inter-Community trade increased more than sevenfold. It follows that the direct impetus to European income imparted by the rise in American national income and transmitted through the growth of US imports from the EEC was limited by the scant value of exports as a percentage of income.[4] In addition, the European countries were unable to use the American recovery as a 'spring-board' for priming their own economies: the increase in currency income they obtained by selling more commodities to the Americans was not sufficient to cover the greater currency outlays they would have to make in the event of an upturn, through an increase in imports from the other European countries (especially in view of the constant high deficit with the OPEC countries). The only way the individual European countries can reflate their economies is through a joint reflation of the European economy as a whole.

The crux of the lack of a joint recovery of the European economy is in turn the lack of recovery in Germany. Indeed, the various European economies are not all equivalent, but are organized in a hierarchical pattern with the German economy at the summit. To mix the metaphor: Germany is the heart of the European economy, while all the other economies are peripheral. Economically, Europe may be defined as a German zone. This zone includes all countries that send a significant share of their exports (15% or more) to Germany and at least half their total exports to the German economic zone, including Germany itself. Germany in turn sends half its total exports to the periphery of its economic zone, but no individual country absorbs more than 5–6% of its exports (except Holland and France, each of which account for about 10% of German exports). This configuration of trade makes economic relations asymmetrical: if a country of peripheral Europe reflates its economy, this recovery is not transmitted to the rest of Europe, because the imports of this country are not

---

[4] A calculation of the direct and indirect income effects among the industrialized economies is in D.A. De Rosa and G.L. Smeal, *The Transmission of Economic Activity Between the Major Industrial Countries.* OASIA Research Papers, Department of the Treasury, Washington 1976; other estimates are presented in H. Howe, *et al.*, 'Assessing International Interdependence With a Multi-Country Model', Board of Governors of the Federal Reserve System, International Finance Discussion Papers, no. 138, April 1979, and F.E. Morris, 'The Transmission of Fluctuations in Economic Activity: Some Recent Evidence', in Federal Reserve Bank of Boston, Conference Series no. 20, *Managed Exchange-Rate Flexibility.*

great enough to draw the other economies along, either cumulatively or individually, country by country. On the other hand, if Germany reflates, the rise in its imports is sufficient to exert both direct and indirect effects on all the other countries: direct effects through the increase of exports of each of these countries to Germany, indirect effects through the increase of exports to all the countries of the German economic zone, which increase their imports in the wake of the increase of exports to Germany. In a word, the European economy throbs with the beat of its German heart.

The transmission of variations in the level of economic activity through trade is reinforced by the slackening of financial constraints on the weak countries. We have seen that these countries cannot hope significantly to increase their cash entries by augmenting their exports to the United States, since these are now too small a share of total exports.[5] They can, however, increase these earnings considerably as a result of a rise of exports within the German zone.

In other words, this process can eliminate the German payments surplus. We have seen that the principal cause of the imbalances in the world economy lies in the difficulties encountered by the European countries in financing their oil deficit. These difficulties are sharpened by the imbalances that prevail within Europe itself, caused by the very existence of a German surplus (and to a lesser extent the small surpluses of Holland, Switzerland, and Belgium). The elimination of the German surplus through the reflation of the German economy would significantly reduce the deficits that would have to be financed by the weak countries, which presently have to finance deficits with both the oil-producing countries and Germany.[6]

Once the German surplus was eliminated, it would probably not be very difficult to finance the rest, especially if the EEC adopted Community measures to raise financial resources on international

[5] For example, only about 7% of Italian exports went to the United States, while more than 20% went to Germany, more than 50% to the EEC as a whole, and more than 60% to Western Europe as a whole.

[6] It should be noted that the reasoning developed in this paragraph refers to the situation immediately before the increase in oil prices in 1979. This new increase had the short-term effect of eliminating the German and Japanese surpluses. Nevertheless, since Germany occupies second position after the United States in trade with OPEC members, the rise in the currency entries of these countries will be reflected, albeit with some delay, in an increase in imports from Germany that will more than compensate for the greater outlay for oil Germany has had to pay as a result of the price increase. Similar considerations apply in the case of Japan.

markets (the Ortoli proposal to increase the medium-term support resources of the European Fund and to augment the capital of the European investment banks) or even proposals of broader scope for the placement of reserves in common and for the creation of a genuine European currency that could be used in competition with the dollar in international payments, even with countries outside the EEC (the Jenkins proposal).[7]

Different considerations apply in the case of the Japanese surplus. It cannot easily be eliminated through policies of expansion, since Japan has a low rate of unemployment (approximately 2%). Unless it assumed a distinctly inflationary flavour, a Japanese reflation would lead only to a diminution of the Japanese surplus, with only indirect effects on the level of activity in Europe, since Japanese imports come primarily from underdeveloped countries and the United States. It therefore seems that the Japanese surplus will have to be eliminated through a further strengthening of the yen, through unilateral measures by importing countries to reduce import levels of Japanese goods, or perhaps in part through extraordinary policies of accumulation of stocks of raw materials on Japan's part. It thus seems clear that the situation of Japan, burdened by an annual current-account surplus of $10 thousand million (the result of the drastic orientation of the Japanese economy toward exports), is now causing great concern among its rulers that the country could be ostracized by its trading partners. The only way to eliminate the Japanese surplus in a lasting and non-inflationary manner would be for Japan to abandon the effectively protectionist practices it has adopted, which make it the industrialized country in which manufactured imports represent the lowest share of national income, apart from the United States. Such a turn would entail heavy costs in restructuration of the economy and re-alignment of the relationship of forces among various sectors of the Japanese bourgeoisie. Japan has therefore adopted a policy similar to Germany's, although with greater subordination to the United States, given the close relations between the two economies. The analysis of German policy presented here can thus be generalized to Japan, although with the appropriate caution,

[7] In chapter 5 we will see why the European Currency Unit actually created by the European Monetary System does not have these features. It should be noted that since Italy has overdone its deflation policy, there is now a problem of an Italian surplus, which amounted to $2 thousand million in 1977, $6 thousand million in 1978, and about $5–6 thousand million in 1979.

for it must be recalled that while Japan cannot act otherwise (because of its productive structure), Germany could shift to a more expansive policy without seriously compromising its ability to restructure its economy. In the German case, political and international financial considerations predominate.

3. The Missed Recovery of the European Economy

It seems clear that German behaviour with regard to its balance of payments is thoroughly aberrant, both in relation to past experience and in relation to the objective responsibilities dictated by the position the German economy occupies internationally. Indeed, in the thirteen years from 1960 to 1972, Germany's current-account surplus averaged the equivalent of $800 million a year, while for the five years beginning in 1973 the annual average rose to about $5 thousand million. It must not be forgotten that for some years now unemployment in Germany has been more than a million (4.5% to 5% of the work force), while more than 600,000 immigrant workers have been repatriated and an undetermined number of school-leavers never absorbed into the labour force. Possibilities of sustained recovery clearly exist, both on the balance of payments side and on the labour-market side. Official German explanations for the refusal to reflate the economy—based on fear of inflation—are not very convincing. The rate of price variation in Germany has actually been quite low. The trade unions have clearly manifested their desire to collaborate in containing increases in labour costs, while dissatisfaction with the high level of unemployment without reflation could impel them to greater militancy. Finally, in no way do the econometric models of the German economy suggest that an increase in the rate of development would entail any outbreak of inflationary fever; these studies simply indicate that an increase in income produced by a rise in foreign demand would be accompanied by an increase in prices inferior to that which would accompany an increase in income generated by public spending—but there is no sign that price increases would be too high even in that case.[8]

These official international considerations have been expressed in

---

[8] See B.G. Hickman, 'International Transmission of Economic Fluctuations and Inflation', in A. Ando, R. Herring, and R. Marston (eds.), *International Aspects of Stabilization Policies*, Federal Reserve Bank of Boston, Conference Series no. 12, 1974.

the famous 'three-locomotives theory'. This approach, championed at one time by the Carter administration, maintains that responsibility for the recovery of the world economy cannot be consigned to the United States alone, but depends on recoveries in Germany and Japan as well. Among other things, a world recovery would favour the rate of the dollar by bolstering it. Indeed, this doctrine was elaborated in the thick of impassioned American defence of the dollar. The US government claimed that it was not responsible for the weakness of the dollar, which was instead attributed fundamentally to the lack of synchronization of the American and international economic cycles.[9] This doctrine, reiterated again and again during a crowded schedule of various types of summit meetings and diplomatic conferences in 1977 and 1978, made no impact on German inertia and even provoked a diplomatic backlash. The Carter doctrine was therefore returned to the drawing board and soon surfaced again, rechristened the 'convoy theory'. According to this new plan, Germany and Japan would not be the only countries compelled to bear the onus of recovery, which was now supposed to be launched simultaneously through the combined efforts of all countries: to begin with even the small countries with surpluses, and later, with a lower stimulation of internal demand, also the countries facing payment difficulties. But the convoy fared no better than the locomotives. At the Bonn summit in the summer of 1978 Germany committed itself to only a modest increase in income, to be brought about primarily through tax relief. Its effect was to raise the rate of growth from 2.7% in 1977 to 3.4% in 1978, and only slightly more in 1979. There were no significant hauling effects on the European economy.

4. The New Depreciation of the Dollar

German economic policy is rooted in the need to combat the effects of the revaluation of the mark. We must therefore quickly review the evolution of competitive relations among the three major capitalist

---

[9] This problem is analysed, especially as far as its currency repercussions are concerned, in T. de Vries, 'In Search of an Exchange-Rate Policy for the Dollar', Banca Nazionale del Lavoro, *Quarterly Review*, June 1978, and B. Balassa, 'Resolving Policy Conflicts for Rapid Growth in the World Economy', ibid., September 1978.

powers: the United States, Germany, and Japan. As we have seen, the deterioration of American competitivity during the post-war period—expressed in the diminution of the US share of world trade in manufactures and in the shift of manufacturing production abroad through multinational investment—had become especially worrying to the US government by the late sixties. The Americans thus decided that the dollar had to be devalued. Chapter 2 discussed the policies through which a rapid depreciation of the dollar was brought about. The currency history of the seventies can be subdivided into four phases, the last of which was still under way as the decade ended. As is shown in table 14, in the ten years of the 1970s the dollar depreciated by 50% relative to the mark and nearly 50% relative to the yen (having dipped as low as 180 yen to the dollar in October 1978).

Table 14

Dollar Quotations in German Marks and Japanese Yen
(annual average of daily rates)

	1961–68	1969	1970	1971	1972	1973	1974	1975	1976	1977	1978	1979*
DM = US $1	4	3.9	3.6	3.5	3.2	2.7	2.6	2.5	2.5	2.5	2.0	1.8
Yen = US $1	361	358	358	349	308	271	282	297	297	265	210	216

* Middle of July.

Source: National Institute for Economic and Social Research.

The first phase of the depreciation process was marked by an excessively expansionary US monetary policy, from 1970 to 1973. The lowering of short-term interest rates, along with negative expectations about the current-account balance, led to enormous outflows of dollars, which were exchanged for currencies expected to be revalued. This was part of the reason for the growth of the Eurodollar market.[10]

[10] To form a direct opinion of the severity and lack of scruple with which the Americans applied their currency strategy, consult the book of C. Coombs, *The Area of International Finance*, New York 1976. Coombs, now retired, was a high official of the Federal Reserve Bank of New York responsible for currency policy in the Federal Reserve System. He describes, with regret, the methods Nixon employed in monetary and currency policy in his efforts to bring about the devaluation of the dollar, methods that violated the spirit and letter of thirty years of international financial co-operation.

The second phase, which began late in 1973 after the definitive abandonment of the system of fixed exchange rates (March 1973) and the rise in the price of oil (November 1973), lasted until the spring of 1977. This phase may be called the period of 'benign neglect', the expression used by US monetary authorities to describe their attitude to the dollar: stand and watch, and allow the market to set the quotation. As is shown in table 14, during the years of benign neglect the dollar recovered slightly relative to the mark and the yen (and even more relative to other currencies). This behaviour changed drastically in 1977, when the United States assumed an aggressive attitude, authorizing high government officials to complain publicly that the dollar was over-valued (or that the mark and yen were under-valued). This 'open mouth' policy lasted from summer 1977 through October 1978. During this period the value of the dollar relative to the trade-weighted average of the currencies of the fifteen major US trade partners fell by more than 10%. The devaluation relative to the mark and the yen in particular was about 20%.[11] The open-mouth phase ended on 1 November 1978, when the US government decided to intervene to support the dollar through a complex combination of credit and currency measures, including the creation of a substantial stock of currency reserves—with which to intervene on exchange markets to support the dollar—made up of the proceeds of sales of public mark-denominated bonds on the German financial market. The period following November 1978 showed that the United States, while not completely accepting the possibility of a return to fixed exchange rates, even in the attenuated form of target rates for the quotations of major currencies relative to the dollar, was inclined to support the dollar in order to prevent a further decline from triggering a wave of financial panic that could result in massive conversions of the dollars held in private and official portfolios into other reserve assets, either other currency or gold.[12]

[11] See Morgan Guaranty Trust, *World Financial Markets*, November 1978.

[12] O. Emminger, president of the Bundesbank, recently commented thus on the new dollar policy: 'Recent interest in a greater stability of exchange rates and in correction of "erratic" levels of exchange rates should certainly not be interpreted as a move toward a target rate for the dollar. But surely it is a significant turn toward stricter control of the dollar's exchange rate, and it shows above all, together with other aspects of the new programme to support the dollar, that the era of the "benign neglect" of the foreign value of the dollar is over.' 'The Exchange Rate as an Instrument of Policy', *Lloyds Bank Review*, July 1979, p. 16.

It is important to examine American currency policy in 1979 carefully, because it graphically expresses the rising contradictions inherent in the attempt to recover American competitivity through depreciation of the dollar. To a considerable extent, us competitivity was indeed restored by successive devaluations. Table 15 shows that by 1977 the cost of labour in American industry was already a good 20% below that in German industry. Because of the very great reduction in the level of hourly wage costs in the United States compared with Germany, American industry is recovering its lost competitivity in many sectors. At a given level of plant productivity, the absolute cost of labour will tend to direct investment wherever costs are lowest. In other words, labour costs are an indicator of medium-term competitivity, unlike the cost of labour per unit of product, which is a short-term indicator. Concretely, we may say that a company that decides on an investment project employing the best technology available will tend, other factors being equal (fiscal conditions, transport costs, excise taxes, etc.), to locate the investment wherever labour costs are lowest, and where their anticipated evolution is lowest too. The United States not only offers lower labour costs than many European countries (not only Germany, but also Holland, Belgium, Switzerland, and Sweden have higher costs than the United States), but can also provide lower energy costs. Most important of all, potential investors are assured that if labour costs, either absolutely or per unit of product, are driven above those of competing countries, fresh competitive devaluations of the dollar can always be effected. Because of all these factors, a reversal of the flow of direct investment occurred: us investment abroad eased, while European investment in the United States rose enormously. Germany was the country hardest hit by this turnabout. Traditionally a net recipient of foreign investment during the post-war period, it made few investments abroad, therefore showing a surplus in the balance of direct investments. In 1975, however, the German balance of direct investments went into deficit. In 1977 foreigners invested a total of 3.5 thousand million marks in Germany, while Germans invested 6.2 thousand million marks abroad.[13] This brought about what the Americans desired: the trend toward the shift of us manufacturing production abroad slackened off, if it did not stop entirely, while the most developed rivals of the United States

[13] See table 16.

were induced to reduce their own rate of industrial growth and increasingly to invest abroad, especially in the United States.

The brilliant effect of the dollar devaluation on direct investment, however, was not accompanied by equally favourable effects on American exports. Figure 1 depicts the sluggish evolution of the American share of world exports. Much of the responsibility for this poor performance is due to special features of German and Japanese

Table 15

Hourly Labour Costs in Industry
(in 1977 DM)

	1977	1979
Germany	18.5	20.9
USA	15.5	16.8
Japan	11.0	11.3

Source: Dresdener Bank.

Table 16

Evolution of Direct Foreign Investment in Germany and of German
Investment Abroad
(in thousands of millions of $)

	(1)	(2)	(3)
1967	3.3	1.3	2.0
1968	2.2	1.9	0.3
1969	2.1	2.8	−0.7
1970	2.2	3.2	−1.0
1971	3.9	3.7	0.2
1972	6.2	5.0	1.2
1973	5.3	4.4	0.9
1974	6.6	5.0	1.6
1975	3.1	4.9	−1.9
1976	3.9	6.2	−2.3
1977	3.5	6.2	−2.7

(1) Foreign investment in Germany.
(2) German investment abroad.
(3) Difference between 1 and 2; a minus sign indicates a net outflow of direct investment.

Source: Bundesbank.

competition, more effectively supported by the national financial systems and by state organization than staunchly free-enterprise-oriented American industry. This situation has provoked increasingly crude insinuations about 'Japan, inc.' and 'Germany, inc.' both in the press and in official American publications. The epithet is intended to refer to the collusion of industry, finance, and the state in German and Japanese commercial penetration of foreign markets. In turn, there has been no lack of explicit references to the behaviour of these countries in the thirties. As I have already mentioned, the

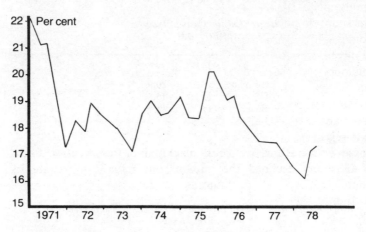

Graph 1. US Share of World Exports of Manufactures

Note: World exports are here defined as the exports of the fifteen major industrialized countries; the values indicated in the graph therefore differ slightly from those of table 12.

Source: Morgan Guaranty.

inadequate dynamic of European demand contributed to keeping the demand for American goods low, while the high American demand during the late seventies encouraged Europeans and Japanese to export to the United States, thus maintaining their shares of world manufactured exports. The American strategy of reducing the income of the other industrialized countries through control of financial channels thus proved self-defeating: Euro-Japanese economic stagnation weakened the dollar. At this point, after almost a decade of continual depreciation, any fresh weakening of the dollar could have threatened the stability of international monetary relations. Indeed, despite the abandonment of the convertibility of the dollar for gold, and even of the official gold price itself (both in the United States and internationally, with the reform of the IMF Articles of Agreement), the dollar is not the uncontested sovereign of international finance. The spectre of gold continues to haunt it through the private market, where the gold quotation soared past $300 an ounce during the summer of 1979. Moreover, holders of funds in dollars could always decide to unload this currency in favour of others, or—an even more frightening prospect—in favour of the accumulation of stocks of raw materials.

This situation of potential currency crisis had effects on American economic policy options, both national and international. The theory of the three locomotives was a first step: the United States abandoned its rigid opposition to European growth, masked under the pretext of aiding the European countries in the struggle against inflation, and turned to the Keynesian language of concerted world recovery. But the Germans refused to budge. And here the United States probably came to regret the loss of its allies in Europe, who felt betrayed by the American financial and petroleum blackmail of the seventies. Then, when Germany declined the gambit and refused to reflate its economy (and Europe's with it), the United States could do little but yield. Indeed, Washington cannot fuel a European recovery by supplying credit unless there is a German recovery too, because this would only worsen the position of the dollar, and the political preconditions for an effort of this type were in any case lacking in the European countries themselves, where the ruling blocs were shifting increasingly to deflationary policies of the German type, in an effort to bring inflation under control, throttle trade-union power, and ape the policy of German production.

To avert a frightful dollar crisis, then, with unpredictable consequences for the entire world economy, the United States was faced with a dilemma: either resign itself to decelerating the growth of its own economy, thus curbing the restoration of its relative strength in the world economy, or come to some agreement with Germany, trading a concerted worldwide recovery for the establishment of more stable exchange rates between the dollar and the European currencies, and possibly even a redefinition of the role of the dollar in the international monetary system, alongside gold and other currencies. The probability that the United States would soon renounce its attempt to maintain the supreme position in all domains—finance, trade, and currency—was heightened by the persistence of American inflation, which was weakening the dollar. This inflation was due in part to the continual devaluation of the dollar throughout the decade. It is true that the inflationary effects of dollar devaluations are far inferior to those of devaluations of other currencies, but the effect does exist nevertheless, and it is cumulative. Chain reactions set in: when the dollar depreciates and then appreciates because other currencies have responded with depreciations of their own, the inflation imparted by the first devaluation, provided a reasonable period of time elapses before the subsequent reappreciation, is not annulled by the restoration of the previous average dollar quotation. The small inflationary impulses of successive dollar devaluations thus accumulate over the course of years, and are reflected in a rate of inflation that, partly because of expectations of yet further devaluations, has not receded to levels comparable to the German rate.

The American difficulty in picking its way through these complex and inter-related problems may well have owed something to the lack of resolution of Jimmy Carter, a rather provincial figure thrust into the White House, but it surely results fundamentally from the special complexity of the international position of the American economy. And the Germans understood this very well.

If the United States opted to decelerate American development, then the recession would have been aggravated, its pressure on the world economy intensified. Even more dangerous, however, would have been a US attempt to bend German will by resorting to operations of a non-economic character, such as, for example, invoking the Soviet threat in an effort to drive Germany back into line and incite it against the other NATO countries.

5. German Deflation

Let us examine the consequences for the German economy. The depreciation of the dollar exerts pressure on Germany,[14] which finds its competitivity threatened. Germany then makes every effort to enhance the technological quality of its products, concentrating investment in advanced sectors (electronics, nuclear power, air transport, military equipment, industrial plant and machinery). On the other hand, it resolves to transfer production of goods of high

[14] The same applies to Japan.

labour intensity abroad, and this is reflected in a rise in capital exports. In addition to maximizing its exports, Germany offers incentives for the concession of credit, granting vast commercial and financial loans to its customers, especially developing countries but also quite a few customers in the developed countries (for example, sales of the Franco-German Airbus in the United States). Indeed, the sectors toward which all the developed countries are now orienting are the new markets of the OPEC countries, the so-called 'medium income' (newly industrializing) countries, and the socialist countries. To break into these markets it is necessary to offer long-term credits (remember that as a whole even the OPEC countries are in debt to the tune of $25 thousand million; the surplus is concentrated in the countries of the Arabian peninsula).

To sustain this enormous outflow of capital in the form of direct investment and export credits, Germany is inevitably compelled to run a current-account surplus and to accumulate reserves. Both of these objectives—increase in the technological level of production and realization of a current-account surplus—require deflationary policies. The low growth rate of the German economy, which is the cause of the stagnation of the European economy, is therefore closely linked to the revaluation of the mark. Let us analyse this phenomenon in more detail.

The revaluation of the mark compels Germany to abandon industrial sectors and products of medium to low technological content, which absorb relatively high quantities of unskilled labour, in order to concentrate on sectors and products of higher technology, which use labour of relatively higher skill. Deflation encourages the abandonment of lines of production rendered uneconomical by the revaluation of the mark and permits the shift of capital and skilled labour to companies operating in the advanced sectors. An examination of the labour market reveals this trend in the modification of German industrial structure: unemployment, which has hovered around a million ever since 1975, affects mainly workers with low skills. Youth under twenty years old and women constitute 49% of the unemployed, whereas in 1968, at a comparable cyclical phase, these categories accounted for only 28.8% of the unemployed. The abandonment of traditional industries has also created many regional imbalances on the labour market.[15] Moreover, in spite of the

[15] This analysis is contained in Deutsche Bundesbank, *Report for the Year 1976*, pp. 35–40.

high level of unemployment, there are some 200–300 thousand unsatisfied requests for skilled workers.

The low level of growth of internal demand, besides encouraging processes of industrial reconversion, also fosters restructuration and rationalization in traditional sectors and products. The pressure of labour costs and the stagnation of demand compel companies to mechanize and automate production. When this does not occur, or occurs insufficiently, the company is driven out of the market, and its market-share is reabsorbed by the surviving enterprises. This process takes place in part through acquisitions and mergers, which have intensified in recent years. The larger companies can introduce more automated productive processes and reduce the unit cost of production in order to remain competitive with foreign products favoured by the revaluation of the mark.

This process of requalification of German production has been accompanied by efforts to increase commercial penetration of the new markets of the OPEC countries and the non-oil-producing developing countries. These countries are absorbing capital imports consonant with the qualitative shifts of German industry: plants, telecommunication apparatuses, machinery, and so on.[16] To sell these products it is necessary to be able to grant long-term credit and therefore to enjoy current-account surpluses that can finance a high volume of reserves and credit. The financial reinforcement of Germany is also required to foster the shift abroad of those sectors of German industry no longer competitive on the basis of national labour costs, through direct investment in countries where labour costs are low: quite significant German investments have also been directed to the United States in order to preserve market shares already achieved by German companies but endangered by the revaluation of the mark.[17]

The need to concede loans and financial investments abroad accounts for the German policy of accumulating currency reserves through current-account surpluses. But these reserves are also required to guarantee future German financial strength. Sooner or

[16] The modification of the composition of German foreign trade, along with its effects on the labour market, is analysed in D. Schumacher, 'Increased Trade with the Third World: German Workers Will Have to Switch Jobs but not Lose Them', *Die Wochenbericht*, February 1977.

[17] A similar explanation of the German surplus is put forward by D. Calleo, *The German Problem Reconsidered*, London 1978, pp. 179–203.

Table 17

Net Financial Assets Abroad of Germany, June 1977
(*thousands of millions of $*)

Federal Bank of Germany	45
(of which reserves: 35)	
Federal Government	8
Commercial Banks	
(net position)	7
Total	60

Note: The brokerage of commercial banks abroad must be added to the total, i.e. the currency loans issued with currency deposits, because these loans can be finalized in German trade; this brokerage is equivalent to $40 thousand million.

Source: Bundesbank, *Monthly Report*, October 1977.

later, the German current-account surplus will inevitably vanish, or at least be substantially reduced, under the protracted effects of the revaluation of the mark. Investments abroad will then be able to be financed only by drawing upon reserves or international capital markets. The so-called base balance, composed of the current-account balance plus long-term capital movements, was in deficit as long ago as 1977. Since Germany does not enjoy the American privilege of issuing international reserve currency, it cannot long afford the luxury of a negative balance of payments, as the United States did for many years. And even to utilize international capital markets fully, Germany requires enough financial power to quell any possible doubts about the solvency of German loan takers.

Apart from these two factors—financing of exports and of direct foreign investment—Germany also has reason to accumulate financial power for subsidiary objectives of commercial and economic policy: great financial power enables Germany to extend its imperialist influence by consolidating its sphere of commercial and political hegemony. It is enough to recall the experience of German loans to countries of southern Europe: Italy, Portugal, and now even Turkey, angry about the US arms embargo. Loans also permit the subordination of weaker countries and prevent them from hampering German plans for the international division of labour. Let us not forget the words of Chancellor Schmidt immediately after the concession of a German loan to Italy: 'We have given Italy enough to keep its head above water. . . . It is necessary that a precise division of labour be brought about in Europe.'[18]

To assess the strength Germany has already attained, it should be noted that $100 thousand million—for such is the full measure of German financial power (see table 17)—is no small sum even by the standards of international finance. Total world reserves, including funds at the disposal of international financial organs (mainly the IMF and the World Bank) and the net amount of the Eurodollar market, and deducting for the many instances of overlap among these items, probably barely exceeded $500 thousand million at the same date.

Moreover, American financial strength is not unlimited. Indeed, as the United States depreciates its currency for commercial reasons, it impoverishes the scope of the dollar as a financial instrument. And there may well be a limit to the depreciation of the dollar: the threshold at which investors no longer desire to hold a currency that loses value continually. If this limit has not yet been reached, it is basically because large portions of official dollar holdings are kept in this form for political reasons. Saudi Arabia, for example, does not diversify its reserves in exchange for American support of the OPEC cartel and, in general, for the political and military protection accorded by its powerful ally. But there is a limit to the American policy. Bonn's efforts to compete with its great ally will not easily be thwarted, and it could be that Germany will succeed in maintaining its share of world trade in manufactures, which is already higher than the US share.

Finally, Germany cannot risk falling prey to inflation. Memories of the two great epidemics of galloping hyper-inflation are often cited as explanations for the determination evinced by German governments in the struggle against inflation. This explanation surely does have some validity, but it must not be forgotten that the entire strategy of the technological advance of German production and trade requires absolute control over price dynamics. To start with, if price increases are inferior to those of the other industrial countries, the revaluation of the mark is proportionally reduced. Second—and this does not contradict the first point, whatever some may say—once it is accepted that it is impossible seriously to oppose the devaluation of the dollar, it makes sense to issue imperious directives to companies:

[18] Cited in M. De Cecco, 'L'economia tedesca e il bastone americano', *La Repubblica*, 22 July 1976.

German corporations must rationalize production and drive ahead into advanced sectors. To reflate internal demand in a situation in which profits are being compressed by revaluations and wages have been practically frozen for years could run the risk of triggering an inflation of costs similar to that which has occurred in other countries. The exchange rate could consequently decline and company policies would be disoriented. In other words, rather than commit itself to a war with the dollar through a suite of devaluations produced by (and causing) inflation, Germany accepts the inevitable fact of revaluation of the mark relative to the dollar but seeks to moderate its real impact by controlling inflation, to regulate its pace in order to prevent steep plunges of the dollar, and above all to avert wild gyrations in the dollar-mark exchange rate. Because of this policy, German industry can be driven to rise to what Chancellor Schmidt has called 'the challenge of new products, new technologies, and new markets'.

6. The Fate of the European Economy

The United States and Germany, antagonists in the realm of the relative competitivity of their commodities, share the desire to open and maintain ever broader markets for their exports. These markets lie in the newly industrializing countries mentioned earlier, which are absorbing commodities in the production of which the United States and Germany have a clear edge over other countries and for the sale of which they command the necessary finance. Moreover, the other developed countries can manage to produce these commodities—and indeed are often already in a position to do so. They thus do not constitute a promising market for the United States and Germany, because any attempt to penetrate these markets provokes reactions from governments and national industries, which are able to organize themselves and to augment the national supply. It is much easier to sell nuclear power plants to Pakistan than to Italy (not to mention France or Britain), because Pakistan stands far below the technological level required to produce even the simplest reactor components. In Italy, on the other hand, the national industry would have to be dealt with, and difficult and costly compromises reached. The United States and Germany thus have a common interest in raising the purchasing power of these countries, and this cannot be assured solely through loans, because there is a limit to the indebtedness any country can tolerate, no matter how free-wheeling it may be. The newly targeted countries must be helped to produce the simple goods they are capable of making, so that they can continue to buy complex products from the United States and Germany. The latter two countries therefore thunder against protectionism whenever the peripheral European countries engage in it. From the German and American point of view, Brazil, Korea, and Hong Kong must increase their sales in Europe (for its part, the United States continues to raise protective barriers for the most backward sectors of the American economy), because Germany and the United States are continuing to increase their sales to these countries. To varying extents, this free-trade policy harms all the European countries, which obtain scant advantages in return, either because they do not produce complex goods as efficiently, or because they lack the financial resources required to sell them. On the other hand, these countries would have an interest in the establishment of the broadest and most generous official financial mechanism. Lack of financing constitutes a significant limitation for the countries that want to augment the share of their exports effected on credit. Here again the preponderance of imperialist interests at the expense of the weak countries is evident. The United States and Germany agree in rejecting any enlargement of official financial mechanisms, which would enable the weak countries to deal more effectively with potential problems related to their concession of credit to newly industrializing countries in order to sell their complex products, or would enable the new countries to go into debt more independently and to select their own suppliers of financing. The various plans to increase official international liquidity have been systematically sabotaged—or in the best of cases sharply reduced in scope—by joint action by the United States and Germany.

The United States and Germany, in conflict over the maintenance of industrial and technological leadership, join together in the commercial exploitation of the rest of the world. The consequence of this imperialist relationship of competition and alliance is the demotion of Europe to conditions of direct subordination to the exigencies of German capitalist development, both internal and multinational. The European countries, subjected to a heavy drain of resources because of the rise in the cost of oil, and unable to increase their exports because of their relative technological backwardness and their poverty of financial resources, are now witnessing the evaporation of their prospects for development of the national income and return to full employment. At the same time, they are faced with mounting competition from new countries, which threatens to plunge entire traditional sectors of their economies into crisis. These states are unable to forge any common action to loosen the grip of German imperialism and instead squander their energies in exhausting conflicts of interest that tend to be resolved, one by one, through the formation of fleeting alliances with Germany. But the inability to form a common front is not solely the result of attempts to maximize short-term national interest; more fundamentally, it reflects the intrinsic weakness of the various bourgeoisies, which, in face of the ongoing reconstruction of the European economy under German hegemony, fragment according to sectors of capital investment and the strength of particular monopolistic groups. Within each country, the strong sectors seek to ally themselves with triumphant German capital, and have no interest in joining with weak national sectors and enterprises. The only terrain of unity among the national bourgeoisies is their attack on the conditions of the workers. Wage controls and the reduction of public spending on social objectives in the broadest sense of the word free resources that the big monopolistic groups can then use in order to line up with German and American capital and compensate for the weak sectors, at least provisionally. The recomposition of the European national bourgeoisies, a prelude to the recomposition of the European bourgeoisie as a whole under the control of German monopoly capital, is occurring against the backdrop of the regression of the living and working conditions of the workers and some layers of the petty-bourgeoisie. The new social factor is the acquiescent behaviour of the popular sectors targeted by this destructive process: never in the past several decades of capitalist history has a shift of power from labour to capital of this proportion occurred with such a low degree of social tension.

Nonetheless, it is hard to believe that this process will fail to generate severe friction in the long run. The individual bourgeoisies are therefore seeking to defend social equilibrium in their countries as far as possible, passing costs on to countries that cannot defend themselves. Italy is probably the weakest country, the one that will pay for German hegemony proportionally more than the others. The sectors in which competition from newly industrializing countries is strongest are the sectors in which the Italian economy has specialized to a large extent. To these must be added the other sectors in which much investment has recently been made: steel, shipyards, basic chemicals. Then there is agriculture, the sacrifice of which to the exigencies of enlargement of the EEC's sphere of influence in the Mediterranean is too well known to require illustration.

Italy faces this highly dangerous phase for its economic vitality and political independence in one of the most unpleasant moments of its political history, with a Communist Party too committed to supplying guarantees of common sense and adherence to the rules of the international game to be able to elaborate a coherent strategy of defence of the interests of the workers and of national economic development. At the same time, the bourgeoisie seems already to have reconciled itself to the new state of affairs, on the whole accentuating the comprador features it has always possessed, the few large sectors and advanced groups appropriating public resources and the patrimony of state participation in preparation for the great imperial banquet.

5
The European Monetary System

1. From the 'Snake' to the EMS

The European Monetary System (EMS) came into effect on 13 March 1979; its formation had been decided by a resolution of the Council of Europe on 5 December 1978.[1] The EMS is the direct descendant of the April 1972 Basle accord on the limitation of the fluctuation margins of EEC currencies—the so-called snake[2]—and entails few novelties compared to the snake.

When the European currency snake was created, the international monetary system was still based on fixed exchange rates in principle, despite the period of free float of the dollar in the second half of 1971. The Smithsonian agreement of December 1971 had redefined par values for the currencies of the Group of Ten—called 'central rates'—and the participating countries agreed to hold the quotation of their currencies relative to the dollar within a band equal to plus or minus 2.25% of the central rates. Under the previous system, the breadth of this band had been ± 1%, and the countries adhering to the European Monetary Agreement[3] had decided to hold the oscillation of their currencies relative to the dollar within a narrower band of ±0.75%, in an effort to limit the maximum gap between the currencies of any two parties to the accord to 1.5% at any given time

[1] For the text of the resolution, see *Bolletino delle Communità europee*, 12, 1978.

[2] The 'snake', creation of which was decided by resolution of the Council of Europe on 21 March 1972, went into effect with the agreement among the central banks of EEC member states on 10 April 1972. For the relevant documents, see *Compendio dei Testi comunitari in materia monetaria*, Brussels, n.d.

[3] The European Monetary Agreement had been stipulated among the OECD countries to create a system of mutual financial aid to replace the European Payments Union. See P. Coffey and J.R. Presley, *European Monetary Integration*, London 1972, chapter 2.

and to $\pm 3\%$ over time. After Washington, the European countries found it useful to reestablish a narrower band of oscillation than that stipulated relative to the dollar. They therefore agreed to hold the oscillation within a band of $\pm 1.125\%$ relative to the central rate of the dollar, and thus to limit the maximum gap between any two Community currencies at any given time to 2.25%. The central banks of the countries that were about to become members of the EEC— Britain, Ireland, and Denmark—immediately joined this accord, although their adherence was brief, since the pound had to be withdrawn from the snake in June of that same year; the Irish pound exited immediately thereafter and was soon followed by the Danish crown.

The agreement to limit the margin of fluctuation was called the snake because the graph traced by the European currencies as they oscillated around the dollar was a sinoidal wave that resembled a snake in a tunnel. When fourteen industrialized countries meeting in Paris in March 1973 decided to abandon the maintenance of parity of their currencies relative to the dollar, the countries that were in the snake decided to continue their joint float, with the exception of Italy, which had begun to allow the lira to float freely in February of that same year. The Swedish and Norwegian crowns were later added to the surviving currencies of the snake, which in the meantime had reabsorbed the Danish crown, although Sweden had no intention of joining the EEC and Norway, which earlier had begun negotiations to join, had by then decided not to do so. Finally, in January 1974 the French franc also abandoned the snake. (The franc rejoined in July 1975, but had to exit once again in March 1976, after the strong depreciation of the lira in January of that year, which had caused a loss of competitivity of French products. Sweden abandoned the snake in August 1977.) The snake thus eventually came to be made up of the German mark and the currencies of a number of weak countries the greater part of whose trade was with Germany.

The snake represented a coupling of the mark and several minor currencies more than a real joint float. The Basle accord had laid down rules for the maintenance of oscillations of member currencies within a limited band nested within a broader band within which all currencies could oscillate relative to the dollar. The accord did not stipulate that European currencies could float freely relative to the dollar. The snake was thus bereft of any mechanisms by which to determine the course of action that should be followed by a country whose currency was appreciating relative to the dollar. In practice, if fixed exchange rates were to be maintained between the countries of the snake, then the minor currencies would have to appreciate with the mark relative to the dollar. For its part, the mark's value soared during this period, rising from an average quotation of 3.18 marks to the dollar in 1972 to an average of 1.88 in December 1978. The currencies that remained in the snake underwent a similar revaluation.

Membership in the snake was not a necessary condition for appreciation relative to the dollar, since other currencies outside the snake—such as the Swiss franc and the Austrian schilling—were revalued as much as or more than the mark relative to the dollar. But for some currencies it was a sufficient condition, especially the crown of Denmark, whose economy proved able to tolerate the sudden appreciation only with enormous effort. The countries party to the agreement maintained parity with the mark, either by obtaining current-account surpluses through reductions in their levels of activity and growth rates, or by maintaining a favourable short-term capital-account balance, posting short-term interest rates above German levels by amounts ranging from 50% to 100%. In other words, Holland, Belgium, and Denmark applied deflationary po-licies. In the particular case of Denmark, this policy and the appreciation of the crown were insufficient to lower the rate of inflation or to reduce the current-account deficit significantly.

Nevertheless, the coordination of economic policies and the manipulation of interest rates were not expressly stipulated in the Basle accord,[4] which concerned only the co-ordination of interven-tions in exchange markets and arrangements to finance them. In other words, the snake was nothing but an exchange agreement, and in my view the European Monetary System is no more than that either. Under the snake the participating central banks were commit-ted to intervene when their currency veered toward the margins of the agreed fluctuation band; infra-marginal interventions were in general ruled out, save by concurrent decision of all the central banks. The Basle agreement guaranteed that unlimited credit would be accorded whichever bank's money fell to the lower margin of the fluctuation band (debtor bank). These credits could be issued either in the form

---

[4] The 21 March 1972 resolution of the Council of Europe refers to co-ordination, but 'in the compass of orientations of economic policy defined by the Council'.

of swaps between the debtor bank and another bank of the snake—in other words, on the initiative of the debtor bank, which would cede a certain quantity of its currency in exchange for money to use in its interventions, committing itself to return the money at the end of the intervention—or in the form of purchases of the weak currency by the other central banks; in that case, after the agreed period had passed, these banks would cede the money acquired on the market to the debtor bank, now a so-called involuntary debtor, which was obliged to hand over an equivalent amount of currency. These credits, which the accord called 'financial operations', fell due one month after the end of the month in which the swap was activated or the market intervention initiated. It was also stipulated that very short-term credit arising from the financial operations could be extended for another three months. This extension, however, applied not to the entire amount, but only to a sum equal to the share of participation of the debtor bank in 'short-term currency support';[5] further extension for the same period and the same amount was also allowed. In April 1973 the European Monetary Cooperation Fund (FECOM) was established to regulate, on a multilateral basis, the balances resulting from financial operations. As a technical instrument of exchange operations, the FECOM was also supposed to officially post the market exchange-rates and to coordinate inframarginal interventions.[6]

The interesting aspect of the experience of co-ordinated interventions under the snake was the limited use of national currencies in these interventions, despite the explicit provisions to the contrary in the official agreements. In reality, the intervention currency was almost exclusively the dollar: interventions on exchange markets in support of currencies that brushed the lower margin of the band from time to time were effected by selling dollars for the weak currency.[7] The countries of the snake therefore did not diversify their reserves,

[5] This is one of the forms of mutual financial assistance in the EEC, described elsewhere. For information on these points, see F. Praussello, *Il Sistema Monetario Europeo*, Florence 1979, pp. 53–57.

[6] In principle the decision to establish the FECOM had been made before the snake, and according to the more optimistic expectations, was supposed to constitute the embryo of a European Federal Bank. For a detailed analysis of the functioning of the FECOM, see F. Masera, 'Finalità e modalità operative del Fondo europeo di cooperazione monetaria', *Moneta e credito*, March-June 1973.

[7] See J. Salop, 'Dollar Intervention Within the Snake', *IMF Staff Papers*, March 1977.

which continued to be held almost exclusively in dollars, gold, and SDRs. The operations to support weak currencies were quite exacting, as may be inferred from the Bundesbank figures on the annual value of the 'intersecting operations' conducted by the bank—in other words, sales of foreign currencies against foreign currencies.

Despite the restrictive economic and monetary policies, the rise of the mark was so strong that some devaluations within the snake were effected, minor currencies being depreciated relative to the mark, although by limited amounts.[8]

The European Monetary System, instituted in December 1978,[9] presents no modifications that would substantially alter the character of the agreement described so far. What are the most important novelties introduced by the Brussels accord?[10] They all amount to the effort to integrate the currency accord into the institutional mechanisms of the EEC more closely—to the point that many observers and participants have claimed that the EMS represents the first stage of the much-coveted unification of European currencies. In the first place, participation in the System now coincides exactly with membership of the EEC: Norway withdrew from the joint float just after the Brussels accord, while Britain, although it does not participate in the joint float, is a full participant in all the decision-making bodies and financial mechanisms of the system.[11] Second, a European Currency Unit (ECU) has been established, which is now employed as the

[8] Modifications of the central rates of the snake were made in June 1973, October 1976, and October 1978. On the entire history of the snake, and more generally on the institutional stages of European monetary unification, see L. Tsoukalis, *The Politics and Economics of European Monetary Integration*, London 1977.

[9] Following the discussions in the Council of Europe in Copenhagen, 7 April 1978, and under the auspices of the Council of Europe in Bremen, 7 July 1978.

[10] Descriptions of the institutional and functional mechanisms of the system are contained in Banca d'Italia, *Relazione all'Assemblea*, Rome 1979, Appendix, 'Il Sistema Monetario Europeo', pp. 151–156; 'Présentation du Système Monétaire Européen', in Banque de France, *Bulletin Trimestriel*, March 1979; with particular reference to the problems of Italy's participation, see also the *Documento presentato dal Governatore della Banca d'Italia alla Commissione Finanze e Tesoro del Senato*, dated 26 October 1978; on the problems of British participation, see the British government's 'green book', *Financial Times*, 25 November 1978.

[11] It must be added, however, that the Swiss franc and the Austrian schilling, although not forming part of the system, are allied to Community currencies by express declaration of the relevant monetary authorities. In the case of the franc, the authorities have declared that they want to prevent its rising above the value of 80 centimes to the German mark. See P. Fabra, 'La Suisse et le SME', *Revue économique franco-suisse*, no. 1, 1979.

numeraire for the mechanism of exchange-rates, as the basis for a divergence indicator, as numeraire for operations relating to the mechanisms of intervention and credit, and as means of settlement among the monetary authorities of the European Community. Formally at least, the central rates of the currencies of the system are posted in ECUs, and from these central rates it is possible to derive the bilateral rates of the various currencies (see table 18). Finally, a better junction has been effected between community credit mechanisms and the credit on demand used in the functioning of the system. The 'financial operations' of the snake have been supplanted by a 'mechanism of very short-term credit', still of limited scope but of a duration of forty-five days from the end of the month in which the intervention took place, and extendable by another thirty days for sums limited to the amount of the debtor's share of 'short-term

Table 18

Compulsory Intervention Points*
(*in national currency units*)

Currency	Mark	French Franc	Florin	Belgian Franc	Lira	Danish Crown	Irish Pound
1 Mark		2.25581	1.05960	15.3665	430.698	2.75960	0.258060
		2.3621	1.10835	16.0740	485,576	2.88660	0.269937
10 French	4.23350		4.58800	66.5375	1,864.900	11,94900	1.117390
francs	4.42850		4.79900	69.6000	2,102.250	12.49850	1.168810
1 Florin	0.90225	2.0838		14.1800	397.434	2.54645	0.238130
	0.94375	2.1796		14.8325	448.074	2.66365	0.249089
100 Belgian	6.22100	14.3680	6.74200		2,740.440	17.55850	1.641980
francs	6.50800	15,0290	7.05200		3,089.610	18,36650	1.717550
1000 Lire	2.05900	4.7560	2.23175	32.3650		5,81300	0.543545
	2.32200	5.3620	2.51600	36.4900		6.55300	0.612801
10 Danish	3.46450	8.0010	3.75425	54.4450	1,526.050		0.914343
crowns	3.62350	8.3690	3.92700	56.9500	1,720.450		0.956424
1 Irish	3.70500	8.5555	4.01450	58.2225	1,631.850	10.45550	
pound	3.87500	8.9495	4.19950	60.9020	1,839.780	10.93650	

* The compulsory intervention points are +2.275% and −2.225% of the central rates. In the ±6% fluctuation band used by Italy, they are +6.18% and −5.82%.

Source: Bank of Italy.

currency support'. 'Currency support' now consists of 15.8 thousand million ECUs in creditor shares;[12] in addition, the 'medium-term financial contribution' was raised to 14.1 thousand million ECUs. Finally, a mechanism has been planned to assure consultation on the functioning of the System regularly every six months, although it does not seem that central exchange rates can be revised on such occasions.

The most important element is the creation of the ECU and its use as 'divergence indicator'. But the ECU is not a genuine currency. In substance, it functions only as a unit of account, replacing the European Unit of Account (EUA)[13] previously used in the compilation of the balance of payments of the EEC and to denominate the financial operations of the European Investment Bank, as well as economic and financial transactions with countries associated with the Community. The ECU also acts as a reserve asset, but in reality the use of the ECU amounts simply to a re-denomination of a portion of the reserves of the Community central banks. The ECU was created by the FECOM against deposit of 20% of the gold and dollar reserves of member countries.[14] In exchanging ECUs, then, the central banks are effectively exchanging the gold and dollars in their possession. The significance of the new currency would have been quite different had it been created by the FECOM without counterpart, as SDRs are created by the IMF, especially if they could be used to settle balances with central banks outside the Community, although assumption of this role would probably require the circulation of ECUs among private individuals. If it had these characteristics, the European currency would expand the available international liquidity of member countries and could usefully contribute to the development and economic recovery of the weakest of them.[15]

---

[12] And of 7.9 thousand million of debtor shares. The creditor shares indicate the total loans the banks can be called upon to finance, while the debtor shares indicate the amount of credit the bank can draw upon.

[13] The EUA, instituted in 1975, is a basket-currency obtained by weighting the nine EEC currencies. The value of the ECU was set equal to that of the EUA at the time the system began functioning, and the same currency composition has been maintained.

[14] In this manner the ECU facilitates the recovery of a monetary function for gold.

[15] Even if the ECU was used only to settle intra-European balances, it would permit the utilization of exchange reserves to settle balances arising from trade with non-European countries. There has been talk about an ECU additional to existing reserves; the anti-unemployment potential of a European currency has been hailed by many. See R. Jenkins, 'European Monetary Union', *Lloyds Bank Review*, January 1978.

The use of the ECU as a divergence indicator is an attempt to remedy one of the defects of the snake: the obligation to intervene on exchange markets whenever a particular currency reached the limits of fluctuation relative to another was imposed indifferently both on the central bank of the relatively stronger currency and on the central bank of the relatively weaker currency, without determining which currency was 'responsible' for the divergence from the central rate. Now, under the EMS, whenever a currency diverges from its central rate in ECUs by more than three-fourths of the permitted oscillation (net of the modifying influence the value of the currency itself exerts on the value of the ECU), a presumption of intervention is created even before the limit of oscillation is reached relative to another currency of the system.[16] Naturally, it can easily happen that the limit of fluctuation relative to another currency may be reached without the threshold of divergence in terms of ECUs being reached. The oscillation permitted an EMS currency relative to the central rate of the ECU and the central rate of the other currencies is $\pm 2.25\%$ (except in the case of the lira, which has been accorded a $\pm 6\%$ oscillation). Because of the superimposition of links between the various pairs of currencies, the exchange rates of all the currencies of the EMS, except the lira, are constantly held within a band equal to the width of the absolute margin allowed, namely $\pm 2.25\%$, as under the old snake.[17]

Attainment of the divergence threshold in ECUs does not entail obligatory intervention, but implies a strong presumption that measures to combat the deviation or eliminate its causes will be taken. These measures may be interventions on exchange markets, changes in monetary policy, or other types of action designed to alter the central rate of a currency. Whenever a currency looks like crossing the threshold of divergence before reaching the maximum oscillation relative to one of the other currencies of the System, the interventions are infra-marginal. Now, on the basis of the accord, only interventions at the margins have to be made in Community currencies; for infra-marginal interventions extra-EEC currencies may be used (namely the dollar). This means that there is no relation

---

[16] On the functioning of the divergence indicator, see M. Tronzano, 'Esame di alcuni aspetti tecnici dello SME', *CEEP Notizie*, no. 5, 1979; M. Tronzano and F. Viglongo, 'Il meccanismo dell'indicatore di divergenza: alcune precisazioni ed una simulazione relative al primo trimestre del 1979', ibid., no. 6, 1979; 'Intervention Arrangements in the European Monetary System', *Bank of England Quarterly Review*, June 1979.

[17] For an explanation of this point, see 'Intervention Arrangements . . .'.

between the evolution of interventions and the monetary conditions of the intervening country, except in the case of a currency that is being strengthened, in other words, one that is deviating at the high end of the band. If, for example, the mark rises and reaches the divergence threshold, then the Bundesbank intervenes. If it were compelled to intervene with Community currency, it would have to sell marks for other currencies and would therefore increase the supply of marks in circulation; a good part of these marks would increase the availability of Euromarks, while the remainder would augment the German money supply. Given the ease with which German residents can resort to the Euromarket, in both cases there would be an improvement in the liquidity situation of the German economy. If, on the other hand, the Bundesbank intervenes in dollars (as the accord permits), then it leaves the supply of marks unchanged while acquiring the weak currency. Moreover, under the former intervention system the mark is weakened and falls into step with the other currencies; under the new system, the other currencies are pulled upward, held in a suffocating embrace by the mark. The intervention, whether it occurs in dollars or an EEC currency, always reduces the quantity of the weak currency in circulation; indeed, it is necessary to buy weak currency in order to strengthen it, and this diminishes the quantity of it in circulation. The divergence indicator therefore aggravates the asymmetrical functioning of the System.

The asymmetry lies in the fact that under the EMS, as under the snake, there are no effective means by which to compel a strong-currency country to weaken its currency, but the weak-currency countries are compelled to strengthen theirs. Indeed, the country whose currency is weak must intervene in the market to purchase its own currency; if the level of its reserves is insufficient, it can obtain credit in the framework of the short-term mechanism, or the other central banks can intervene to buy its currency, making it an involuntary debtor. When it comes time for restitution of these credits, the country in question can obtain extensions if its reserves are insufficient, but in the end it will have either to repay the debt or to consolidate it through resort to short-term currency support or medium-term financial contributions. To obtain these loans it will have to commit itself to adopt particular measures of monetary and fiscal policy, if these have not already been imposed earlier, within the compass of the controlling bodies of the System. The obligation to carry out adjustments thus falls predominantly on the weak currencies. The defect of the System is that it does not identify the causes of currency weakness. A country like Italy, for example, which imports raw materials from countries outside the EEC and exports manufactures to Community markets, can encounter balance of payments difficulties because of the stagnation of European demand. In that event, the solution to the weakness of the lira ought to be a reflation of the Community economy. The mechanism of the System, however, would impose the adoption of deflationary measures in Italy.

This defect is exacerbated by the fact that the System always imposes deflation on the weak-currency country, even when the strong-currency country could expand without upsetting its balance of payments—in other words, when it has a high current-account surplus, as has been the case for Germany in recent years.

The EMS is more asymmetrical than the snake, thanks to the possibility of infra-marginal interventions in extra-EEC currencies at the attainment of the divergence threshold. Under the snake, interventions occurred generally only at the margins, and since they were carried out in national currency,[18] they entailed a widening of the supply of strong currency, with an expansive-inflationary effect, at least potentially. Under the EMS, on the other hand, authorization to effect infra-marginal interventions in extra-EEC currencies, which is automatic when the divergence threshold is reached, enables the strong-currency country to seal off the supply of national currency from the interventions, and above all to ensure that the other currencies will follow the strong currency upward and that the strong currency does not weaken. In addition, to limit the interventions in national currency is to limit the creation of Eurocurrency (Euro-marks, in the event) which could trigger reactions from the United States, concerned about the possibility that monetary authorities and non-resident individuals could use these Euromarks to diversify their own liquidity reserves.[19]

---

[18] In practice, even in the snake the interventions were almost always in dollars.

[19] It is difficult to say which concern ranks higher in the minds of the German monetary authorities, that the growth of the money supply could cause inflation or that too many Euromarks could be placed in circulation. In the light of what is known about the relation between money and inflation in Germany (see G. Fels, 'Inflation in Germany', in L.B. Krause and W.S. Salant (eds.), *Worldwide Inflation*, Washington 1977), it seems to me that the monetarist explanation is largely a pretext. In reality, the authorities are more interested in not allowing an excessive expansion of the international role of the mark, and at the same time in ensuring that the other

The asymmetry of the System is further aggravated by the lack of a common policy toward the dollar and by the lack of clear rules on how to modify the central rates of the various currencies. Because of the lack of a common policy toward the dollar, there is concern that in the future the dollar could undergo fresh devaluations relative to the mark and that Germany may not effectively oppose these devaluations, which would draw all the Community currencies upward with the mark.[20] The lack of statutes for devaluation within the System is also cause for concern, since national inflation rates vary widely and can entail strong variations in competitivity among the countries of the EMS, and these can be corrected only through devaluations. Both these questions must now be considered more closely.

2. The Problem of Asymmetry

The problem of asymmetry in the distribution of the burdens of balance of payments settlements is not new in discussions of systems of fixed exchange rates. Only the gold standard was a symmetrical system of fixed exchange rates, at least in that the national money supply was genuinely regulated by variations in reserves, and the level of prices and income corresponded, as prescribed in quantitative theory, to variations in the money supply. When the Bretton Woods system was founded, the participants in the negotiations were well aware of the danger of establishing a system that would impose settlement burdens only on deficit countries. As we know, the American view prevailed: that the United States should not be automatically driven to expansionary policies in order to facilitate the economic recovery and growth of its partners. Formally, the only concession made to the notion of symmetrical obligations was the inclusion in the IMF

---

currencies are hitched to the mark. The supposed refusal of the Bundesbank to renounce its monetarist objectives and its alleged independence of the executive are a convenient diplomatic expedient by which the German chancellor can make Germany's partners accept the most distasteful technical mechanisms of the System. German concern about the loss of control of allied currencies as a result of the EMS are expressed in W. Steruer, 'Le SME laisse les Allemands sceptiques', *Euroépargne*, no. 2, 1979.

[20] On policy towards the dollar, see P. de Grauwe and T. Peeters, 'The EMS, Europe and the Dollar', *The Banker*, April 1979.

Article of Agreement of the so-called currency-shortage clause. This stipulated that whenever members encountered difficulties in acquiring a currency because of a continual surplus in the balance of payments of the issuing country, the Fund would be empowered to declare a 'shortage' of this currency, authorizing the other countries to take administrative measures of trade restrictions against the indicated country.[21] In fact, when the feared American surplus materialized in the early fifties and what came to be called the 'dollar gap' arose, the currency-shortage clause was never invoked.

Nevertheless, the Bretton Woods system did empower member countries to vary the par value of their currencies within a range of 10% without having to ask the IMF for authorization. Although the surplus countries were naturally reluctant to revalue, nothing prevented the deficit countries from devaluing.[22] And indeed, many countries freely resorted to devaluations, with gratifying results, as shown by the French experience. The EMS, on the contrary, rules out unilateral variations of the central rate of a currency, and does not even specify what conditions must be met to permit or impose a variation in the central rate of a currency by the 'appropriate Community organs'.

The Bretton Woods system, then, did not function in a purely deflationary direction, because the United States made sure that it was interpreted very broadly and with a proper sense of responsibility. Indeed, the drift toward the dollar gap was counteracted by the promotion of a broad programme of credits and aid (the Marshall Plan), by permitting the European countries to postpone the declaration of foreign convertibility of their currencies until 1958, and by enabling them to establish a mechanism that would discriminate against US imports and thus permit them to economize reserves, the European Payments Union.[23] These expedients, in addition to encouraging post-war reconstruction, allowed the European countries more rapid growth than the American economy during the 1950s. Then, in the sixties, the US economy began to impart

[21] A lively reconstruction of the discussions on this clause is contained in T. Balogh, 'Keynes and the International Monetary Fund', in A.P. Thirwall (ed.), *Keynes and International Monetary Relations*, London 1976.

[22] Except, of course, for the reluctance of the United States to devalue in the second half of the seventies, in order to avert the dethroning of the dollar.

[23] On the functioning of the international monetary system in those years, see R. Triffin, *Europe and the Money Riddle—From Bilateralism to Near-Convertibility, 1947–1956*, New Haven 1957.

vigorous expansive impulses to the world economy. In the first half of the decade there was a healthy expansion, sustained by the increase in the public deficit effected by the new Democratic administration and bereft of inflationary effects, thanks to the determined income policy that accompanied it. The American balance of payments deficit also remained within reasonable dimensions, and competitivity was preserved by inflationary good conduct. Later, as war spending was superimposed on public spending and the consent that had made the incomes policy possible evaporated, the American economy continued to impart expansive impulses, but this time accompanied by excessive creation of international liquidity and an inflation rate higher than that of the rest of the world; this, by raising the price ceiling of goods traded internationally, encouraged the spread of inflationary trends worldwide.

Is it legitimate to compare Germany's position in the EMS to the US position in the Bretton Woods system? German national income is the greatest of the EEC, although the gap separating it from that of the other countries is not as wide as that between the United States and the rest of the industrialized world at the time of Bretton Woods. Nevertheless, the German economy is far more exposed to the outside than the American, and therefore exercises proportionally greater influence on the rest of the world (and is itself proportionally more influenced). Indeed, Germany is now the world's leading exporter, having overtaken the United States. Germany's share of world exports of manufactures is more than 20%, while that of the United States oscillates between 15% and 16%. Germany is the country of Western Europe with the greatest levels of income, exports, and imports. In addition, the entire system of commercial connections among the countries of Western Europe is such that the evolution of the national income of the minor countries is closely linked to the evolution of German national income. To recreate a system of fixed exchange rates between the mark and the other European currencies would render the dependence of European on German development even stronger. Indeed, it should be noted that Western Europe as a whole has become relatively independent of the United States, to which it now sends a minimal portion of its own exports. The European economic cycle has therefore tended to be relatively little influenced by the favourable American conjuncture in recent years.

It is therefore not unreasonable to compare the functioning of the

EMS dominated by Germany to the functioning of the Bretton Woods system dominated by the United States. Given the absence of any mechanism by which to create fiduciary reserves within the EMS,[24] trade with Germany is the only way the European countries can acquire reserves; at most, it may be conjectured that the deficits with the OPEC countries are compensated by the surpluses Europe manages to run with other areas: North America, the developing countries, and the socialist countries.[25] The European countries tend to set their imports from other European countries at a level that equals their exports to these countries. In the final analysis, the rate of development of German imports from the rest of Europe determines the growth of the exports, and therefore of the imports, of the other European countries. Therefore, since the relationship between rate of growth of the national income and rate of growth of imports is roughly similar in the various European countries, the growth rate of German income determines the growth rate of the European economy. The countries of southern Europe, which rank high in the export of services to Germany (primarily tourist services and labour, which are not compensated for by imports of services), are partially exempt from this constraint. If the southern European countries continue to register rising service surpluses, they can achieve growth rates relatively independent of Germany's.[26]

Because of the importance of the German for the European growth rate, the probable evolution of the German economy in the medium term must be estimated if we are to conjecture about whether the EMS will function like the Bretton Woods system in the fifties, in the first half of the sixties, or in the second half of the sixties—in other words, to judge whether it will have deflationary, expansive, or expansive-inflationary effects on the European economy. There is no doubt that all indications are that Germany will exert a deflationary influence.

[24] We have seen that the ECU does not represent an addition to reserves.

[25] Europe also runs a large deficit with Japan. In evaluating the effect of the configuration of balances on reserves it must also be kept in mind that deficits with OPEC are settled in cash, while surpluses with the developing countries and the socialist countries are financed with medium- and long-term credit. Even equilibrium in the European accounts with the rest of the world thus entails a worsening of the financial situation of the European countries.

[26] As was done by Greece (whose invisible items are also enormous, partly because of maritime charter fees), which maintained full employment and a good rate of growth throughout these years, and as Italy could do if the high tourist balance of these years, which helped to create a current inflow of $2 thousand million in 1977 and $6 thousand million in 1978, continued.

For several years now the German economy has exhibited a growth rate hovering at about 3–3.5% a year, and there is no reason to assume that this rate will rise substantially soon.[27] The previous chapter sought to explicate the factors inflecting the German economy in a deflationary direction. Briefly, we can distinguish factors relating to the technological upgrading of the German productive apparatus, to Germany's international financial position, and to the struggle against inflation—in short, all motivations typically linked to German interests, without concern for the more general interests of the European economy.[28]

3. Consequences of the EMS for the European Economy

The lack of any mechanism encouraging Germany to eliminate its surplus is causing a generalization of deflationary trends throughout the European economy.[29] Deflation, combined with the prospect of the appreciation of national currencies along with the mark, is impelling the various economies to a requalification of production similar to the process now under way in Germany. Instances of the reconversion and the restructuration of industry, accompanied by concentration of firms and acute shortages of skilled labour, are now evident in nearly all the countries whose currency was revalued along with the mark, whether they were formal participants in the snake or remained outside it—in other words, in what are usually called the strong countries of Europe, from Switzerland to Norway.[30]

Now, the extension of the joint float to Italy and France[31] raises

[27] In the course of the negotiations on the EMS, the German authorities refused to accept any commitment to raise the rate of development of their own economy beyond the modest percentages conceded the previous summer, at the Bonn summit.

[28] For a detailed examination of the deflationary propensities of economic policy in Germany, see chapter 4.

[29] Because of the 1979 rise in the price of oil, the German current-account could record a zero balance. Nevertheless, since Germany controls a very large share of the OPEC market, any increase in the buying power of these countries will be reflected, with some delay, in an increase in German sales to them, the income from which will more than compensate for the increase in the price of oil. The German surplus will thus inevitably reappear.

[30] For a review of these tendencies, see United Nations, *Structure and Change in European Industry*, New York 1977.

[31] The following argument applies to Britain too, which also applied a policy designed to strengthen the pound, although it did not join the EMS exchange accord.

the question of whether these countries—whose structure of production is less advanced than Germany's, not to mention Holland's or Switzerland's—will be able to effect a similar requalification of their industry too. In other words, can they succeed rapidly enough in abandoning the sectors for which demand is most sensitive to price competition and shift to more sophisticated sectors for which demand is relatively price inelastic. Speed is required because the recession and the upward pressure on exchange rates have caused a further loss of employment, concentrated in the traditional sectors, on top of already high unemployment levels. Without a reflation of demand, this unemployment can be reabsorbed only if job openings are created in the new industries. Even Germany, which has been able to begin this process of requalification of production on the best possible basis,[32] sees no prospect of reducing unemployment over the next several years. What will happen in a country like Italy?

Even in the absence of the requisite in-depth studies,[33] it may reasonably be doubted that deflation and a rising exchange rate are helpful to the Italian economy. These negative trends could be partially combated if the EMS directed considerable financial flows to the weakest areas, as the Bretton Woods system did in its early days. These would have to consist primarily of aid grants, and would have to be used to prime demand without incurring balance of payments difficulties. Either balance of payments financing or development project financing would do. The only effect of the former would be to increase reserves, thus allowing the national government the choice of reflating the economy by stimulating consumption or investment. The latter would serve directly to augment national productive capacity. Naturally, this financing could be accompanied by a total or partial spending constraint on the purchase of European products. Financing such as this would make it possible to avert the worst effects of the EMS; the strong countries would be free to continue an 'intensive' development policy accompanied by deflation, while the weaker ones could pursue an 'extensive' development policy, which

[32] German technical level is such that Germany can move into the nuclear industry, electronics, and aeronautic construction (along with France) while maintaining its primacy in machine tools, special steel, many branches of secondary chemicals, and other sectors as well.

[33] See F. Onida, *Industria italiana e commercio internazionale*, Bologna 1978. This work, naturally, relates the problem to discussions about Italian industrial policy. For an introduction to the debate, see AREL, *Industria in crisi: soluzione europea o nazionale*, Bologna 1978.

would at the same time encourage the rationalization and reconversion of industry, through legislative measures that might possibly draw on the same European financing. But plans for financial transfers on a grand scale have remained a dead letter within the EEC,[34] and the Brussels accord stipulated only the allocation from the Community budget of a sum designed to facilitate interest payments, at the rate of 3%, on loans granted to 'less prosperous states' by the European Investment Bank and other Community institutions, up to a maximum of one thousand million ECUs.

It seems obvious that a great opportunity was lost. The requisites of both the more and the less advanced countries could have been composed to serve the common goal of European development and the expansion of employment. In the event, the Germans feared to place excessive burdens on their reserves, while German banks and industrialists held that their accumulated dollars had to be used to finance the expansion of German trade and industry throughout the world. And it could be that these concerns were legitimate. But the fact remains that the tragedy of European history is being repeated: the continent has the misfortune of having at its centre a country too great to take no interest in its neighbours, but too weak to afford the luxury of generosity.

In the absence of adequate financial recompense, adherence to the EMS by the less prosperous countries, Italy in particular, presents no clear benefits, but only drawbacks that will become evident sooner or later. The EMS does, however, present considerable advantages for the German economy.

4. Germany and the EMS

We have seen that the snake ensured that participating currencies

---

[34] These projects, born of the need to narrow the gap in per capita incomes of the various areas, had been set out in the famous McDougall Report (Commission of the European Communities, *Report of the Study Group on the Role of Public Finance in European Integration*, Brussels 1977), the recommendations of which were not implemented. Other projects brought up in the course of the EMS negotiations emphasized the need to reassess the costs and benefits of the Common Agricultural Policy. Still others called outright for an increase of the Regional Fund in the Community budget. For information on the budget and Community policies, see D. Swann, *The Economics of the Common Market*, Harmondsworth, 1978.

would be revalued relative to the dollar, along with the mark. The EMS makes it even easier for participating currencies to follow the mark upward. The depreciation of the dollar relative to the mark over the past decade has been stunning. From 1969 to 1978[35] the quotation of the dollar in terms of the mark fell 55%. Nominal wages rose much faster in Germany than in the United States during the same period; the real depreciation of the dollar relative to the mark, then, computed by combining the variation of currency quotations with the differential in the variation of wages in the two countries, was more like 80%. Since productivity rose more rapidly in German industry, however, we should also correct for the differential increment in labour costs per unit of output, which would reduce the real depreciation of the dollar somewhat, bringing it to about 70% since 1969.[36]

These data show that the loss of German competitivity to the United States was dramatic over this decade. Moreover, the revaluation of the mark relative to the currencies of Germany's major trading partners taken as a whole was even greater. According to an estimate of the IFO (the authoritative German Institute for Study of the Economic Cycle), in the nine years from 1969 to 1977 the mark was revalued in nominal terms by an average of about 60% relative to the currencies of the twelve countries (including the United States) that absorb 70% of German exports. Correcting for unit labour costs, the revaluation falls to 20%; it was especially strong relative to the lira (28%), the pound sterling (47%), and the French franc (32%). On the other hand, the mark remained stationary in real terms, or even depreciated, relative to the currencies of the snake: it depreciated 4% relative to the Belgian franc, 3% relative to the Dutch florin, and appreciated only slightly (6%) relative to the Danish crown. The snake thus served to preserve the competitivity of the German

[35] The period may be said to have opened in 1969 because that was the year in which the mark was revalued, in the framework of the system of fixed exchange rates. The data used to calculate the depreciation, corrected for various indices, are taken from the *National Institute Economic Review*, various issues.

[36] The depreciation would be lower still if it were compared with the consumer price index: then the dollar would have been devalued by only 30%. This diversity simply means that real wages declined in the United States—in other words, nominal wages rose less rapidly than the cost of living, while in Germany they rose slightly faster than the cost of living.

economy relative to the other economies of the snake, which together absorb 21% of German exports.[37]

For its part, the United States absorbs only about 7% of German exports, but the mark-dollar exchange rate is much more important to the German economy than this figure would indicate. The structure of German industry is now similar to that of US industry, and the two countries consequently compete on all the world's markets. The process of industrial reconversion and rationalization now under way in Germany should enable the German economy to keep pace with the American in the future, recovering competitivity both through a more rapid rise in productivity and through the greater technical sophistication of its products. Committed as it is to this effort, which is vital to the country's survival as an independent economic power, the German government has to guard its flank against competition from its major trading partners: France, Italy, and Britain, which together absorb 25% of German exports. By enlarging the arc of currencies anchored to the mark, the creation of the EMS prevents sudden variations in the competitivity of the German economy relative to the countries to which nearly 40% of German trade is directed.[38] Germany can thus continue undisturbed its process of industrial fortification, which, as I have sought to demonstrate, includes a powerful deflationary propensity within the German economy itself. If Germany became less competitive, its imports would rise and its exports decline, which would increase unemployment. This extra unemployment, added to that which has already been caused by deflation and restructuring, would probably render the social costs of the entire process of requalification of industry intolerable. Repatriation of immigrant workers has kept the cost in unemployment within 1 million, many of whom are women. But if Italy, France, and Britain continued to become more competitive, the loss of jobs in traditional sectors would become unbearable.

[37] Even without the snake these currencies would have been revalued relative to the dollar, which is what happened to the Swiss franc and the Austrian schilling. The Danish crown, on the other hand, surely would have depreciated by amounts similar to the lira and the pound.

[38] If we add Britain, which has not yet joined the EMS, and Switzerland and Austria, which are indirectly connected to it, the area of currency stability covers about 60% of German trade.

With the formation of the EMS, Germany has sheltered its economy from the devaluations of its European trade partners.[39] Of course, the economies that devalued their currency in past years paid a high price in the form of an acceleration of inflation: the rise in national price levels largely wiped out the devaluation;[40] but the figures cited above demonstrate that this compensation was not proportional relative to all currencies. Indeed, since 1969 the lira, franc, and pound have depreciated considerably relative to the mark in real terms, while they depreciated little or not at all relative to the average of all currencies. Moreover, in the eighteen months prior to the formation of the EMS, some countries—Sweden and Italy in particular[41]—had been applying an exchange policy that was extremely dangerous for Germany: appreciating their currencies relative to the dollar and depreciating them relative to the mark and the other strong currencies. The effects in the case of the Italian economy were described as follows by the Bank of Italy: 'the gradual appreciation of the lira relative to the dollar (5% between December 1977 and December 1978) . . . exerted a downward effect on the rate of inflation by the fraction of Italian imports constituted by oil and raw materials (about 30% of the total), which are invoiced essentially in dollars and generally price inelastic. . . . At the same time, the depreciation of the lira's exchange rate relative to the European currencies, which rose significantly relative to the dollar, permitted Italy to acquire advantages of competitivity in the export of manufactures directed primarily toward the Community area.'[42] In other words, while holding the exchange rate of the lira almost unaltered (as measured by the appropriate index, in which the currencies of the snake have more or less the same weight as the dollar),[43] Italy succeeded in becoming more competitive relative to

[39] Although it did not join the EMS exchange system at the beginning in 1978, Britain is pursuing a strong-pound policy, facilitated by its high oil income.

[40] The sequence was often reversed: inflation produced devaluation, which more than corrected for competitivity, leading to a fresh acceleration of inflation.

[41] Sweden officially adopted a policy of maintaining the value of the crown stable relative to an index composed of a weighted average of the currencies of Sweden's major trading partners. The policy was inaugurated when Sweden left the snake in August 1977. In Italy a substantially similar exchange policy was applied by monetary authorities, although it was never officially declared.

[42] *Relazione all'Assemblea sul 1978*, pp. 157–58.

[43] For information on the construction of the index, see 'Nota metodologica del tasso di svalutazione della lira', Bank of Italy, *Supplemento al Bollettino*, no. 27, July 1975. The weights of the index were subsequently adjusted in accordance with the shares of Italian foreign trade in 1977 by area and by value.

the countries of the snake and suffered scarcely any inflationary effect. The effects of this policy on the evolution of the Italian-German trade balance are obvious; they are represented in table 19.[44] There was also a hefty diminution of inflation in 1977 and 1978.[45]

Table 19

Commercial Trade Between Italy and West Germany, 1971–78
(thousands of millions of $)

	(1)	(2)	(3)
1971	3.3	3.6	0.3
1972	3.9	4.4	0.5
1973	5.7	5.3	−0.4
1974	7.2	5.8	−1.4
1975	6.6	7.0	0.4
1976	7.6	7.5	−0.1
1977	8.1	8.9	0.8
1978	9.8	10.6	0.8

(1) Italian imports from Germany (c.i.f.).
(2) Italian exports to Germany (f.o.b.).
(3) Balance of 1–2; a minus sign indicates that the balance was to Italy's disfavour.

Sources: GATT and Bank of Italy.

The exchange policy applied by Sweden—and by Italy before its adherence to the EMS—is perfectly legitimate by the standards of the present organization of international monetary relations. Indeed, the new Article IV of the International Monetary Fund stipulates that a member country can fix the foreign value of its own currency with reference to 'SDRs or other denominations other than gold'. The indices of the foreign value of currencies, such as that adopted for the

---

[44] The data of table 19 must be interpreted cautiously. First, imports are c.i.f., while exports are f.o.b. The real balance is therefore more favourable to Italy by the cost of insurance and freight for the transport of imports, which can run as high as 5–6% of the value of the imports themselves. In addition, we have to distinguish the income effect exercised by de-synchronization of the economic cycle from the price effect produced by variations of competitivity. Since the growth rates of the two economies have been similar since 1976, it is not unreasonable to assume that the surplus of about a thousand million dollars in Italy's trade with Germany is due largely to the rising competitivity of Italian products, in large part because of the depreciation of the lira.

[45] Halting the devaluation of the lira was a precondition for reducing the inflation rate, on which various factors act, some of them fiscal.

lira by the Bank of Italy, are constructed according to the principles of a weighted currency basket—the same procedure as is used to determine the value of SDRs (and now also ECUs), except that the currencies and weights employed are referenced not to world trade, as in the case of the SDR (or inter-Community trade in the case of the ECU), but to the foreign trade of the country in question.

Nevertheless, if Italy had not joined the EMS and if the dollar had continued to weaken relative to the mark, it would have been quite difficult for Italian monetary authorities to continue to improve the competitivity of the Italian economy relative to its Community partners without provoking reactions. The formation of the EMS turned the situation around completely. The lira is now anchored to the mark, and the Italian economy is fated to lose competitivity either if the mark appreciates relative to the dollar or if the Italian inflation rate continues to exceed the European average. In the former case competitivity will be lost relative to outside areas, in the latter relative to other EEC members. Nothing prevents both cases from occurring simultaneously. The loss of competitivity can only reinforce the tendency of the EMS to exert deflationary effects on the Italian economy. As the Italian balance of payments surplus is eroded by the loss of competitivity, it will become indispensable to hold imports down through controls on income.

The deflationary tendency of the EMS could be attenuated if measures were adopted to counter the loss of competitivity or to allow for a more rapid rise in income, consigning the task of reducing inflation to direct controls. The problem with the first option is that the variation of the central exchange rates is automatic, a problem similar to that of the freedom of variation of par values under the Bretton Woods system. The second would raise the problem of reflating the German economy and altering the Community budget in Italy's favour. This could be done by revising the overall operation of the Community's budget policy, especially the management of agricultural policy. It has been calculated that Italy contributed between 1500 and 2000 thousand million lire to the Community budget in the 1970s,[46] even though it has the second-lowest

---

[46] See Bank of Italy, *Relazione sul 1978*, p. 45. To these figures must be added the greater outlays Italy had to make to purchase agricultural commodities within the EEC instead of outside it. The prices of Community agricultural products have been pretty consistently higher than world averages, producing a burden of several million million lire a year on Italy's balance of payments.

per capita income in the EEC (after Ireland). As has been observed, Italy's adherence to the EMS was a lost opportunity to revise the mechanisms by which the Community operates.[47]

5. The Future of the EMS

The future of the EMS will be dominated by two factors: the relation between the mark and the dollar and the relative evolution of inflation in the EEC countries. As far as the dollar is concerned, there is little doubt that objective conditions will tend to maintain its downward trend relative to mark, at least for several years. The US rate of inflation continues to be higher than the German, and it will be no simple matter to bring about a convergence of the two: this will not be achieved soon.[48] The rate of increase of industrial productivity in the United States continues to be disappointingly low: even though the gap during the seventies was somewhat narrower than during the previous twenty years, American productivity growth is still the lowest in the industrialized world.[49] The narrowing of the gap in the seventies was due to the fall of demand in the other countries, which gave rise to instances of 'labour hoarding'. The United States, which continued to pursue policies of expansion, thus continued to register increments of slightly more than 2% a year. Taken as a whole, these factors make it likely that the dollar will remain relatively weak for a long period.

As for the possibility that the United States might commit itself to a consistent and sustained defence of the dollar, in the absence of specific international commitments, this can surely be excluded. To start with, defence of the dollar does not mean defence of any particular dollar-mark exchange ratio, and that is the factor that, at bottom, will affect the evolution of the EMS most decisively. It could well be that in the future the United States will want to hold its

[47] See L. Spaventa, 'Queste ragioni sconsigliavano un ingresso affrettato', *Rinascita*, 15 December 1978.

[48] The difficulties encountered by anti-inflation policies in the United States are sharply highlighted in a collection of essays: A.M. Okun and G.L. Perry (eds.), *Curing Chronic Inflation*, Washington 1978.

[49] See table 10. For a more detailed analysis of the evolution of American productivity, see National Centre for Productivity and Quality of Working Life, *The Future of Productivity*, Washington 1977.

currency stable relative to the average of the currencies of the countries with which it trades, but this objective in no way excludes a devaluation relative to the currencies of the European bloc, compensated for by a revaluation relative to the major US trading partners: Canada, Mexico, and Brazil, whose total weight in US trade equals that of the EEC as a whole. The decisive initiative to support the dollar in autumn and winter 1978–79, launched with the 1 November 1978 measures,[50] cannot in my view be said to mark the end of the era of the devaluation of the dollar. In fact, in autumn 1978 the United States faced a currency crisis that threatened to demolish the entire framework of monetary relations, despite the existence of flexible exchange rates. Moreover, the dollar had already suffered a hefty depreciation during the preceding eighteen months, so that US exports were stimulated sufficiently.[51] It therefore cannot be concluded that the United States is inclined to resuscitate a system of fixed exchange rates (which in practice would be dominated by a dollar-mark axis) so soon after floating exchange rates were made official in the international monetary system through statutory modifications of the IMF promoted by the United States itself. The recent observation of P.A. Volker, president of the Federal Reserve System, seems still valid: 'A nation, especially a great world power, does not want its policies, international security, or political objectives to be impeded by external economic constraints'.[52] Nevertheless, since there has already been one fundamental shift in the dollar-mark exchange rate in recent years, it is probable that future depreciations of the dollar relative to the mark will be comparatively minor, substantially limited to correcting for the different inflation rates in the two countries. Since Italian inflation will be superior to German, and since the lira will be revalued along with the mark relative to the dollar, Italy is condemned to become less competitive relative to the American economy on all markets.[53]

[50] On the November 1978 measures, see Bank of Italy, *Relazione*, chapter 1, and *World Financial Markets*, November 1978.

[51] On the deferred effect of the dollar devaluation on US exports, see R. Brusca, 'United States Export Performance', *Federal Reserve Bank of New York Quarterly Review*, winter 1978–79.

[52] 'The Political Economy of the Dollar', ibid.

[53] The indispensability of a common policy toward the dollar if intra-Community currency stability is to be assured is exhaustively argued by R. Triffin, 'La Communauté face au désordre monétaire mondial', *Moneta e credito*, March 1975.

Apart from relations with the dollar, the problem of greatest concern for the future of the EMS is the evolution of national inflation rates. This is also the problem most thoroughly considered in the theoretical literature on the subject: all recent contributors to the 'theory of optimum currency areas' insist that inflation rates in the countries—or regions—making up an optimum area must be equal.[54] The differences arise between those who believe that the diverse inflation propensities of various countries are reducible in substance to the varying shapes of the Philips curve in these countries and to the effects of different expectations about inflation,[55] and those who instead hold that differences in the evolution of inflation ultimately result from differences in the growth of the money supply (or other monetary and credit aggregates), which can be eliminated through the adoption of common policies.[56]

Table 20 shows that inflation rates in the EEC vary widely. In 1978 the Italian inflation rate was twice the European average (computed without Italy) and more than quadruple the German rate. In 1971, on the other hand, the year before the snake went into effect, the Italian inflation rate was lower than the European average, and also lower than the German rate. Despite this, Italy was unable to sustain participation in the snake, because external shocks (mainly the increase in the prices of raw materials, especially oil) powerfully accelerated its inflation rate. The vast literature on optimum currency areas and on the virtues of common monetary policies in achieving a convergence of inflation rates has very little to say about the problem

---

[54] A not very up to date review of the copious literature on this question is Y. Ishiyama, 'The Theory of Optimum Currency Areas: A Survey', *IMF Staff Papers*, July 1975. It is important to note that only two of the contributors considered in the review deal with the problem of the relation between the currencies participating in an exchange agreement and external currencies.

[55] This position has been most thoroughly defended by G. Magnifico, *European Monetary Unification*, London 1973, although recently this author seems to have joined those who believe that the adoption of a common monetary standard can facilitate the homogenization of monetary policies and therefore the convergence of inflation rates. See 'Exchange Rates, Interest Rates, and the European Parallel Currency', Banca Nazionale del Lavoro, *Quarterly Review*, March 1978.

[56] For this point of view, see M. Parkin, 'Unione monetaria e politica di stabilizzazione nella Comunità Europea', *Moneta e Credito*, September 1976. The monetarist point of view is subjected to sweeping criticism by F. Onida, 'Obiettivi e strategie per l'integrazione monetaria europea', *Moneta e credito*, December 1975. Many essays evincing the monetarist approach may be found in Movimento Europeo, Movimento Federalista Europeo (ed.), *L'unione economica e il problema della moneta europea*, Milan 1978.

Table 20

Evolution of Consumer Prices in the Major Countries of the European Monetary System
(increase in %)

	1971	1978
Belgium	4.3	3.9
France	5.5	9.3
Germany	5.3	2.6
Britain	9.4	8.5
Holland	7.5	3.9
Italy	4.8	12.1

Sources: IMF and Bank for International Settlements.

of external shocks. But there is no reason to assume that the sort of events that have shaken the world economy in recent years will not recur. Since the various economies respond to these external shocks in different ways, the future of any exchange agreement seems highly sombre.[57]

But even if the possibility of exogenous shocks is ruled out in a fit of quite unjustified optimism, there remains the problem of the differences in inflation rates at the starting point. The solution accepted when the EMS was formed was to bring the highest rates down to the levels of the lowest, whereas the possibility could have been considered of insisting that the less inflationary countries reflate and thus encourage a moderate increase in prices, allowing a middle ground to be struck. From the standpoint of inflation, however, the

[57] These differences of reaction can be due to objective factors (greater dependence on foreign supplies, and therefore the impossibility of controlling the price of raw materials on the national market) or institutional factors (greater oligopolization of markets, greater role of expectations of inflation). The hypothesis has recently been advanced that revaluation is the most effective response to these shocks. Alliance with the mark, which has reacted this way in the past, would thus allegedly make it easier to bring inflation under control through revaluation. See S. Biasco, 'Nuove strategie contro l'inflazione', *Mondo economico*, 4–11 August 1979. This strategy, however, did not work very well for Denmark, which even today, after six years of revaluation, has a rate of inflation in excess of 7%, triple the German rate. Moreover, revaluation harms exports, which in a country like Italy are price elastic. The British experience in this regard is tragic. In 1977–78 the pound was strongly revalued, which resulted in a stagnation of exports in the first half of 1979 and a phenomenal rise in imports, aggravating the already lamentable condition of employment. It thus seems that the strategy of lowering inflation through revaluation can be applied only by countries whose foreign trade is not price elastic or that are prepared to subsidize exports.

automatic convergence mechanisms of the System favour the most inflationary countries. Indeed, since it is impossible for the less inflationary countries to revalue, they are compelled to import inflation, because of the price increases of imports from the more inflationary countries. But the strength of this mechanism is limited, for it depends both on the weight of the exports of the high-inflation country in the income of the low-inflation country and on the price elasticity of these exports. Since alternative supplies from newly industrializing countries are available, it does not seem that much store can be set on this mechanism.

If the automatic mechanism is too slow and feeble to bring about a convergence of inflation rates, the high-inflation countries (Italy in the first place) will find it necessary to reduce their inflation rate as rapidly as possible, under pain of a heavy loss of competitivity,[58] which would be transformed, through a deterioration of the trade balance, into a rise in unemployment. When Italy joined the EMS, it was assumed implicitly that the future evolution of inflation would cause a loss of competitivity of about 5% a year, assuming that profit margins on exports remained unchanged.[59] This erosion of competitivity could have been compensated, in part by diminishing profit margins, in part through budget controls.[60] If this were done incompletely, there would be a definite erosion of Italy's current-account surplus. In any event, adherence to the EMS ruled out any possibility of priming the economy by relying on the large current-account surplus and the accumulation of reserves. In the course of 1979, it became clear that the government hypotheses on which Italian adherence had been based were far too optimistic. The Italian inflation rate in 1979 was nearly 20%. As a result, despite some acceleration of inflation in the other countries too, the absolute gap between Italian inflation and the European average (and the German rate) will widen far more than expected. The loss of competitivity consequently threatens to approach 10% a year. Given the strong

---

[58] The loss of competitivity can be attenuated by the price policy of the export industries. In that case, however, profit margins are reduced. The reduction of profits when firms are facing financial difficulties can discourage investment and thus contribute to recession.

[59] The hypotheses are contained in the so-called three-year plan, the economic programme for 1979–81 presented by the president of the Council to Parliament on 15 January 1979.

[60] For example with the modification of social security and welfare contributions.

current-account surplus and the high level of international reserves,[61] no possible worsening of the trade balance is likely to
provoke exchange-rate difficulties so severe as to place Italy's
continued adherence to the system in doubt. Nevertheless, a picture
of a gradual slackening of the strength of exports has been taking
shape over the past several years, and exports have been the only
dynamic segment of demand. The effect of the weakening of
exports—above all through a shift in expectations, which may well
come before an actual decline in exports—will be to discourage
corporate investment, thus contributing to depressing economic
activity even further. It is quite difficult to see how public spending
could compensate for this, for fear of further worsening the trade
balance and bringing the lira's moment of truth even nearer. A period
of continuing stagnation of economic activity is therefore likely, in
which persistent inflation will cause a progressive decline of the
competitivity of the Italian economy. Loss of competitivity will
inevitably tend to bring about the absorption of the current-account
surplus and the depletion of reserves to the very limit of the lira's
resistance capacity within the EMS. The longer this period lasts, the
more serious will be the damage to the Italian economy caused by
both the loss of accumulation and the loss of export markets to
competitors, which could prove difficult to recover. The strategy of
the monetary authorities thus seems correct under the circumstances:
to liberalize capital movements as much as possible, abolishing some
of the constraints on effectuation of payments in Italy's foreign trade
and some of the restrictions on the ability of the banks to operate on
exchange markets. The market will then be able to supply indications
about the anticipated rate of the lira, which can guide the authorities
in the formulation of policy toward the EMS so as to ward off the worst
of its consequences for the Italian economy.

[61] Equal to $32.7 thousand million at the end of May 1979.

6
The Extension of the World Market

1. The Ambivalence of the Crisis

The unfolding of the world crisis compels the rehabilitation of views of capitalism that had been far too hastily declared out of date. The great contributions of Marx, Lenin, and Schumpeter to the understanding of the role of crisis in the development of capitalism allow us to organize the complex of events now occurring in the world economy into a coherent whole. In the view of these theorists, crisis is not a purely negative phenomenon, a disequilibrium of the system that slows production and accumulation. Instead, it is ambivalent. Schematically, we may say that these thinkers see a crisis as performing three functions. First, it creates a new relationship of forces between capitalists and workers more favourable to the former (Marx). Second, it strengthens the great oligopolistic groups to the detriment of small producers, encouraging processes of modernization and reorganization of industry as a whole (Schumpeter). Third, it sharpens conflicts between the various national capitalisms for control of market outlets and supplies of raw materials (Lenin). Of course, these distinctions are somewhat arbitrary, for all three dimensions of crisis were present in the thought of all three authors, although the emphasis ascribed to each factor in analytic elaboration differed. In the view of Keynes, on the other hand, crisis represented a net loss for the economy: loss of production, employment, and accumulation. Crisis, he held, has no inherent place in the dynamic of capitalism, but is the product of the irrationality of the people who make up the society of capital. As such, crisis can be expunged from capitalism, if only the various coalitions of interest groups into which society is divided would forego pursuit of their own immediate interests and delegate the task of regulating the level of demand to the state and its institutions. During the post-war period, the Keynesians held that the irrationality that had to be combated was the firm determination of the working class to take advantage of the rising position of strength offered it by full employment, and Keynes's disciples were the exponents and promoters of 'incomes policies'. The entire scientific and intellectual work of Keynes himself may be read as an unrelenting attempt both to discourage irrationality and selfishness on the part of the great imperialist powers, which, he held, precludes the establishment of the free conditions propitious for the development of international trade and investment, and to combat the industrial and financial interests—in a word, the interests of private property—that stand opposed to those institutional reforms required to permit more active state intervention in the management of the economy.

2. Characteristics of Post-War Development

Now, the practical composition of these conflicting interests during the post-war period was made possible by two universally noted factors: the victory of American imperialism and the formidable fortification of the socialist countries. The United States generally renounced full exploitation of the advantages American capitalists could have seized upon because of the predominance conferred on them by military victory and strove, though not without contradiction, to constitute a system that would afford all countries the most nearly equal opportunities for trade and development.[1] The very existence of a strong socialist bloc made the capitalists much more flexible in accepting that modicum of institutional reform and state intervention required to maintain full employment and avert the formation of any link between discontent among the proletarian masses and the power of the socialist countries. On the one hand, fresh international opportunities benefited many countries, which achieved rates of growth of income and industrial production much higher than the United States; on the other, as we have already noted, the maintenance of conditions of full employment engendered a tendency toward redistribution of income to the detriment of profits.

---

[1] For an account of the initiatives and limitations of the US reconstruction of the international order, see R.N. Gardner, *Sterling-Dollar Diplomacy*, second edition, New York 1969.

Moreover, the accelerated development achieved by all the industrialized capitalist economies had a number of important consequences. This development was, on the average, higher than that of the non-industrialized countries, thereby giving rise to a dangerous counterposition of developed and developing nations, aggravated by demographic factors that made the per capita income gap even wider. On the other hand, the development of the capitalist countries was exceeded by that of the socialist countries of the Comecon, such that in spite of their limited starting point, these countries succeeded until recently in maintaining a military potential that could compete with that of the capitalist countries while simultaneously attenuating pressure on private consumers.

At the same time, the rapid growth of individual incomes led to the beginning of a profound transformation of the composition of production in the capitalist countries. Several decades ago, the economist C. Clark had predicted that the growth of the developed economies would be accompanied by a more than proportional expansion of the tertiary sector (services) to the detriment of the secondary sector (manufacturing), just as the initial phases of growth had seen a more rapid development of manufacturing than of agriculture.[2] With the rise of incomes, individuals—and in aggregate, collectivities—demand services as a rising percentage of their own consumption. Indeed, the countries with the highest per capita incomes are also those in which the service sector is most developed. In 1973, for example, 64% of the work-force was employed in services in the United States, 56% in Sweden, and 57% in Holland, compared to 49% in Japan and 43% in Germany.[3] Moreover, the rise of employment in this sector was more rapid than the growth of per capita income, since in 1950 the equivalent figures had been 53% in the United States, 39% in Sweden, 48% in Holland, 30% in Germany, and 30% in Japan. Of course, services grew more slowly as a percentage of national income, because productivity rises more slowly in services than in industry.[4] Apart from potential effects on

[2] C. Clark, *The Conditions of Economic Progress*, third edition, London 1957.

[3] Today the differences in per capita income among the countries considered here have been considerably reduced, if not inverted, because of variations in exchange rates.

[4] OECD, *Labour Force Statistics*, various years. On structural modifications in the developed capitalist economies, see J. Cornwall, *Modern Capitalism: Its Growth and Transformation*, New York 1977.

the rate of growth of national income,[5] the growth of services entails another consequence that has rarely been emphasized: the expansion of services narrows the natural growth areas of the large corporations. Indeed, although they are highly heterogeneous, services are generally more apt to be supplied by small companies or even individual firms, given the scant importance of economies of scale, and sometimes even the existence of drawbacks of scale. Even where economies of scale do exist, and therefore where services lend themselves to being supplied by large companies (retail distribution or brokerage banking), there is often powerful political resistance to the expansion of giant corporations. Consider, for example, the limited spread of supermarkets in the European countries, or the severe regulations against banking concentration in almost all countries. In addition, services are often supplied by public entities (railroad transport, for instance), while other sorts of services (education and sanitation, for example) are generally provided by the state or by individuals or small companies. In particular, the state's redistribution of income tends to sustain a higher demand for this type of service than the market would otherwise bear in the absence of public transfers or subsidies, given the same per capita income.[6]

There are, then, few sorts of services that can conveniently be provided by large private corporations: in particular, some types of transport and telecommunications, tourist services, some varieties of show business. The sweeping development of services in the sixties thus attracted the great corporations, which tried to penetrate the most dynamic market sectors,[7] often with unsatisfactory results. The trend of the composition of production is a serious problem for the prosperity of big capital, since it reduces the total share of the market it can control and therefore the total share of profits it garners. These negative aspects of the growth of services are worsened by the expansion of social services: since the role of the state is decisive in promoting the development of these services, there has been an un-

[5] The reference is to Kaldor's famous thesis that a high proportion of services in income tends to lower the growth rate of the economy, because of the low rate at which productivity rises. See N. Kaldor, 'Causes of the Slow Rate of Economic Growth in the United Kingdom', reprinted in *Further Essays. . . .*

[6] The role of the state in the demand for services is analysed in OECD, *Expenditure Trends in OECD Countries, 1960–1980*, Paris 1972.

[7] This behaviour has been noted by M. De Cecco, 'Determinanti internazionali della politica economica italiana negli anni sessanta', in P. Vitale (ed.), *L'ordinamento del credito tra due crisi, 1929/1973*, Bologna 1977, pp. 101–102.

paralleled campaign against public spending for social purposes in recent years, the inspiration of which (leaving aside the well-known intellectual influences) can easily be traced back to important centres of corporate power.

The long wave of post-war capitalist development has been gradually undermined by a complex of contradictions—economic, political, and social. The conflict between capital and labour has sharpened, albeit in its 'economistic' form; conditions conducive to clashes between the various state monopoly capitalisms have again arisen;[8] a profound conflict between industrialized and developing countries has taken root; the relative strength of the socialist countries has remained unaltered, and they are prepared to take advantage of the mounting conflicts between industrialized and developing countries; a trend toward de-industrialization dangerous to the interests of the large economic groups has been developing.[9] It is my opinion that all these contradictions are being resolved, or at least eased, through the grave crisis that has racked the capitalist economy for nearly a decade now. Indeed, to some extent the crisis is the result of the deliberate attempt to dissolve some of the contradictions of world capitalist development.

The devaluation of the dollar, for example, is at the root of the dyscrasia in the international economy that results in a lack of co-ordination of national economic policies, which is in turn largely responsible for the slowdown in the growth of the other countries.[10] The countries targeted by the American currency offensive have an interest in keeping their own economies in low gear: to control inflation and attenuate the impact of the revaluation of their currency, to foster processes of reconversion and reconstruction of production, and finally to accumulate the foreign surpluses required to finance both the shift of productive activity abroad and the sales of their industrial products. Moreover, they are often compelled to retard growth because of stifling balance of payments constraints. In

---

[8] By state monopoly capitalism —an expression coined by Lenin—is meant the organization of the national economic system according to the interests of the great corporations, which subject the administrative and military powers of the state to themselves.

[9] On the subject of de-industrialization, with particular reference to Britain but also including some material on the United States, see R.W. Bacon and W.A. Eltis, *Britain's Economic Problem: Too Few Producers*, second edition, London 1978, and F. Blackaby (ed.), *De-industrialization*, London 1979.

[10] See chapter 2.

addition to these factors, it is important to note that the modification of the international division of labour, produced by an evolutionary change in the relations between industrialized and developing countries, contributes to lending the contradictions enumerated above a new stamp, aggravating the crisis of employment and income in the industrialized countries.

3. The Development of the Developing Countries

The past decade has seen significant development in a wide range of developing countries. Beginning in 1969–70 all indicators relating to the developing economies in aggregate point to more rapid growth. We find accelerated growth of national income, production and industrial employment, gross investment, internal formation of savings, and exports. (The data are summarized in tables 21 through 24.) Partly because of the crisis in the industrialized countries, the rate of growth of the national income of the developing countries has widely exceeded that of the industrialized countries for the first time in history, narrowing the gap between the two areas (although the gap in per capita income has not been proportionally reduced, because of the faster population growth in the developing countries). This result is surprising, because not even in the sixties, when the efforts of international organizations and aid from the industrial countries were at a peak, did the developing countries succeed in achieving such high rates of growth.[11]

If we examine the phenomenon in more detail, we may note that not all the developing countries benefited from this acceleration of development. To begin with, we must distinguish between the oil-producing and non-oil-producing countries. The former have enjoyed an acceleration of growth because since 1973 they have been able to register a greater mass of investment than before, as a result of the enormous increment in their currency income consequent to the rise in the price of oil. A similar phenomenon occurred in some of the other developing countries, since in the early seventies there was a strong rise in the prices of raw materials, which make up the greater

---

[11] On the features of development of the developing countries in the sixties and early seventies, with particular reference to their international position, see K. Morton and P. Tulloch, *Trade and Developing Countries*, London 1977.

Table 21

Growth of World Income by Area, 1960–75
(*rate of annual variation in % of GNP or GDP*)

	1960–70	'60–65	'65–70	'71	'72	'73	'74	'75
Industrialized countries	4.8	5.1	4.5	3.7	5.7	6.0	0	−1.5
Less advanced industrialized countries*	5.8	5.9	5.8	5.7	5.6	6.2	4	1.6
Developing countries	5.5	5.1	5.8	5.3	5.4	7.1	6.2	4.2

* Includes: Australia, Finland, Greece, Iceland, Ireland, Malta, New Zealand, Portugal, South Africa, Spain, Turkey, and Yugoslavia.

Source: IMF.

Table 22

Growth of Production and Employment in Manufacturing Industry by Area, 1960–76
(*annual rate of variation in %*)

	1960–69	1970–73	1974–76
Production			
World	7.0	6.2	2.6
Industrialized Countries	6.5	4.7	0.0
Developing Countries	6.2	8.2	6.1
Socialist Countries	9.1	8.6	8.4
Employment			
World	2.7	2.5	n.a.
Industrialized Countries	1.8	0.2	−1.7
Developing Countries	3.6	5.5	n.a.
Socialist Countries	3.8	3.3	n.a.

Source: GATT.

portion of the exports of these countries. Despite the subsequent levelling out of raw materials prices and the strong increase in the price of the manufactured products exported by the industrial countries, even today the terms of trade are slightly better for the developing countries than they were in the sixties, and expectations are that they will continue to improve slightly in the medium term,

Table 23

Gross Formation of Fixed Capital by Area, 1960–76
(annual rate of variation in %)

	1960–69	1970–73	1974–76
Industrialized Countries (excluding residential construction)	7.2	4.6	−2 (app.)
Developing Countries	6.4	8.6	9 (app.)

Source: R. Blackhurst, N. Marian and J. Tumlir, *Trade Liberalization, Protectionism and Interdependence*, GATT Studies in International Trade, no, 5, Geneva 1977.

Table 24

Growth of World Trade by Area, 1960–76
(annual rate of variation of volume in %)

	1960–70	'71	'72	'73	'74	'75	'76
World trade	8.5	6	9.5	13	5	−4.5	11.5
Industrialized countries							
imports	9	6.5	11.5	12.5	1	−7.5	14.5
exports	8.5	6.5	9	14	8	−4.5	10.5
Non-oil producing developing countries							
imports	6	6.5	1	15	8	−6	1.5
exports	6	8	10.5	8	4.5	0	13

Source: IMF.

putting an end to the pessimism that was fashionable in the sixties.[12]

Nevertheless, the fastest growing of those of the developing countries that do not produce oil were able to achieve what they did largely thanks to a very powerful increase in their foreign debt. Because of the financing provided by foreign loans, a large number of developing countries were able to reach a very high volume of investment, made up of imported capital and intermediary goods.

[12] For an analysis of the long-term evolution of the terms of trade of the developing countries and for an interpretation of the role of international finance in shaping the dependence of these countries on the industrialized countries, which is in many respects similar to that presented here, see W.A. Lewis, *The Evolution of the International Economic Order*, Princeton 1978.

What was once called the Third World is no longer the homogeneous reality it generally was in the past, but is now profoundly diversified; within it a new grouping of countries have emerged that have probably completed the phase of economic 'take-off'.[13] A good number of the countries of OPEC and a dozen or so non-oil-producing developing countries are now entering the world market as producers of manufactures and have already attained sufficiently high levels of per capita income to permit a high formation of national saving. In current terminology, these countries are variously called advanced developing countries (ADCs), medium-income countries, or newly industrializing countries. Apart from the OPEC countries, they are concentrated primarily in Southeast Asia and Latin America: Taiwan, South Korea, Singapore, Hong Kong, the Philippines, Malaysia, Argentina, Brazil, Mexico.[14] These countries have crossed—often by a long shot—the threshold of an average annual per capita income of $1,000. Their total population exceeds 300 million. With the addition of many of the OPEC countries, the population that has left under-development behind comes close to 500 million. Now, the aggregate data on the entire Third World listed in the statistical tables above are heavily influenced by the behaviour of these countries. If they were able to maintain the high growth levels of the last several years, they would soon be catching up to the industrial countries. South Korea, for example, which is one of the best-placed of these countries, is expected to attain the present per capita income of Japan by 1990, provided world trade continues to grow at least 6% a year and provided the industrialized countries do not intensify the present level of protection of their own markets.

What is of interest to us here, however, is not the general development prospects of the ADCs, but the relation between their development and that of the industrialized countries. The past

---

[13] It is too early to tell whether this situation will continue to prevail. According to the most authoritative observers of the economies of these countries, the failure to modernize the agricultural sector—because of the political inability to enact profound agrarian reforms that would lead to structures adequate to assimilate high-productivity techniques—constitutes a weighty mortgage on their future. As recent experience in Iran has shown, when the failure of an agrarian reform is combined with other deep social tensions created by industrialization, political situations can arise whose end result can paralyse growth, at least of the type delineated here.

[14] Actually, Mexico has become an important oil producer, and it would be more appropriate to place it among the countries of OPEC, although it does not belong to that organization.

several years have seen a shift in the system of worldwide accumulation in accordance with the emergence of a new pattern in the international division of labour.[15] The modification of the international division of labour now under way renders the crisis of the industrialized countries chronic: it is therefore correct to say that the interminable crisis suffered by the European and Japanese economies is structural. In other words, it is largely impervious to policies of control of aggregate demand, whether fiscal or monetary. As will become clear in the analysis, however, any attempt to resolve the crisis through structural policies (abandoning the struggle for full employment) aimed at improving the qualitative composition of production and augmenting its efficiency—in other words, policies of restructuration and reconversion of the apparatus of production— would mean accepting *this* particular modification of the international division of labour as an accomplished fact, along with all the consequences for both international and internal social and political relations.

4. The Role of International Finance

The impressive development registered by the new markets over the past decade was made possible by the abundance of international finance, which enabled these countries to accelerate the growth of manufactured imports required for the realization of investment plans. A good part of this finance was made available by the improvement of the terms of trade for primary products against manufactures, but an even larger portion was supplied by international credit operations. Indeed, the level of public debt and public securities with due date of more than one year of the non-oil-producing developing countries had climbed to nearly $270 thousand million by the end of 1978. To this figure must be added the approximately $60 thousand million in debts of residents of these countries not guaranteed by the state. Now, it is estimated that the

[15] This is the opinion of one of the most acute students of 'dependency', Samir Amin. See his 'Quale alternativa alla dipendenza', colloquium in 'Crisi economica, Terzo Mondo, nuovo ordine internazionale', *Politica Internazionale*, October-November 1978, and especially 'I termini nuovi della lotta di liberazione nazionale e sociale dentro la crisi del "Nuovo ordine economico internazionale"', *Unità Proletaria*, no. 2, 1979.

public debt of these countries in 1960 totalled only $20 thousand million; in 1969 it neared $70 thousand million, which means that over the past decade the public debt of these countries has risen by about $200 thousand million, tripling. Moreover, this indebtedness is concentrated in the few countries mentioned above, which have often multiplied their debts by an even higher factor. Even if we discount for inflation and measure the debt in real terms, the increase is still enormous; since the overwhelming majority of these loans are expressed in dollars, the decline of their buying power must be calculated with reference to the rate of variation of American wholesale prices. During the period in question, the loss of value of the dollar, calculated according to this index, was about 60%. Examining the debt position of the various countries in more detail, we find the following dizzying figures: Brazil $40 thousand million; Mexico $25 thousand million; Argentina $16 thousand million; South Korea, Malaysia, Taiwan, and the Philippines more than $30 thousand million.[16] To these debts should be added the short-term debts, which are difficult to calculate.[17] These were used partly to finance the increase in the price of oil, partly for consumption (especially foodstuffs), and partly for military spending; but the mass of indebtedness also serves to finance the purchase of producer goods. (See tables 25, 26, and 27.)

[16] By way of comparison, when its foreign debt was greatest Italy owed a total of about $21 thousand million, including public and private, long- and short-term debts. In face of these debts, however, Italy always registered considerable assets, in the form of currency reserves, credit abroad, or gold reserves (among the largest in the world). Moreover, Italian national income at the time (1977) was about $200 thousand million dollars. Today a country like Brazil, whose national income is about $140 thousand million, is more than $40 thousand million in debt, against which it has almost no foreign assets. Moreover, its exports are less than a quarter of Italy's. There are two possibilities. Either the notion of the great 'Italian risk' lacked any economic foundation and was bandied about only as part of a (successful) 'strategy of financial alarm'. Or it did have some foundation, in which case it is hard to see why this sort of risk was not invoked against countries like Brazil, unless we admit that international finance follows rules that are not strictly economic and, in the case at hand, bends to the strategic exigencies of big capital.

[17] The figures cited are based on the analytic data published by the World Bank in its *World Debt Tables (External Public Debt of Developing Countries)*, Washington 1977, which, however, go up to 1975 only. For successive years there is an estimate of the net Eurocredits issued the developing countries. The debt situation of various countries is frequently analysed in the specialized press. See in particular *Amex Bank Review*, March 1977 and May 1978. Information on the bank loans of the various countries is provided by the Bank for International Settlements. More up to date information may be found in OECD, Development Assistance Committee, *Development Cooperation, 1978 Review*, Paris 1978.

Table 25

Total Debt of Developing Countries (actually granted) Broken Down by Creditor: Size at Year End, 1970–77
(thousands of millions of $)

Sources of Credit	1970	1971	1972	1973	1974	1975	1976	1977
1. DAC Country*	57.9	64.9	69.5	77.5	90.2	110.4	124.7	137.9
ODA**	22.6	24.0	25.2	27.5	30.2	33.5	36.0	38.4
Total Export Credit	23.8	27.5	28.5	31.0	34.0	43.4	50.2	57.5
Other (private)	11.5	13.4	15.8	19.0	26.0	33.5	38.5	42.0
2. International Financial Markets***	0.5	1.9	5.0	12.0	17.5	24.2	37.8	47.3
3. International Organizations	9.2	10.6	12.6	14.9	18.1	22.5	27.5	33.0
4. Planned Economies	5.6	6.2	6.8	7.6	8.5	9.2	9.8	10.6
5. OPEC countries	—	—	0.1	0.9	3.5	6.0	7.9	10.0
6. Other Developing Countries	0.9	1.0	1.2	1.5	2.1	2.5	2.9	3.4
7. Others	—	—	—	—	—	0.5	1.5	1.8
Total	74.1	84.6	95.2	114.4	139.9	175.3	212.2	244.0
Growth rate (%)	14	14	13	20	22	25	21	15

*   Development Assistance Committee, composed of 17 members of the OECD plus the European Commission.
**   Official Development Aid.
***   Including credit issued by institutions posted in offshore financial centres located in developing countries.

Sources: OECD, DAC, 1978 *Review*.

Table 26

Net Flow of Financial Resources to Developing Countries: Breakdown by Type
(thousands of millions of $)

Type	1961–63	1966–68
Aid and credit facilities, state, private, supra-national institutions	5.47	6.29
Direct credit and investment	3.29	5.47
Total	8.76	11.76
Direct investments of DAC countries	1.64	2.44

Source: K. Morton and P. Tulloch, *Trade and Developing Countries*.

Table 27

Net Annual Flow of Resources to Non-Oil-Producing Countries by Type, 1969–77
(thousands of millions of $)

Type	1969–71	1972	1973	1974	1975	1976	1977	1969–71	1975–77
Aid and credit facilities, from state, private, supra-national institutions	8.0	9.4	11.4	14.9	19.3	18.6	19.2	51.9	38.2
Direct credit and investment	7.4	10.2	15.4	17.5	27.2	29.1	36.2	48.1	61.8
Total	15.4	19.6	26.8	32.4	46.5	47.7	55.4	100.0	100.0
Direct investments of DAC countries	3.3	4.2	4.7	1.1	10.5	7.8	8.7	21.4	18.0

Source: See table 25.

The powerful rise of debt of a selected group of developing countries is a completely new feature of international finance. Moreover, the majority of these loans were issued through private financial channels—in other words, through big banks operating on the Eurodollar market. The official loans—i.e. country to country, or those issued by international financial organs like the World Bank and the various regional development banks—while they rose in absolute terms, diminished considerably as a share of the total.[18] As a whole, then, the Eurodollar banks rechannelled the great mass of funds injected into the international financial market by the US balance of payments deficit after 1970 (and by the European deficits in some years after 1973) toward developing countries, and a few of these countries in particular. The annual flow of new credit to these countries now totals about $30 thousand million. It is estimated that about half of all credits to the developing countries are held in the portfolios of just thirty banks.[19] The preponderant role of private finance will inevitably rise still further; according to estimates of the World Bank, the foreign finance requirements of the developing countries supplied through credit in 1985 will amount to some $208 thousand million in current prices, of which 67% will be furnished by

[18] See table 25.
[19] World Bank, *World Development Report*, Washington 1978, p. 24.

private markets. In other words, the annual flow of fresh Eurocredit should rise from the present \$30 thousand million to about \$140 thousand million.[20]

As the role of private finance has expanded compared with official credits, the relative importance of international aid furnished by the industrial countries, the members of the Development Assistance Committee of the OECD, has been much diminished. Aid from these countries rose from about \$6 thousand million annually in the 1960s to about \$10 thousand million annually in the 1970s, remaining almost unaltered as a percentage of the income of the donor countries. The industrial countries are committed to furnishing aid to the developing countries to the tune of 0.7% of their own gross national product. In reality, because of the failure of the biggest countries to fulfil this pledge (the United States, Germany, and Japan), aid actually hovers around 0.35% of their GNP.

In short, the development of the Third World is being financed by private international finance. The flow of official credit and aid has become insignificant compared with the private loans issued by a handful of big banks, many of them American and British, but more and more of them Swiss, German, and Japanese. A similar phenomenon has occurred in relation to the socialist countries of the Comecon, whose indebtedness, estimated at about \$55 thousand million, is largely made up of debts to private institutions, although in a lesser percentage than the debt of the developing countries.[21] The reflection of the increased importance of international private financing is its rising politicization.[22]

5. The Historical Precedents

Through their control of the flow of finance, the great imperialist powers are seeking to control the economic development of the debtor countries, forcing them to open their markets and to abandon

[20] Ibid., pp. 26–33. Requirements, however, include the refinancing of debts fallen due.

[21] See R. Portes, *West-East Capital Flows: Dependence, Interdependence, and Policy*, Seminar Paper no. 72, Institute for International Economic Studies, University of Stockholm 1977.

[22] The politicization of the role of the banks results in the politicization of posts. When Henry Kissinger left the government, he assumed the position (among others) of

control of multinational investment within their borders; they are also seeking to influence the foreign policy of the debtor countries. But the prime factor that has induced the industrialized countries to supply the developing countries with unprecedented volumes of funds is that the former countries need a wider market for the sale of their own industrial products, especially capital goods. As we shall see, foreign demand from the developing countries is now supplanting internal demand, tending to raise the share of manufactured production in national income. Second, the manufactures produced by the developing countries with equipment purchased from the industrialized countries are flowing back to the latter's markets and eliminating the most inefficient products of the backward sectors, releasing a labour force that will fill the unemployment queues and reduce the bargaining power of the working class.

Now, it is important to emphasize that the use of private finance to enlarge the world market is not a peculiar characteristic of our epoch; it occurred previously in the history of capitalist development.

The obvious precedent is Britain's long-term export of capital in the nineteenth century, especially in the second half of the century. The growth of British capital exports was strictly linked to a modification in the composition of British exports. During the first half of the century these exports were predominantly made up of textiles, but with the spread of industrialization in the European continent and the United States, the role of textiles was gradually reduced. Capital goods, especially railroad equipment, began to become the most important item in British exports. Britain began to export increasing quantities to the emerging countries of the time, the European colonies of the temperate zone, whether members of the Empire or not: the United States, Argentina, Australia, South Africa. These same countries were the biggest recipients of capital flows from Britain.

British capital movements have been investigated in many studies,

vice-president of a big international bank and consultant on international credit for another large banking group. Other former US officials have made similar transitions, taking on important positions in banks active in international finance. In the past, people of this sort would have become university rectors or board members of some large Wall Street brokerage house. It is no accident that in the early seventies, when this process began, a politician of the standing of Robert MacNamara was designated president of the World Bank by the United States.

and there have been many attempts at statistical reconstruction.[23]
The results of this research converge on several points. To begin with,
far the greatest share of these capital movements were made up of
credits and not direct investment.[24] These credits took the form of
debenture stock—in other words, loans issued directly (without any
brokerage by financial institutions) by possessors of British capital to
foreign mutuaries. The foreign debtors were almost always public
bodies (governments, municipalities, administrations of territories)
or commercial companies assisted by public guarantees (railroad or
mining companies),[25] and the guarantee of the foreign government
was often backed by a further guarantee from the British government. Although there were no explicit clauses in this regard, the funds
supplied by these loans were generally used to buy British commodities. When the debtor was the ruling authority of a colony or
British possession this was stipulated; in the other cases it was quite
probable, since Britain held a technical monopoly in the production
of the goods required to develop the economies of the emerging
countries (material for railways, heavy machinery like marine
engines, pumps, mining equipment, and so on). The interest rates on
these loans were not much different from the interest rates on
domestic debentures; since every profit differential corresponded to a
risk differential, the savers of the time evidently considered this sort
of financial investment to be low risk.[26] In effect, these loans were

[23] The basic text, a descriptive historical account, is H. Feis, *Europe: The World's
Banker, 1870–1914,* Yale University Press 1930. A good review of the many works on
the subject, even though it is not completely up to date, is M. Barratt Brown, *The
Economics of Imperialism,* Harmondsworth 1974, which states (p. 179): 'the export of
capital is closely associated with the export of capital goods. These became increasingly
important in Britain's total exports.' For more general aspects of the functioning of these
flows in the payments system, see M. De Cecco, *Money and Empire: The International
Gold Standard, 1890–1914,* Oxford 1974. For the evolution of British trade relations, see
S.B. Saul, *Studies in British Overseas Trade, 1870–1914,* Liverpool 1961.

[24] Nevertheless, a very recent review of all the available statistical evidence tends to
heighten the share constituted by direct investment. See P. Svedberg, 'The Portfolio-
Direct Composition of Private Foreign Investment in 1914 Revisited', *Economic
Journal,* December 1978.

[25] Government guarantees covered more than three-fourths of British investment in
1890, since about half of it was made up of public bonds and another third of shares in
railroad companies and other public-service firms backed by government guarantees.
J.E. Rippy, *British Investment in Latin America,* Hamden 1959.

[26] 'Rates of return overseas could not then have been the attraction. The aim of
such holdings [foreign shares] was security of income . . . even where the state did
not provide direct protection for capital at home, it did provide it or obtain it abroad.'
(Barratt Brown, pp. 175–7.)

guaranteed by foreign states—with a super-guarantee from the British government. On some occasions, if the foreign state failed to honour its commitments, the plenitude of Her Majesty's power was mobilized against the insolvent country. This was, after all, the epoch of gunboat diplomacy; interference of creditors in the life of the debtor countries was so powerful as to be manifested in coups d'etat and even changes of the political system. The most famous case was the ephemeral adventure of Maximilian of Austria, named emperor of Mexico by a consortium of European creditors.

In the end, the historical and statistical evidence supports the hypothesis that the private international financial flows were designed to sustain an active world demand for the sophisticated manufacturing products of British industry. In the authoritative judgement of Feis, 'the principal industries of the country [Britain] relied increasingly on foreign trade and held that this would be fuelled by English capital investment abroad. . . . Since the greater part of investment was made in sectors such as railroad construction, mining, maritime transport, and the exploitation of land, the income, in the form of orders for British industry, was direct and obvious'. And also: 'whether this is explained by the reasons claimed [promoting the development of the community of nations in the context of free trade] or whether it was a matter of pure and simple financial calculation, there is no doubt that in general the evolution of English investment abroad harmonized with the objectives of national policy. . . . Capital was directed above all to those lands from whose development the nation hoped to benefit—in terms of new sources of raw materials and foodstuffs, and new markets. Likewise, it chose primarily those uses that brought profits, in the form of orders for English industry '[27]

The worldwide predominance of British finance enhanced the supremacy of national industry. As the countries of the European continent industrialized, they not only closed their own markets to British goods in an effort to encourage nascent national industry, but also began to compete with British goods on third markets. To penetrate these markets, Germany and France also began granting loans, often on favourable terms. These two countries, which lacked developed financial systems of the British type, relied especially on direct state-to-state loans, which drew protests from the British, who

[27] H. Feis, pp. 75–6, 79.

saw this state interference as a violation of the principles of free trade.
Nihil novi . . .

6. Lack of Finance and Underdevelopment

During the period after the Second World War, international
financial activity has acquired many features profoundly different
from those described above. The thirty years ending with the close of
the war were the most convulsive of all world history, punctuated by
two world wars, revolutions, and the most serious economic crisis
ever. During this period many countries declared their inability to
pay foreign debts, without the dominant powers being able to do
anything about it. In particular many countries of Latin America
declared bankruptcy, causing very serious losses to their creditors.

International loan activity never fully recovered from that blow.
After the Second World War, private financial flows were channelled
almost exclusively through banks. Moreover, many countries
(among them the United States itself for a long period) enacted more
or less rigorous restrictions on the freedom of movement of funds.
Even the recovery of the market of foreign bonds and Euro-bonds,
which began in the middle of the 1960s, seems due to the efforts of
financial firms more than savers: the securities—except those of
specially guaranteed debtors, like the World Bank or the European
Investment Bank—were often held in the portfolios of banks and
insurance companies. Even today, in practice long-term securities are
issued exclusively by public or private corporations of the industrialized countries. As for international banking activity, which
consists in the brokering of short- or medium-term funds, it has
flowered luxuriantly since the middle of the 1950s. Nevertheless, until
the end of the seventies, the Eurodollar banks had financed primarily
trade and investment among the industrialized countries.

The developing countries obtained funds only through official
credit or aid channels, and even then in a measure quite inadequate to
their needs. Even direct investment failed to provide them very great
amounts of funds (see table 26).

The usual justification for this operation of the financial system to
the detriment of the developing countries has been that these
countries represent excessive risks, because of the general insecurity
of political and social conditions caused by decolonization and the

spread of the Communist movement. Actually, besides this factor there is a more decisive cause: during the post-war period the developing countries were allocated a subordinate role in the international division of labour. They were thus condemned to specialize in the production of raw materials, while the industrial base of the developed countries was fortified. The political imperative of the post-war period was the reconstruction and strengthening of the capitalist economies in order to maintain full employment and bring about the rising prosperity of the citizenry in an effort to attenuate or eliminate the powerful drive toward profound social transformations that had been unleashed by the crisis of the thirties and the Second World War. National financial mechanisms, both public and private, were manipulated—not without contradictions, of course—so as to intensify the role of the developing countries as producers of raw materials and to limit their possibilities of industrial growth. Thus, for example, in some industrial countries mechanisms to insure direct investment abroad were enacted, but only in raw materials and not manufacturing sectors. Moreover, the entire financial structure the developing countries inherited after political independence continued to foster their dependence on the old metropolises, draining funds abroad.[28] Finally, the promised aid programme fell far short of the needs of these countries, and even then, as we have seen, was only half implemented anyway. The only source of currency open to these countries was therefore the production and sale of raw materials, for which capital was indeed available.[29] In the final analysis, the effort of these countries to augment their earnings through exports of raw materials was largely self-defeating, since the relatively abundant supply of these goods on the market brought their prices down compared with the prices of manufactured goods, thus causing a tendential deterioration of the terms of trade for these countries, one that continued until recent years. This is the historical background against which the colossal debt of the developing countries cited at the beginning of this chapter must be viewed (see table 25). The

[28] See the magnificent study of T. Balogh, 'The Mechanism of Neo-Imperialism', *Oxford University Institute of Statistics Bulletin*, August 1962.

[29] Both by assuring direct investments (which is, however, only partly effective) and by finalizing loans from the World Bank and other regional banks to finance investment projects in the primary and transport sectors in order to carry these goods to the international market more easily. On these points, see T. Hayter, *Aid as Imperialism*.

watershed between the two panoramas delineated—extreme economic dependence and specialization in primary production on the one hand, rapid industrial growth on the other—is marked by the explosion of private international liquidity at the end of the sixties. The net dimension of the Eurodollar market (excluding inter-bank deposits), which at the end of 1968 was estimated at $30 thousand million, had reached $400 thousand million exactly ten years later. It is beyond the scope of this book to analyse the causes of this explosion of the Euromarket. Surely it cannot be explained solely by US current-account deficits, but must be connected primarily to the American decision to support the growth of this market by abolishing all control on the foreign loans of US banks. In addition, the rise in international loan activity by the industrialized countries, both through direct credits and through placing official reserves at the disposal of commercial banks for foreign credit, was itself reflected in support to the expansion of the market. In sum, except for the very first years of the boom in the debt of the developing countries between 1969 and 1972, the growth of the Euromarket seems to be a consequence more than a precondition of the rise in this debt, in the sense that the financial practices of the industrialized countries allowed the sustained growth of the market.[30]

7. The End of Non-Alignment

Nevertheless, only about a dozen countries really profited from this relaxation of previously severe international financial discipline. The rest of the Third World—India in the first place—continues to be generally excluded from international private credit. In reality, the countries that have gone into debt and have thereby created an industrial structure that makes them dangerous competitors of the industrial countries in some sectors are the ones that had tried to obtain a subordinate insertion into the capitalist world market even in previous decades. We have seen that the great option of the imperialist centres in the post-war period was to restrict the developing countries to the role of producers of raw materials. This

[30] This observation, if it were confirmed, could remove all doubt about the future capacity of the market to continue to maintain and increase financial flows of the scope described above.

design was not wholly achieved, in large part thanks to the existence of the socialist countries, which favoured the aspirations of the national bourgeoisie of the Third World to construct an independent industrial base. Once the phase of decolonization was concluded towards the beginning of the sixties, the development prospects of the Third World were strengthened with the intervention of the United Nations, which sought to remove some of the most constricting bottlenecks to development. The greatest of these was obviously the limited size of the internal market. The developing countries were regarded with suspicion by the industrialized countries as they strove to industrialize, for the latter feared that the former would eventually invade their own markets. But for the most part, the developing countries would have been unable to initiate a process of self-sustaining growth if they had limited themselves to their own markets.[31] The role of the United Nations was to moderate these divergences of interests, helping the developing countries to create regional markets extensive enough to render investment in the mass production of manufactures economical. A series of regional markets were thus constituted in the sixties, which came to include nearly all the Third World: the Latin American Free Trade Association, the Central American Common Market, the Caricom, the West African Community, the Association of Southeast Asian Nations, the Andean Pact, and others. The existence of these regional markets assured the industrialized countries that they would not be swamped with cheap manufactures consequent to the industrialization of the Third World, but also assured the emerging nations themselves that they would be able to attempt industrialization without being compelled to accept a subordinate role in the international division of labour in manufacturing industry. With the option to form regional markets, the countries of the Third World rejected export-fuelled development, for such a model would have had great difficulty permitting the rise of a balanced industrial structure. At the same time, united in regional association they were better able to control

---

[31] This was done just after the Second World War, especially by some countries of Latin America that tried to construct their own industrial development by relying on 'import substitution'—in other words, supplanting manufactures imported from the industrialized countries. For an evaluation of the policies of import substitution, see J. Ahmad, *Import Substitution, Trade and Development*, Greenwich 1978. See also P. Pasca, 'I paesi arretrati tra politica di sostituzione delle importazioni e politica d'espansione della esportazioni', *Rassegna economica*, March-April 1977.

multinational investment in their own markets, for at the first sign of industrialization the giant corporations sought to penetrate the market in order to corner predominant positions.

In substance, the regional markets were an attempt to generalize the Indian model of development to the entire Third World. Indeed, India is so large as to constitute a largely self-sufficient market. After independence, the Indian ruling class attempted an ambitious development programme designed to generate a sector producing capital goods. India thus maintained a considerable degree of protection against foreign goods and capital, and has now succeeded, on the whole, in becoming the tenth industrial power of the capitalist world.[32] This type of independent development may be said to correspond to what the countries of the Third World call 'non-alignment'. This option, taken in the 1950s at the Bandung Conference, is not merely the rejection of incorporation into a system of political-military alliances, but is also the selection of a type of development independent of the international division of labour imposed by imperialism.

The close association between independent development and non-alignment permits us to understand—negatively—the dependent development achieved during the sixties by a small, gradually expanding nucleus of developing countries. In the interstices of this division of the Third World into vast regional entities, small countries emerged that were completely aligned with the great imperialist metropolises, either because they were still colonies or dependencies, or because they had escaped revolutionary attempts that had convinced the local bourgeoisie to abandon all national reserve in exchange for the support of imperialism against revolution. These countries were Hong Kong, Singapore, Malaysia, Taiwan, the Philippines. They opened their markets to foreign capital and began to become peripheral producers of manufactures. The choice of production sectors was made not by them but by the metropolises, either in the direct form of multinational investment or in the indirect

[32] This does not mean that no great clouds menace the future of the Indian economy, primarily because of the inability to resolve the problem of agriculture adequately. It is nevertheless significant that in 1978 India was the only country of the Third World not to be in debt to foreign private institutions. India has debts only to international agencies and foreign states, while its position with respect to the foreign banks is one of surplus: it has $1.8 thousand million on deposit against $0.5 thousand million in loans. See Bank for International Settlements, *L'evoluzione dell'attività bancaria internazionale–secondo trimestre 1978*, Basle, 1 December 1978, table 7.

form of trade concessions that partially opened the Euro-American market to their products.[33]

It is interesting to note that the economic role of these countries was later generalized to nearly all countries that had brushes with revolution: Thailand, Brazil, Argentina, up through Pinochet's Chile. When they found themselves facing the danger that the aspirations of the people (peasants for the most part) could merge with national forces for independent development, effectively embodied in movements that often claimed allegiance to Marxism, the national bourgeoisies of the various countries reacted with fury, destroying democratic organizations and embracing the perspective of industrial development in whatever form, provided that it would consolidate a social stratum opposed to communism—in other words, provided a middle layer would arise slavishly devoted to Western consumption models and capable of providing a mass base for anti-communism. When these countries abandoned non-alignment, they opted for economic subordination. Or rather, to put it in the language of economists, they liberalized their markets by abandoning the straitjacket of currency controls, investment controls on the multinationals, import restrictions, and investment planning.

The opening of these markets coincided with a new stage in the evolution of metropolitan capital. In the 1960s the conflict between capital and labour in the metropolitan countries had become increasingly sharp. Capitalist firms tried to escape the pressure of the workers by transferring productive facilities, either in whole or in part. Initially, this process occurred largely within the so-called developed world, as investment flowed from the United States to Europe, and gradually came to include peripheral countries like those of the Mediterranean and Ireland. Soon, however, capitalist firms recognized the possibilities offered by the emerging countries and began transferring production to them, either in the form of direct multinational investment or in the form of subcontracting. The phenomenon known in the literature as 'runaway industries' burgeoned.[34] American industries were not alone in this process of transference: European countries followed suit, Germany in the lead.

[33] On the dependent industrialization of these countries, see D. Nayyar, 'Transnational Corporations and Manufactured Exports from Poor Countries', *Economic Journal*, March 1977.

[34] See H. Plaschke, 'Le industrie "runaway" e la ristrutturazione della divisione internazionale del lavoro', *Problemi del Socialismo*, 6–7, 1977.

The dependent developing countries thus became export bases. Since their labour costs were but a fraction of those of the developed countries (sometimes as low as one-twentieth of American levels), they produced commodities far in excess of their ability to absorb them in their own markets, and the excess products flowed to the markets of the industrialized countries. Clarity on this point is essential: the independent developing countries would also like to export to Western markets, but not to concentrate their development on technologically backward industries being abandoned by the metropolitan centres. These countries, in other words, aspire to a sort of balanced development, and to finance this they would like to export a portion of the production of those sectors in which they enjoy cost advantages, but not to concentrate their development in those sectors.

To sum up, then, there was a profound divergence between the dependent and independent countries in the seventies. The former were rewarded for their subordination to the international division of labour imposed by the metropolitan countries and received considerable foreign investment and credit financing. With the explosion of international liquidity at the end of the sixties, their capacity to go into debt became immense, and they were favoured with credit issued by the big Eurodollar banks. Their rate of growth of investment, income, and exports accelerated tremendously, in some cases to figures of more than 10% a year. In the space of a decade, these countries were able to cross the threshold of development. Nevertheless, their industrial structure is highly unbalanced, and they are integrated into the world market in a subordinate position.

On the other hand, the other developing countries were excluded from international private finance. In part—and this applies especially to India—the exclusion was self-imposed,[35] since these countries are well aware that at the first sign of difficulties in the servicing of their foreign debt, they would fall into the clutches of the International Monetary Fund and of the club of their creditors. These, in

[35] In reality, the non-aligned developing countries (India in the lead) have always requested international financing, but through official channels: credit and aid through supra-national agencies administered in a non-discriminatory manner, or better still through automatic mechanisms like the issue of Special Drawing Rights to developing countries only (the 'link'). The socialist countries, on the other hand, have generally not been in a position to provide financing in sufficient quantity to constitute an alternative, even in the rare cases (Egypt and India) in which the effort to extract political advantages was greatest.

exchange for refinancing or rescheduling the debts, would impose grievous conditions on economic policy, the aim of which would be to sweep away the barriers protecting the market and control of national industry. The sad experience of the present national-progressive regime in Peru is a lesson to them all.

In effect, the International Monetary Fund has now begun to fulfil a function that has been little noted so far: liberalizing capital markets instead of commodity markets alone. The philosophy that underlies the IMF, of course, as well as all the other international economic and financial organizations, (like the World Bank and the GATT), is one of the laissez-faire, of open markets, of abolition of all controls on the free movement of commodities. And the Fund has never missed an opportunity firmly to oppose any protectionist attempts by its members, naturally being more severe with the industrialized countries, more accommodating with the developing countries. But the laissez-faire principle has never been seriously applied to capital movements, especially in regard to developing countries. Indeed, nearly all these countries have drawn up more or less complex codes limiting the penetration of foreign capital into their own structures of production. It is clear to all these countries that it would not be possible to develop a truly national industry if foreign firms were allowed to set themselves up in key sectors of the national economy at will. Journalistic sources now seem to suggest that the IMF is assuming an uncharacteristically severe attitude toward restrictions on direct investment. Following the financial press, one notes more and more cases in which developing and partially developed countries announce measures liberalizing control of direct investments during or immediately after loan negotiations with the IMF: Portugal, Peru, Sudan, and Turkey. The Turkish case was particularly serious. The conditions imposed by the Fund in the spring of 1979 were so onerous that the Turkish government, although compelled to accept them, obtained an agreement from the Fund that the final letter of intent would be kept secret. One month after it was signed, the barriers to foreign investment were removed in all sectors.

No 'conspiracy theories' of international finance are required to explain why the dependent developing countries were favoured with concessions of credit at the expense of the others. No one would want to claim that the Rockefellers, Rothschilds, Hambros, and the other dynasties of international high finance do not know very well to whom money should be given, especially in view of the high degree of integration between high finance and big industry.[36] It is indeed difficult to see how these banks would issue loans that conflicted with the interests and development plans of the big Euro-American firms. But the technical operation of the system itself guarantees that credit goes to the dependent developing countries and not to the others. Indeed, however much the enormous increase in international bank deposits has driven the Eurobanks to less prudence in evaluating 'debtor risk', i.e. to lower their standards in assessing the credit ratings of the developing countries, all banks nevertheless do rank the various debtors on a risk scale. In other words, credit to the developing countries was generally considered less risky in the seventies than in the sixties, but the various countries were still rated on a scale of rising riskiness. In international finance, risk is assessed for the most part on the basis of the relation between exports and indebtedness. Now, countries whose ratio of exports to national income is high tend to have better relations between debts and national income. In other words, they tend to obtain proportionally more money than the others. Indeed, the amounts of currency generated by exports reassure the banks that they will be able to recover their credits. Since the dependent countries were the Third World countries best integrated into the world market at the end of the sixties, they were also the ones that, on the average, had the greatest exports as a share of national income. They were therefore able to go further into debt, in both absolute and relative terms.

Indebtedness through private channels has now reached proportions such that it can no longer continue to rise without coordination by public authorities. The IMF is thus assuming a new function as the supervisor of the financial behaviour of debtors in the last resort. On the other hand—and this is the more interesting aspect—the individual imperialist states are now concerned to co-ordinate and direct the flows of private finance. In other words, every country is striving to capture the greatest share of the 'new markets'; towards this end they seek either to grant direct state-to-state credit or to encourage their own banks to grant credit consonant with the interests of national industry. In the latter case, the state makes part of its international reserves available to its own banking system, thus increasing the basic funds with which these banks operate. Germany,

[36] On the integration of banks and industry in the United States, see D.M. Kotz, *Bank Control of Large Corporations in the United States*, London 1978.

Japan, and Switzerland have been the leading countries in this regard. Other, less fortunate countries, like Italy, France, and Britain, lack sufficient financial strength to cede reserves to their own banks. These countries react in two ways. On the one hand, they apply much more restrictive economic policies in order to achieve current-account surpluses and augment their financial assets abroad; on the other, they urge their own banks and financial institutions tc go into debt on international financial markets in order to be able to issue credit to developing countries. To make the entire process easier and safer, both categories of country, the strong and the weak, have perfected systems to insure export credits: in Italy the SACE, in Britain the ECGD, in Germany the Hermes, and so on in nearly all countries.[37] At the same time, the state subsidizes export credits through contributions that reduce the interest demanded of debtors.

The expansion of the world market sharpens competition among national capitalisms: the financial, bureaucratic, and military apparatuses in all countries are increasingly subordinated to the development exigencies of the big companies. State monopoly capitalism is again becoming the model of capitalist development. This is reflected in the more specific domain of currency relations: the dollar's role as reserve currency, which secures enormous advantages

---

[37] In reality, methods of insuring and financing export credits have been available in the major countries for more than fifty years. In Italy insurance for some export credits was introduced in 1927; in Britain the Export Credit Guaranty Department was created in 1919; in the United States the predecessor of the present Eximbank was created in 1934. For information on the Italian system, see *Il finanziamento e l'assicurazione all'esportazione*, Mediocredito Regionale Lombardo, Studi e ricerche, no. 3, Milan 1977; for Britain, see ECGD Services, London 1979; for the United States, see Export-Import Bank of the United States, *Report to the US Congress on Export Credit Competition and the Export-Import Bank of the United States*, Washington 1979. In the latter publication we find, among other things, an up-to-date review of the systems in force in various countries. It seems clear that since 1970 there has been a gradual intensification of support to exports through the extension of public guarantees and the facilitation of interest rates for credit. Even Italy has not been immune to this tendency, with successive measures culminating in the noted Ossola law and the creation of the Special Section for the Insurance of Export Credits (SACE), on the British model. Competition in this field has become so intense that the financial press has begun to speak of 'commercial credit wars'. At US insistence, the countries of the OECD reached a 'gentleman's agreement' (which was ratified in 1978 and thus became a genuine pact) for the adoption of common rules on terms for these credits, especially the due dates and interest rates. Nevertheless, violations of the agreement occur frequently, and even the United States is beginning to show more aggression, departing from its traditional concern to maintain conditions of free trade without intervention by public agencies. See 'Eximbank Finance Drive', *The Financial Times* (London), 17 May 1979.

for the United States, is now increasingly questioned. The temptation for strong-currency countries to use their own money in extending international credits is too great to resist. Although the dollar continues to be the predominant means of payment in international exchange, the volume of foreign and international transactions expressed in marks, yen, and Swiss francs is rising steadily, a prelude to a future diversification of the instruments of international reserves.[38]

Now, the United States is trying to curb the most inflamed flare-ups of renascent economic nationalism, in part even renouncing full exploitation of the enormous advantages it commands because of its monetary and military supremacy. In other words, the United States is striving to preserve a multilateral framework of international trade and payments in order to prevent the disruptive nationalism of the various bourgeoisies from undermining the system as a whole. It would be too time-consuming to analyse US international economic policy from this vantage point, but there are surely signs of a growing awareness of the need to preserve the unity of the capitalist world by curbing antagonisms: the Carter administration made particular efforts in this direction.

The preservation of the internal unity of the capitalist world is more necessary than ever, because the new developments in the international division of labour are bringing about the disintegration of the very concept of the Third World. Indeed, the availability of international finance and the possibility of development, however dependent, represent alluring temptations for a great number of developing countries. The model of dependent development is spreading. A rising number of countries are modifying their political attitude in an effort to cut a slice of international credit, proclaiming the end of controls and state planning, in other words, the end of the project of independent development. The latest and most illustrious case is that of post-Nasserist Egypt.

In sum, the very foundations of non-alignment are crumbling. In my opinion, this explains why the Soviet Union, abandoning its traditional restraint in international politics, is augmenting its intervention capacity, bolstering its fleet, and extending military support, either directly or indirectly through other countries of the

---

[38] See chapter 1, section 9.

socialist bloc, to the revolutionary regimes in Angola, Ethiopia, South Yemen, and Afghanistan. It is the end of an era: the development exigencies of world capital are destroying the dream of the neutrality, peace, and independent development of the Third World.[39] War is again becoming a permanent feature of capitalism. The aggressivity of the various state monopoly capitalisms must therefore be directed against the main enemy: the socialist bloc (Comecon). All the more reason why the tension among capitalist countries must be held in low gear, why supra-national must prevail over national concerns. The most appropriate definition of this phase is supra-national state monopoly capitalism, which recalls that the general process of enlargement of the capitalist market and containment of the socialist countries is occurring along supra-national lines: multilateralism is maintained by allowing the equal participation of all the capitalist countries in the profits of the new markets.

The decision to promote the development of China becomes comprehensible in this context, as an attempt to create a further obstacle to the Soviet Union. The development of China is occurring through use of the same instruments that favoured the dependent countries: once again international credit is in the forefront.

Deng Xiaoping's 'four modernizations' call for the investment of $600 thousand million in the Chinese economy over the ten years beginning in 1979; $350 thousand million of that is to be imported. Exports, remissions from overseas Chinese, and tourism are slated to cover three-fourths of these currency requirements; the remaining $90 thousand million is to be supplied in the form of credit from capitalist countries. The race to finance China has already begun: $1 thousand million from Italy, $1.2 thousand million from Britain, $600 million from France, $4 thousand million from Germany, and $8 thousand million from Japan, while the United States is hastening to modify its own legislation, which prohibits concession of credit to countries that have seized property from US citizens without compensation.[40]

[39] Trends toward the end of non-alignment clearly emerged at the World Conference of the Non-Aligned Movement in Havana at the beginning of September 1979.

[40] As of 30 June 1979 the total credit conceded China exceeded $30 thousand million.

8. Modifications of the International
Division of Labour

All countries that receive international credit must make sure that they will be able to repay their loans. This means that the products of the investments made by these countries with foreign credit must find market outlets in the industrialized countries. It is through this market connection that the modification of the international division of labour in the interests of the big monopolies is occurring.

Before analysing how great is the return flow of goods produced by the developing countries and which sectors are involved, let us cite the general assessment of a leading German banker: 'The [Eurodollar] market needs a solid basis if the growing need for international finance, particularly by the emerging countries, is to be satisfied with facility in the future. . . . To ask how the debtors will stand is to ask whether they will be credit worthy. Will the emerging countries that have access to financial markets be able to repay their rising debt, which far exceeds their export earnings? The answer to this question depends on the line the industrialized countries follow in their trade policy. It appears necessary to open markets to the industrial products of the most dynamic of the emerging countries, which are among the major debtors on the Euromarket—and not only in the commercial interests of the industrialized countries, which in 1975 sold about 30% of their exports of industrial products to the emerging countries (for a total value of $123 thousand million, while the trade flow of industrial products in the opposite direction was only $26 thousand million). At the same time, liberal import policies are now the principal precondition for maintaining the solvency and credit worthiness of many emerging countries, and therefore, in the final analysis, for the regulation and continued operation of the international financial system. The general rule must be to keep the market open to those countries that present real cost advantages. At the Bonn summit, the major industrialized countries decided, in general, to behave in this manner.'[41]

General studies have been made of the characteristics of the manufactured products of the developing countries, prepared mainly

[41] H.J. Abs, 'Problemi monetari ed economici attuali', *Bancaria*, September 1978.

by international organizations like the ILO, GATT, and OECD.[42] From these studies it is clear that the developing countries have specialized mainly in textiles, clothing, fur and leather goods, light machinery, and electronic components. They are now beginning to move into shipbuilding, steel, and petrochemicals. Probably the most sophisticated product of these countries is the South Korean black-and-white television set, which has conquered 50% of the American market. Information from journalistic sources and specialized reports indicates that although the industrialized countries have delivered capital goods to these countries (often so-called key-in-hand factories), they have carefully refrained from ceding advanced technology. Thus, in chemicals, for example, none of the plants sold to the developing or socialist countries produce new fertilizers and pharmaceutical products, for which great market possibilities are anticipated. In general, one gets a clear impression that the shift of investment from North to South is occurring according to a definite schema: plants, equipment, and know-how are sent for the production of manufactures for which demand is rising relatively slowly.[43] The industrialized countries thus reserve for themselves production in electronics, refined chemicals, machine tools, arms, aircraft, and even lines of products of greater sophistication and higher value-added among traditional sectors.

It may be thought that this choice is in part simply a result of the way things are, since the developing countries are probably deficient in the skilled personnel and, in general, the organizational and cultural infrastructure required to put sophisticated technology to use. But this consideration must be subject to numerous qualifications, as is demonstrated by the energetic political campaign of the Group of 77[44] for access to advanced technology.

---

[42] See H.F. Lydall, *Trade and Employment*, International Labour Office, Geneva 1975; S. Mukherjee, *Restructuring of Industrial Economies and Trade With Developing Countries*, ILO, Geneva, 1978; and especially the up-to-date report of the OECD secretariat, *L'incidence des nouveaux pays industriels sur la production et les échanges des produits manufacturés*, Paris 1979.

[43] The evolution of demand is measured by the income elasticity of sales of the products; goods with an elasticity greater than 1 are considered goods of high development potential.

[44] The Group of 77, the number of whose members now actually exceeds 100, is an organization of developing countries that seeks to promote their interests in the financial, economic, and commercial organs and conferences of the United Nations (GATT, IMF, World Bank, Conference on Rights of the Sea, and so on). In recent years the Conference on a New International Economic Order (the so-called North-South

In any event, the manufacturing exports of the developing countries as a whole rose 12.3% a year between 1960 and 1975, while manufacturing exports worldwide rose 8.9% a year during the same period, and world manufacturing production 6% a year. Manufactured exports from developing countries, which constituted 5.9% of the imports of the industrialized countries in 1960, rose to 8.9% in 1975, and are expected to reach 13.6% by 1985.[45] These figures, already significant enough, become even more impressive when it is recalled that the exports of the developing countries are concentrated in just a few sectors. In sum, the present and potential threat to employment in the traditional sectors of the industrial countries is serious. And as we have already noted, the growth rates of exports listed above refer to the Third World as a whole. The exports of some of the dependent countries, like South Korea and the Philippines, have risen at rates approaching 20–25% annually in recent years. The urgent demand that the borders of Europe be kept open to Third World goods—which the press, dominated by big capital, and neo-free-enterprise ideologues are repeating ever more insistently— is misleading in reality. What is now taking place is not a process of the economic and social advance of foreseaken humanity, but a conscious and cold effort to widen the world market to a handful of countries that have sold their own liberty and economic independence in order to accede to a subordinate position in the market controlled by big capital, and have contributed to sabotaging the great attempt at autonomous and equal development of the entire Third World, which had achieved a first timid realization in the UN's attempt to broaden the markets of the Third World.

9. Structural Features of the Crisis

Since investment in a cluster of developing countries is concentrated in just a few sectors, in which these countries have an overwhelming

---

Conference) has been convened at its urgings. The Group of 77, whose aims are primarily economic, should not be confused with the Non-Aligned Movement, whose membership is smaller (about eighty countries) and whose aims are primarily political (decolonization, struggle against imperialism, Zionism, and so on), although recently it has begun to pay more attention to economic themes.

[45] The growth rates are taken or calculated from the *World Development Report 1978*, and GATT, *International Trade 1976–77*.

advantage in labour costs, the corresponding sectors in the industrial countries are now doomed. It is this sweeping dislocation of manufacturing investment from North to South—which is continuing, and indeed will continue—that has made the present crisis of the industrial countries structural in character. Capital no longer sees any future for the traditional sectors, which are being abandoned to the new countries now taking their place in the world market. Investment is instead being directed to the more advanced industries producing high-technology manufactures: electronics (especially telecommunications and micro-electronics), aerospace construction, special steel, machine tools (especially computer-controlled), atomic reactors, secondary chemicals, the nascent biology industry, and armaments. The giant corporations carefully refrain from ceding the means of production—and especially the scientific and technical knowledge—required to manufacture these products. World industry is being restructured, the hierarchy among nations intensified: the United States, Germany, and Japan at the top; a second level of small countries highly specialized in a few sectors: Belgium, the Netherlands, Switzerland, and Sweden; then a group of countries seeking either to avert the descent in the hierarchy that will occur if they remain trapped in declining sectors or to maintain the impetus that brought them rapid growth and promotion in the international hierarchy in recent years: Britain, France, Italy, Canada; the remainder of the industrialized countries, which are seeking to turn their remaining advantages in unit labour costs into greater technological capacity: Spain, Greece, Ireland, and Turkey; and finally, the new countries, South Korea, the Philippines, Brazil, Taiwan, Mexico, and others.

Since the countries of this last group hold immense advantages in labour costs, it is probable that the differential in their favour will persist for many years to come. In the older industrialized countries, the sectoral shift of investment is partially spontaneous, a response to the impetus of demand from the new countries: the hundreds of thousands of millions of dollars worth of orders that have been accumulated over the past several years—from the developing countries, OPEC members, and the socialist countries—have enabled the great machine-tool industry to garner staggering gross profits and thus to accumulate the financing required to initiate its own restructuration. In part this process is encouraged by the state. In many countries, then, there has been a modification of public intervention in the economy. Attempts are being made to reduce public assistance to companies in difficulty in order to grant incentives—in the form of orders, aid for mergers, or direct infusions of public capital—to the most efficient companies of the dynamic sectors.[46] In short, public industry is taking the Japanese road. Of course, this trend is not equally strong in all countries, for it depends on local traditions and the resistance from the entrepreneurs and workers of the declining sectors. But Japanese-style industrial policy seems to have won the day—at least on paper—in France, Britain, and Norway. What could be more symbolic of the new course than the decision of the Norwegian government to cut off subsidies to the shipbuilding sector, traditional backbone of national industry?

Italy and Germany are significant exceptions. Italian big industry believes that it lacks the strength to wage a battle to allocate priority to the fast-growing sectors and is afraid to fall victim to the patronage that riddles the political system. It is therefore requesting aid, but equal aid for all, thereby hoping to cut itself a hefty slice of the pie without shouldering national responsibilities (apart from a behind-the-scenes struggle for export credits).[47] German industrial policy continues to be based mainly on public orders in a context of lack of formal and direct state intervention. In any event, big industry is so powerful and so steeped in cartel practices that it can carry out restructuration itself.[48] At the same time, Germany favours the export of laissez-faire policies, to prevent the other European countries from being able, through state intervention, to restructure their own industries to the detriment of Germany.

The system of insurance and facilitation of export credits is also a powerful instrument in fostering the restructuration and reconversion of industry. Big industry is receiving foreign orders guaranteed by the state and acquired in the first place thanks to the facilitation of interest rates. The management system of these credits represents the

[46] For an analysis of these trends in the French economy, see C. Stoffaes, *La grande menace industrielle*, Paris 1978. A panorama of the trends of industrial policy in various industrialized countries is contained in S.J. Warnecke (ed.), *International Trade and Industrial Policies*, London 1978.

[47] See AREL, *Industria in crisi*.

[48] Observers of the German economy are increasingly convinced that the abolition of cartelization by the occupying powers after the war (in any case limited to a few great holdings) did not have genuinely profound effects and was unable to alter mental attitudes and behaviour patterns whose roots stretch back nearly a century.

epitome of the close link between finance, industry, and bureaucracy: every year, thousands of millions of dollars are handed over to a few corporations by technical organs impervious to public control, and the boards of directors of these organs are staffed by high-ranking bureaucrats and financiers with close links to big industry. The mechanism of state-guaranteed financial flows is distorting the very principles underlying the parliamentary order: three centuries of European parliamentary life have been founded on the evolution of the principle 'no taxation without representation'. Anyone who thinks this is an exaggeration would do well to reflect on what would have happened a dozen or so years ago if the parliaments of the industrialized countries had been asked to sanction the transfer of thousands of millions of dollars a year to a few developing countries so that these countries could purchase products of big industry in order to make investments with which to produce low-cost goods that could subsequently be thrown on to the markets of the industrialized countries themselves. And yet this is what was accomplished through private credit. When private credit began to wear thin, the state intervened, issuing guarantees of foreign credit. Given the great unknowns—the ability of the debtor countries to pay back these loans and the capacity of the Euromarkets to handle rising flows of funds in the future—state support is now indispensable in effecting any further modification of the international division of labour. But no one has ever discussed exactly how this division of labour should be modified, and in whose interests.

The profound structural modification now under way in the industrialized economies contributes decisively to world recession. First, investment is diminished in order to increase the productive capacity of sectors of high labour intensity threatened by competition from the emerging countries. Second, if concentration and rationalization of companies in older sectors are to be facilitated, along with the shift of resources to technologically advanced sectors, then it is well that markets not be 'choked' by full employment. Such is the German road to industrial restructuration and reconversion. Third, in order to remain competitive on the markets of the Third World, the various countries must be able to furnish financial assistance. This makes it attractive to pursue the goal of a balance of payments surplus, and the only way to register a surplus is to ensure a current-account surplus by reducing imports through a reduction of income.[49]

The only country that continued to apply a policy of expansion after mid-1978 was the United States, which has an industrial structure profoundly different from Europe's. Indeed, the United States is the country with the greatest industrial concentration and the largest average size of companies. For years now the prevailing opinion has been that mergers and acquisitions in the United States do not correspond to genuine gains in efficiency or economies of scale. Moreover, given the enormous external dis-economies, it is easier to achieve mobility of companies than mobility of labour. An expansive policy facilitates the creation of new industrial projects in the depressed zones of the South, where trade unions are weak, and permits the abandonment of obsolete plants in congested urban areas. At the same time, a satisfactory anticipated rate of market growth further encourages foreign manufacturing investment already attracted by the depreciation of the dollar. In other words, the United States has a problem of re-industrialization. Finally, many American economists are convinced that only a rapid growth rate in manufacturing production will be able to lift the rate of growth of productivity, which is still terribly low.

Nevertheless, both because of an exhaustion of expansion and because of the need to defend the dollar (as analysed in chapter 4), even the United States entered a recession in 1979. The American recession, coming on top of the European, will aggravate the crisis of the industrialized world. Only the developing countries will continue to maintain a high demand for manufactures. The struggle for control of these markets will remain lively, and will rekindle Europe and Japan's desire to acquire greater weight in the international financial system in order to exert more effective control of the process of financing of these countries.

10. The New Laissez-Faire Wave

The world economy is passing through a phase of genuinely qualitative change. The transition is not yet complete. The processes analysed in this book have yet to come to fruition. It is therefore still

---

[49] Capital can also be imported and thus act as financial intermediary, but without a strong base of reserves this policy is impractical in the long run.

possible to negotiate control of the transformation of the international division of labour. The interests of both workers and capitalists in the traditional sectors are quite strong; they often encompass entire nations fearful of being left behind in the new economic alignment. One reflection of these conflicts is the ambiguous character of the results of multilateral trade negotiations, the last phase of the Tokyo Round, concluded in Geneva in spring 1979.

Many European countries were reluctant to agree to a further extension of the trade privileges granted the developing countries through the system of 'generalized preferences'.[50] Protectionist clauses and other limitations were imposed that resulted in the refusal of most of the developing countries to ratify the Geneva accord.

Nevertheless, the forces of big capital continue to press ahead everywhere, for the obstacles to trade are being swept away. If the developing countries encounter problems in selling their goods and therefore in repaying the debts they have contracted, then the process of the further expansion of the world capitalist market could be slowed or even halted. In that event, many banks could find themselves in trouble and—even if we exclude the possibility of a very severe international financial crisis—they would have to seek aid from their respective governments or monetary authorities, either on the basis of the formal guarantee of export credits or simply to forestall going under with the national deposits as well. At that point the entire system would be subjected to public scrutiny: parliaments, public opinion, and trade-union forces would have to express their views on how appropriate the present worldwide restructuration is.

The new laissez-faire wave does not stop at foreign trade alone, but involves all the aspects of economic and social life in capitalist societies that impede the extension of the ability to make profits and the predominance of the great economic groups. Public spending is the first target in big capital's sights. We have seen that because of sales of capital goods abroad there is a tendency for the share of manufactured products in national income to rise; at the same time, the consumers in the newly emerging countries are reaching income levels at which the elasticity of demand for manufactures (especially durable consumer goods) is becoming quite high. New prospects of

[50] The 'preferences' were granted the developing countries in 1971, at the beginning of the process of enlargement of the world market in manufactures. For an assessment of their effects, see R.E. Baldwin and T. Murray, 'MFN Tariff Negotiation and LDCs Under the GSP', *Economic Journal*, March 1977.

development are opening up in the new countries for automobiles, refrigerators, air conditioners, etc—and many of these opportunities are being seized upon by Euro-American big industry, either directly (through trade or the formation of local subsidiaries) or indirectly (through the sale of more sophisticated parts for these manufactures). The necessary complement of this strategy is the reduction of social spending in the industrial countries, which tends to direct resources toward social services, and a redistribution of income that will increase the differential between rich and poor social strata, in order to create high-income market sectors to which to sell highly complex and costly consumer goods, such as those made possible by the development of microchips, and to increase the saving propensity in order to make room for exports.

Naturally, not all these tendencies can come to fruition. Some even conflict with others. The need to maintain social peace, for example, makes it necessary to continue sizable expenditures in public budgets. Nevertheless, it must be emphasized that capital has seized the initiative, and is now seeking to free itself of all the 'traps and snares'[51] in which the popular classes have sought to entangle it over the past thirty years. No aspect of the condition of the working class—or of the popular layers—will be spared in this offensive: jobs, the organization of labour, security, the dignity and tranquillity of life, consumption. A long phase in the history of capitalism is drawing to a close, that of capitalism with a human face, of benevolent capitalism concerned with full employment, equitable distribution, and protection of the dignity of citizens through social spending. Now it is back to the wildcat capitalism of the industrial revolution, of unbridled cartelization, of imperialism, of world wars.

The breadth of this restoration of the complete domination of capital over society is generating counter-reactions, and forces are now organizing that can combat the trends now under way. These developments are undermining the very basis of the existence of Social Democracy, the bankruptcy of which lies not in the fact that it has failed to transform capitalism into a different system, but in that it did not even succeed in controlling the system's most aggressive tendencies, which are now challenging the social pact on which the Social Democratic administration of society is based. It is probable

[51] The phrase is taken from Guido Carli, former director of the Bank of Italy, who coined it in complaining about restrictions on capitalist practices.

that we will soon see a radical crisis of consciousness throughout European Social Democracy, once it becomes definitively clear to everyone that the high unemployment of the last half of the seventies will persist for another ten or fifteen years.

On the basis of the recovery of consciousness of the antagonistic character of capitalist development, it may be possible to weave the threads of an alternative strategy and society that can encompass, side by side, the workers of the West, the new proletarian masses of the Third World, and the socialist countries.